GENEVA
CYMBELINE REFINISHED
GOOD KING CHARLES

LONDON

PUBLISHED BY

Constable and Company Ltd.

10–12 ORANGE STREET, W.C.2

•

INDIA

Longmans, Green and Company Ltd.

BOMBAY   CALCUTTA   MADRAS

•

CANADA

Longmans, Green and Company Ltd.

TORONTO

GENEVA, CYMBELINE REFINISHED, & GOOD KING CHARLES: BY BERNARD SHAW

LONDON
CONSTABLE AND COMPANY
LIMITED

First collective publication
1946

PRINTED IN GREAT BRITAIN
BY R. & R. CLARK, LIMITED, EDINBURGH

CONTENTS

	PAGE
Preface to GENEVA	3
Hoodwinked Heroism	3
England Frightened and Great	5
England Secure and Lazy	6
History Stops Yesterday: Statecraft Works Blindfold .	7
We Split the Atom	9
An Amoral Victory	9
Civilization's Will to Live Defeated by Democracy .	12
Incompetent Governments are the Cruellest . .	16
Hitler	18
Pseudo Messiah and Madman	20
Democracy Misunderstood	23
"Great Men"	24
We Can and Must Live Longer	25
The Next Discovery	26
Foreword to CYMBELINE REFINISHED . . .	133
The Jacobean Compulsory Masque . . .	134
Nullity of the end without the Masque . . .	135
Shakespear anticipates Ibsen and rewrites Lear .	135
Variations of Masterpieces Legitimate . . .	137
Preface to GOOD KING CHARLES	153
Stage Chapters of History	153
Newton's Rectilinear Universe	154
Charles's Golden Days	155
The Future of Women in Politics	157
The Coupled Vote	157

GENEVA

ANOTHER POLITICAL EXTRAVAGANZA

XLV

1938

PREFACE

WHEN I had lived for 58 years free from the fear that war could come to my doorstep, the thing occurred. And when the war to end war had come to a glorious victory, it occurred again, worse than ever. I have now lived through two "world wars" without missing a meal or a night's sleep in my bed, though they have come near enough to shatter my windows, break in my door, and wreck my grandfather clock, keeping me for nine years of my life subject to a continual apprehension of a direct hit next time blowing me and my household to bits.

I cannot pretend that this troubled me much: people build houses and live on the slopes of Etna and Vesuvius and at the foot of Stromboli as cheerfully as on Primrose Hill. I was too old to be conscripted for military service; and the mathematical probabilities were enormously against a bomb coming my way; for at the worst of the bombardments only from ten to fifteen inhabitants of these islands were killed by air raids every day; and a dozen or so out of fortyfive millions is not very terrifying even when each of us knows that he or she is as likely as not to be one of the dozen. The risk of being run over by a motor bus, which townsmen run daily, is greater.

HOODWINKED HEROISM

It was this improbability which made pre-atomic air raiding futile as a means of intimidating a nation, and enabled the government of the raided nation to prevent the news of the damage reaching beyond its immediate neighborhood. One night early in the resumed war I saw, from a distance of 30 miles, London burning for three hours. Next morning I read in the newspapers that a bomb had fallen on the windowsill of a city office, and been extinguished before it exploded. Returning to London later on I found that half the ancient city had been levelled to the ground, leaving only St Paul's and a few church towers standing. The

3

wireless news never went beyond "some damage and a few casualties in Southern England" when in fact leading cities and seaports had been extensively wrecked. All threatening news was mentioned only in secret sessions of parliament, hidden under heavy penalties until after the victory. In 1941, after the Dunkirk rout, our position was described by the Prime Minister to the House of Commons in secret session as so desperate that if the enemy had taken advantage of it we should have been helplessly defeated; and it is now the fashion to descant dithyrambically on the steadfast heroism with which the nation faced this terrible emergency. As a matter of fact the nation knew nothing about it. Had we been told, the Germans would have overheard and rushed the threatened invasion they were bluffed into abandoning. Far from realizing our deadly peril, we were exulting in the triumph of our Air Force in "the Battle of Britain" and in an incident in South America in which three British warships drove one German one into the river Plate. Rather than be interned with his crew the German captain put to sea again against hopeless odds; scuttled his ship; and committed suicide. The British newspapers raved about this for weeks as a naval victory greater than Salamis, Lepanto, and Trafalgar rolled into one.

Later on our flight from Tobruk to the border of Egypt did not disturb us at home: it was reported as a trifling setback, whilst trumpery captures of lorries or motor bicycles by British patrols figured as victories. After major engagements German losses were given in figures: Allies' losses were not given at all, the impression left being that the Allies had killed or taken prisoner tens of thousands of Axis troops without suffering any casualties worth mentioning. Only by listening to the German broadcasts, similarly cooked, could the real facts and fortunes of the war be estimated. Of course the truth leaked out months later; but it produced only a fresh orgy of bragging about our heroic fortitude in the face of the deadly peril we knew nothing of.

All this was necessary and inevitable. It was dangerous to tell the truth about anything, even about the weather. The signposts on the roads had to be taken down and hidden lest they should help an invader to find his way. It was a crime to give an address with a date, or to scatter a few crumbs for the birds. And it was an act of heroic patriotism to drop a bomb weighing ten thousand pounds on dwellings full of women and children, or on crowded railway trains. Our bombing of foreign cities not only in Germany but in countries which we claimed to be "liberating" became so frightful that at last the word had to be given to two of our best broadcasters of war reports to excuse them on the ground that by shortening the war they were saving the lives of thousands of British soldiers.

Meanwhile nobody noticed how completely war, as an institution, had reduced itself to absurdity. When Germany annexed Poland in 1939, half of it was snatched out of her jaws by Soviet Russia. The British Commonwealth, having bound itself to maintain inviolate the frontiers of Poland as they were left after the fighting of 1914–18 with a Polish corridor cut right through Prussia to the Baltic, was committed to declare war on Germany and Russia simultaneously. But the British people and their rulers were in no mood to black out their windows and recommence the Four Years War in defence of this distant and foreign corridor. Being, as usual, unprepared for war, we tried to appease Germany and yet keep the peace with Soviet Russia.

ENGLAND FRIGHTENED AND GREAT

Nations should always be prepared for war, just as people with any property to leave should always have made their wills. But as most of them never do make their wills, and the rest seldom keep them revised and up to date, States, however militarist, are never fully prepared for war. England will do nothing outside her routine until she is thoroughly frightened; but when England is frightened England is capable of anything. Philip II of Spain frightened her. Louis XIV of France frightened her. Napoleon frightened her. Wilhelm II of the German Reich frightened her. But instead of frightening the wits out of her they frightened the

5

wits into her. She woke up and smashed them all. In vain did the Kaiser sing *Deutschland über Alles*, and Hitler claim that his people were the Herrenvolk created by God to rule the earth. The English were equally convinced that when Britain first at Heaven's command arose from out the azure main she was destined to rule the waves, and make the earth her footstool. This is so natural to Englishmen that they are unconscious of it, just as they cannot taste water because it is always in their mouths. Long before England first sang Rule Britannia at Cliveden she had annihilated Philip's Invincible Armada to the music of the winds and waves, and, after being defeated again and again by General Luxemburg, made hay of the French armies at Blenheim, Ramilies, and Malplaquet to the senseless gibberish of Lillibullero-bullenalah. She not only took on Hitler singlehanded without a word to the League of Nations nor to anyone else, but outfought him, outbragged him, outbullied him, outwitted him in every trick and turn of warfare, and finally extinguished him and hanged his accomplices.

England Secure and Lazy

The drawback to England's capacity for doing impossible things when in danger is her incapacity for doing possible things (except repeating what was done last time) in security. The prefabrication in England of harbors for France and planting them there as part of the baggage of the allied invading armies, was a feat which still seems incredible even now that it has actually been achieved; yet during the 20 years armistice England could not bridge the Severn below Gloucester, harness the Pentland tides, nor tap the volcanic fires of the earth's boiling core, much less mechanize the coalmines or even design an alphabet capable of saving billionsworth of British time, ink, and paper, by spelling English speech sounds unequivocally and economically. The moment the Cease Fire is sounded England forgets all the lessons of the war and proves the truth of Dr Inge's old comment on the Anglo-Irish situation as illustrating the difficulty of driving in double harness people who remember nothing with people who forget nothing. Still, as forgetful people who act in the present can master vindictive people who only brood on the past there is much to be said for England's full share of human thoughtlessness. It is sometimes better not to think at all than to think intensely and think wrong.

Statesmen who know no past history are dangerous because contemporary history cannot be ascertained. No epoch is intelligible until it is completed and can be seen in the distance as a whole, like a mountain. The victorious combatants in the battle of Hastings did not know that they were inaugurating feudalism for four centuries, nor the Red Roses on Bosworth Field and the Ironsides at Naseby know that they were exchanging it for Whig plutocracy. Historians and newspaper editors can see revolutions three centuries off but not three years off, much less three hours. Had Marx and Engels been contemporaries of Shakespear they could not have written the Communist Manifesto, and would probably have taken a hand, as Shakespear did, in the enclosure of common lands as a step forward in civilization.

HISTORY STOPS YESTERDAY: STATECRAFT WORKS BLINDFOLD

This is why history in our schools stops far short of the present moment, and why statesmen, though they can learn the lessons of history from books, must grope their way through daily emergencies within the limits of their ignorance as best they can. If their vision is vulgar and vindictive the guesses they make may be worse than the war. That vision has not widened nor that ability grown of late. But the perils of the situation have increased enormously. Men are what they were; but war has become many times more destructive, not of men, who can be replaced, but of the plant of civilization, the houses and factories, the railways and airways, the orchards and furrowed fields, and the spare subsistence which we call capital, without which civilized mankind would perish. Even the replacement of the slain is

7

threatened because the latest bombs are no respecters of sex; and where there are no women there will soon be no warriors. In some of the air raids, more women were killed than men. The turning point of the war was the siege of Stalingrad, written up by the newspapers more dithyrambically than any siege in history since the siege of Troy. But when the Greeks captured Troy they had the city for their pains as well as the glory. When the Red Army triumphed at Stalingrad they had nothing but festering corpses to bury, heaps of rubble to clear away, and a host of prisoners to feed. Meanwhile the British and American armies were "liberating" French cities, Dutch cities, Belgian cities, Italian cities: that is, they were destroying them exactly as they were destroying German cities, and having to house and feed their surviving inhabitants after wrecking their water mains, electric power stations, and railway communications. From the national point of view this was conquest, glory, patriotism, bravery, all claiming to be necessary for security. From the European wider angle it was folly and devilment, savagery and suicide. The ready money collected for it (wars cannot be fought on credit) was called Savings: a barefaced wicked lie. All the belligerents have been bled white, and will find, when they claim their "savings" back from their governments, that their Chancellors of the Exchequer will reply, like the juvenile spendthrift exhorted to pay his debts by Richelieu in Lytton's play, "Willingly, your Eminence: where shall I borrow the money?"; for not a farthing of it (say 12 millions shot away every day for six years) remains; and all of it that achieved its purpose of ruin has imposed on us the added burden of repairing what we have destroyed.

So much for England frightened into fighting. The question now is has war become frightful enough to frighten her out of it? In the last months the bombs launched by young British warriors from airplanes at the risk of their lives grew to such prodigious weight and destructiveness that they wrecked not merely houses but whole streets, and scattered blazing phosphorus and magnesium on such a scale that the victims, chiefly women with children who could not escape by flight as a few of the men did, were stifled by having nothing to breathe but white hot air, and then burnt to cinders and buried under the piles of rubble that had been their houses. We rained these monster bombs on Germany until the destruction of their railways and munition factories made retaliation in kind impossible. Our flame throwing from tanks finished the fugitives.

WE SPLIT THE ATOM

But the resources of decivilization were not exhausted. When we were exulting in our demolition of cities like Cologne and Hamburg we were very considerably frightened by the descent on London of new projectiles, unmanned yet aimed and guided, which demolished not only streets but districts. And when we and our allies "liberated" German-occupied territory (blowing its cities to smithereens largely in the process) we discovered that the manufacture of these new horrors had been planned for on such a scale that but for their capture in time the tables might have been turned on us with a vengeance.

But we had another card up our sleeve: this time a trump so diabolical that when we played it the war, which still lingered in Japan, was brought to an abrupt stop by an Anglo-American contrivance which may conceivably transform the globe into a cloud of flaming gas in which no form of life known to us could survive for a moment. That such explosions have visibly occurred on other stars (called novas) is vouched for by our astronomers, who have seen them with their naked eyes and studied their photographs and spectrographs for years past. When England and the United States of North America got ahead of Germany and Japan with this terrific weapon all their opponents at once surrendered at discretion.

AN AMORAL VICTORY

This time there could be no sustainable pretence of a moral victory, though plenty were made as usual; for nothing yet discovered has cured mankind of lying and boasting. It was what Wellington called Waterloo, a very near thing; for had the Germans not concentrated on the jet propulsion of pilotless aeroplanes instead of on the atomic bomb, they might have contrived it before us and made themselves masters of the situation if not of the world. They may yet cheapen and improve on it. Or they may discover a gas lighter than air, deadly but not destructive. And then where shall we be? Ethical victories endure. Discoveries cannot be guaranteed for five minutes.

Still, though the victory was not a triumph of Christianity it was a triumph of Science. American and British scientists, given *carte blanche* in the matter of expense, had concentrated on a romantic and desperate search for a means of harnessing the mysterious forces that mould and hold atoms into metals, minerals, and finally into such miracles as human geniuses, taking some grains of metal and a few salts purchasable at the nearest oilshop and fashioning with them the head of Shakespear, to say nothing of my own. It is already known that the energy that makes uranium out of molecules, escapes by slow radiation and both kills and cures living organisms, leaving behind it not radium but lead. If this disintegration could be speeded up to instantaneousness it would make a heat so prodigious that a couple of morsels of uranium dropped from a plane and timed to collide and disentegrate above a city could convert that city and its inhabitants into a heap of flaming gas in a fraction of a second. The experiment was tried on two Japanese cities. Four square miles of them vanished before the experimenters could say Jack Robinson.

There is no getting away from the fact that if another world war be waged with this new weapon there may be an end of our civilization and its massed populations. Even for those philosophers who are of opinion that this would not be any great loss there is a further possibility. An atomic bomb attached to a parachute and exploded in the air would devastate only as many square miles as it was meant to; but if it hung fire and exploded in the earth it might start a continuous process of disintegration in which our planet would become a *nova* to astronomers on Mars, blazing up and dimming out, leaving nothing of it and of us in the sky but a gaseous nebula.

It seems that if "the sport of kings" is to continue it must be fought under Queensberry rules classing atomic bombs with blows below the belt, and barring them. But it was the British refusal to bar aerial bombardment that made the air battles of the world war lawful; and these air battles had already reduced war to economic absurdity before the atomic bomb came into action. War had become logical: enemies were massacred or transported: wayleave was abolished. Thus the victors were left with the terror of their own discovery, and the vanquished with the hope that they may soon discover for themselves how to disintegrate uranium or perhaps some other element with ten times its energy. And two of the great allies, England and America, flatly refuse to share the secret of the new bomb with Russia, the third. Villages in India are still wiped out to "larn" their mostly harmless inhabitants not to snipe at British soldiers. The alarm is general: the cry of all hands, the triumphant even more than the subjugated, is that there must be an end of war. But all the other cries are as warlike as ever. The victorious Allies agree in demanding that Germans and Japanese must be treated as Catholic Ireland was treated by England in the seventeenth century.

Some of them are now consoling themselves with the hope that the atomic bomb has made war impossible. That hope has often been entertained before. Colonel Robinson, in *The Nineteenth Century And After*, has given a list of previous discoveries, dating back to B.C., which have developed the technique of killing from the single combats of the Trojan war, fought man to man, to artillery operations and air raids in which the combatants are hundreds of miles apart on the ground or thousands of feet up in the air dropping bombs and flying away at a speed of ten miles per second, never seeing one another nor the mischief they do. At every development it is complained that war is no longer justifiable as a test of heroic personal qualities, and demonstrated that it has become too ruinous to be tolerated as an institution.

War and imperialist diplomacy persist none the less.

Civilization's Will to Live Always Defeated by Democracy

Mankind, though pugnacious, yet has an instinct which checks it on the brink of selfdestruction. We are still too close to the time when men had to fight with wild beasts for their lives and with one another for their possessions, and when women had to choose fighters for their mates to protect them from robbery and rapine at their work as mothers, nurses, cooks, and kitchen gardeners. There are still places in the world where after tribal battles the victors eat the vanquished and the women share the feast with the warriors. In others foreign explorers, visitors, and passengers are killed as strangers. The veneer of civilization which distinguishes Europeans from these tribesmen and their wives is dangerously thin. Even English ladies and gentlemen "go Fantee" occasionally. Christmas cards will not prevent them from using atomic bombs if they are again frightened and provoked. But the magnitude of the new peril rouses that other instinct, stronger finally than pugnacity, that the race must not perish. This does not mean that civilization cannot perish. Civilizations have never finally survived: they have perished over and over again because they failed to make themselves worth their cost to the masses whom they enslaved. Even at home they could not master the art of governing millions of people for the common good in spite of people's inveterate objection to be governed at all. Law has been popularly known only as oppression and taxation, and politics as a clamor for less government and more liberty. That citizens get better value for the rates and taxes they pay than for most other items in their expenditure never occurs to them. They will pay a third of their weekly earnings or more to an idle landlord as if that were a law of nature; but a collection from them by the rate collector they resent as sheer robbery: the truth being precisely the reverse. They see nothing extravagant in basing democracy on an assumption that every adult native is

either a Marcus Aurelius or a combination of Saint Teresa and
Queen Elizabeth Tudor, supremely competent to choose any
tinker tailor soldier sailor or any goodlooking well dressed
female to rule over them. This insane prescription for perfect
democracy of course makes democracy impossible and the adventures of Cromwell, Napoleon, Hitler, and the innumerable conquistadores and upstart presidents of South American history inevitable. There never has been and never will be a government
which is both plebiscitary and democratic, because the plebs do
not want to be governed, and the plutocrats who humbug them,
though they are so far democratic that they must for their own
sakes keep their slaves alive and efficient, use their powers to
increase their revenues and suppress resistance to their appro-
priation of all products and services in excess of this minimum.
Substitute a plebeian government, and it can only carry on to the
same point with the same political machinery, except that the
plunder goes to the Trade Unions instead of to the plutocrats.
This may be a considerable advance; but when the plebeian government attempts to re-organize production collectively so as to
increase the product and bring the highest culture within the
reach of all who are capable of it, and make the necessary basic
material prosperity general and equal, the dread and hatred of
government as such, calling itself Liberty and Democracy, re-
asserts itself and stops the way. Only when a war makes collective organization compulsory on pain of slaughter, subjugation,
and nowadays extinction by bombs, jet propelled or atomic, is
any substantial advance made or men of action tolerated as Prime
Ministers. The first four years of world war forced us to choose
a man of action as leader; but when the armistice came we got
rid of him and had a succession of premiers who could be trusted
to do nothing revolutionary. Our ideal was "a commonplace type
with a stick and a pipe and a half bred black and tan." Even
Franklin Roosevelt won his first presidential election more by a
photograph of himself in the act of petting a baby than by his
political program, which few understood: indeed he only half
understood it himself. When Mr Winston Churchill, as a man

of action, had to be substituted for the *fainéants* when the war was resumed, his big cigars and the genial romantic oratory in which he glorified the war maintained his popularity until the war was over and he opened the General Election campaign by announcing a domestic policy which was a hundred years out of fashion, and promised nothing to a war weary proletariat eager for a Utopia in which there should be no military controls and a New World inaugurated in which everybody was to be both employed and liberated.

Mr Churchill at once shared the fate of Lloyd George; and the Utopians carried the day triumphantly. But the New World proved the same as the old one, with the same fundamental resistance to change of habits and the same dread of government interference surviving in the adult voter like the child's dread of a policeman.

It may be asked how it is that social changes do actually take place under these circumstances. The reply is that other circumstances create such emergencies, dangers, and hardships, that the very people who dread Government action are the first to run to the Government for a remedy, crying that "something must be done." And so civilization, though dangerously slowed down, forces its way piecemeal in spite of stagnant ignorance and selfishness.

Besides, there are always ancient constitutions and creeds to be reckoned with; and these are not the work of adult suffrage, but inheritances from feudal and ecclesiastical systems which had to provide law and order during the intervals between dominating personalities, when ordinary governments had to mark time by doing what was done last time until the next big boss came along and became a popular idol, worshipped at the polls by 99 per cent majorities.

All the evidence available so far is to the effect that since the dawn of history there has been no change in the natural political capacity of the human species. The comedies of Aristophanes and the Bible are at hand to convince anyone who doubts this. But this does not mean that enlightenment is impossible.

Without it our attempts at democracy will wreck our civilization as they have wrecked all the earlier civilizations we know of. The ancient empires were not destroyed by foreign barbarians. They assimilated them easily. They destroyed themselves: their collapse was the work of their own well meaning native barbarians. Yet these barbarians, like our own at present, included a percentage of thinkers who had their imaginations obsessed by Utopias in which perfectly wise governments were to make everybody prosperous and happy. Their old men saw visions and their young men dreamed dreams just as they do now. But they were not all such fools as to believe that their visions and dreams could be realized by Tom, Dick, and Harriet voting for Titus Oates, Lord George Gordon, Horatio Bottomley, Napoleon, or Hitler. My experience as an enlightener, which is considerable, is that what is wrong with the average citizen is not altogether deficient political capacity. It is largely ignorance of facts, creating a vacuum into which all sorts of romantic antiquarian junk and cast-off primitive religion rushes. I have to enlighten sects describing themselves as Conservatives, Socialists, Protestants, Catholics, Communists, Fascists, Fabians, Friends (Quakers), Ritualists, all bearing labels which none of them can define, and which indicate tenets which none of them accept as practical rules of life and many of them repudiate with abhorrence when they are presented without their labels. I was baptized as a member of the then established Protestant Episcopal Church in Ireland. My religious education left me convinced that I was entitled to call myself a Protestant because I believed that Catholics were an inferior species who would all go to hell when they died; and I daresay the Roman Catholic children with whom I was forbidden to play believed that the same eternity of torment awaited me in spite of Pope Pius the Ninth's humane instruction to them to absolve me on the plea of invincible ignorance. We were both taught to worship "a tenth rate tribal deity" of the most vindictive, jealous, and ruthless pugnacity, equally with his Christlike son. Just so today Conservatives know nothing of the Tory creed, but are convinced that the rulers of Russia are bloodstained tyrants, robbers and murderers, and their subjects slaves without rights or liberties. All good Russians believe equally that the capitalist rulers of the Western plutocracies are ruthless despots out for nothing but exploiting labor in pursuit of surplus value, as Marx called rent, interest, and profit. They group themselves in political parties and clubs in which none of them knows what he or she is talking about. Some of them have Utopian aspirations, and have read the prophets and sages, from Moses to Marx, and from Plato to Ruskin and Inge; but a question as to a point of existing law or the function of a County Council strikes them dumb. They are more dangerous than simpletons and illiterates because on the strength of their irrelevant schooling they believe themselves politically educated, and are accepted as authorities on political subjects accordingly.

Now this political ignorance and delusion is curable by simple instruction as to the facts without any increase of political capacity. I am ending as a sage with a very scrappy and partial knowledge of the world. I do not see why I should not have begun with it if I had been told it all to begin with: I was more capable of it then than I am now in my dotage. When I am not writing plays as a more or less inspired artist I write political schoolbooks in which I say nothing of the principles of Socialism or any other Ism (I disposed of all that long ago), and try to open my readers' eyes to the political facts under which they live. I cannot change their minds; but I can increase their knowledge. A little knowledge is a dangerous thing; but we must take that risk because a little is as much as our biggest heads can hold; and a citizen who knows that the earth is round and older than six thousand years is less dangerous than one of equal capacity who believes it is a flat groundfloor between a first floor heaven and a basement hell.

Incompetent Governments are the Cruellest

The need for confining authority to the instructed and capable has been demonstrated by terrible lessons daily for years past. As I write, dockfulls of German prisoners of war, male and

PREFACE

female, are being tried on charges of hideous cruelties perpetrated
by them at concentration camps. The witnesses describe the
horrors of life and death in them; and the newspapers class the
accused as fiends and monsters. But they also publish photographs of them in which they appear as ordinary human beings
who could be paralleled from any crowd or army.

These Germans had to live in the camps with their prisoners.
It must have been very uncomfortable and dangerous for them.
But they had been placed in authority and management, and
had to organize the feeding, lodging, and sanitation of more
and more thousands of prisoners and refugees thrust upon them
by the central government. And as they were responsible for the
custody of their prisoners they had to be armed to the teeth
and their prisoners completely disarmed. Only eminent leadership, experience, and organizing talent could deal with such a
situation.

Well, they simply lacked these qualities. They were not fiends
in human form; but they did not know what to do with the
thousands thrown on their care. There was some food; but they
could not distribute it except as rations among themselves. They
could do nothing with their prisoners but overcrowd them within
any four walls that were left standing, lock them in, and leave
them almost starving to die of typhus. When further overcrowd-
ing became physically impossible they could do nothing with
their unwalled prisoners but kill them and burn the corpses they
could not bury. And even this they could not organize frankly
and competently: they had to make their victims die of illusage
instead of by military law. Under such circumstances any mis-
cellaneous collection of irresistibly armed men would be demoralized; and the natural percentage of callous toughs among them
would wallow in cruelty and in the exercise of irresponsible
authority for its own sake. Man beating is better sport than bear
baiting or cock fighting or even child beating, of which some
sensational English cases were in the papers at home at the time.
Had there been efficient handling of the situation by the authorities (assuming this to have been possible) none of these atrocities

would have occurred. They occur in every war when the troops get out of hand.

HITLER

The German government was rotten at the centre as well as at the periphery. The Hohenzollern monarchy in Germany, with an enormous military prestige based on its crushing defeat of the Bonapartist French Army in 1871 (I was fifteen at the time, and remember it quite well) was swept away in 1918 by the French Republic. The rule of the monarch was succeeded by the rule of anybody chosen by everybody, supposed, as usual, to secure the greatest common measure of welfare, which is the object of democracy, but which really means that a political career is open to any adventurer. It happened that in Munich in 1930 there was a young man named Hitler who had served in the Four Years War. Having no special military talent he had achieved no more as a soldier than the Iron Cross and the rank of corporal. He was poor and what we call no class, being a Bohemian with artistic tastes but neither training nor talent enough to succeed as an artist, and was thus hung up between the bourgeoisie for which he had no income and the working class for which he had no craft. But he had a voice and could talk, and soon became a beer cellar orator who could hold his audience. He joined a cellar debating society (like our old Coger's Hall) and thereby brought its numbers up to seven. His speeches soon attracted considerable reinforcements and established him as a leading spirit. Much of what he spouted was true. As a soldier he had learnt that disciplined men can make short work of mobs; that party parliaments on the British model neither could nor would abolish the poverty that was so bitter to him; that the Treaty of Versailles under which Germany, defeated and subjected far beyond the last penny she could spare, could be torn up clause by clause by anyone with a big enough army to intimidate the plunderers; and that Europe was dominated economically by a plutocracy of financiers who had got the whip hand even of the employers. So far he was on solid ground, with unquestionable facts to support him. But he mixed the facts up with fancies such as that all plutocrats are Jews; that the Jews are an accursed race who should be exterminated as such; that the Germans are a chosen race divinely destined to rule the world; and that all she needs to establish her rule is an irresistible army. These delusions were highly flattering to Hans, Fritz, and Gretchen at large as well as to the beer drinkers in the cellar; and when an attempt was made to silence the new Hitlerites by hired gangsters, Hitler organized a bodyguard for himself so effectively that the opposition was soon sprawling in the street.

With this stock in trade Hitler found himself a born leader, and, like Jack Cade, Wat Tyler, Essex under Elizabeth Tudor, Emmet under Dublin Castle, and Louis Napoleon under the Second Republic, imagined he had only to appear in the streets with a flag to be acclaimed and followed by the whole population. He tried the experiment with a general from the Four Years War at his side and such converts to his vogue and eloquence as his beer cellar orations had made. With this nucleus he marched through the streets. A rabble gathered and followed to see the fun, as rabbles always will in cities. In London I have seen thousands of citizens rushing to see why the others were rushing, and to find out why. It looked like a revolutionary *émeute*. On one occasion it was a runaway cow. On another it was Mary Pickford, "World's Sweetheart" of the old silent films, driving to her hotel in a taxi.

For a moment Hitler may have fancied that a success like that of Mussolini's march to Rome (he went by train) was within his grasp. He had the immediate precedent of Kurt Eisner's successful *Putsch* to encourage him. But Eisner was not resisted. When Hitler and his crowd came face to face with the Government troops they did not receive him as the grognards of the Bourbon army received Napoleon on his return from Elba. They opened fire on him. His rabble melted and fled. He and General Ludendorff had to throw themselves flat on the pavement to avoid the bullets. He was imprisoned for eight months for his escapade, not having frightened the Government enough to be considered worth killing as Cade, Tyler, and Essex were killed. In prison, he and his companion-secretary Hess, wrote a book entitled *Mein Kampf* (My Struggle, My Program, My Views or what you please).

Like Louis Napoleon he had now learnt his lesson: namely, that *Putsches* are a last desperate method, not a first one, and that adventurers must come to terms with the captains of finance and industry, the bankers, and the Conservatives who really control the nations wherever the people choose what rulers they please, before he can hope to be accepted by them as a figure head. Hitler had sufficient histrionic magnetism to strike this bargain even to the extent of being made perpetual chancellor of the German Realm with more than royal honors, though his whole stock-in-trade was a brazen voice and a doctrine made up of scraps of Socialism, mortal hatred of the Jews, and complete contempt for pseudo-democratic parliamentary mobocracy.

Pseudo Messiah and Madman

So far he was the creature and tool of the plutocracy. But the plutocracy had made a bad bargain. The moment it made Hitler a figure head, popular idolatry made a prophet and a hero of him, and gave him a real personal power far in excess of that enjoyed by any commercial magnate. He massacred all his political rivals not only with impunity but with full parliamentary approval. Like St Peter on a famous earlier occasion the German people cried "Thou art the Christ", with the same result. Power and worship turned Hitler's head; and the national benefactor who began by abolishing unemployment, tearing up the Treaty of Versailles, and restoring the selfrespect of sixty millions of his fellow countrymen, became the mad Messiah who, as lord of a Chosen Race, was destined to establish the Kingdom of God on earth—a German kingdom of a German God—by military conquest of the rest of mankind. Encouraged by spineless attempts to appease him he attacked Russia, calculating that as a crusader against Soviet Communism he would finally be joined by the whole Capitalist West.

But the Capitalist West was much too shortsighted and jealous to do anything so intelligent. It shook hands with Stalin and stabbed Hitler in the back. He put up a tremendous fight, backed by his fellow adventurers in Italy and Spain; but, being neither a Julius Cæsar nor a Mahomet, he failed to make his initial conquests welcome and permanent by improving the condition of the inhabitants. On the contrary he made his name execrated wherever he conquered. The near West rose up against him, and was joined by the mighty far West of America. After twelve years of killing other people he had to kill himself, and leave his accomplices to be hanged.

The moral for conquerors of empires is that if they substitute savagery for civilization they are doomed. If they substitute civilization for savagery they make good, and establish a legitimate title to the territories they invade. When Mussolini invaded Abyssinia and made it possible for a stranger to travel there without being killed by the native Danakils he was rendering the same service to the world as we had in rendering by the same methods (including poison gas) in the north west provinces of India, and had already completed in Australia, New Zealand, and the Scottish Highlands. It was not for us to throw stones at Musso, and childishly refuse to call his puppet king Emperor. But we did throw stones, and made no protest when his star was eclipsed and he was scandalously lynched in Milan. The Italians had had enough of him; for he, too, was neither a Cæsar nor a Mahomet.

Contemplating the careers of these two poor devils one cannot help asking was their momentary grandeur worth while? I pointed out once that the career of Bourrienne, Napoleon's valet-secretary for a while, was far longer, more fortunate, easier and more comfortable in every commonsense way, than that of Napoleon, who, with an interval of one year, was Emperor for fourteen years. Mussolini kept going for more than twenty. So did Louis Napoleon, backed by popular idolization of his uncle, who had become a national hero, as Hitler will become in Germany presently. Whether these adventurers would have been happier in obscurity hardly matters; for they were kept too busy to bother themselves about happiness; and the extent to which they enjoyed their activities and authority and deification is unknown. They were finally scrapped as failures and nuisances, though they all began by effecting some obvious reforms over which party parliaments had been boggling for centuries. Such successes as they had were reactions from the failures of the futile parliamentary talking shops, which were themselves reactions from the bankruptcies of incompetent monarchs, both mobs and monarchs being products of political idolatry and ignorance. The wider the suffrage, the greater the confusion. "Swings to the Left" followed by "swings to the Right" kept the newspapers and the political windbags amused and hopeful. We are still humbugging ourselves into the belief that the swings to the Left are democratic and those to the Right imperial. They are only swings from failure to failure to secure substantial democracy, which means impartial government for the good of the governed by qualified rulers. Popular anarchism defeats them all.

Upstart dictators and legitimate monarchs have not all been personal failures. From Pisistratus to Porfirio, Ataturk, and Stalin, able despots have made good by doing things better and much more promptly than parliaments. They have kept their heads and known their limitations. Ordinary mortals like Nero, Paul of Russia, our James the Second, Riza Khan in Iran, and some of the small fry of degenerate hereditary tribal chiefs like Theebaw in Burma have gone crazy and become worse nuisances than mad dogs. Lord Acton's dictum that power corrupts gives no idea of the extent to which flattery, deference, power, and apparently unlimited money, can upset and demoralize simpletons who in their proper places are good fellows enough. To them the exercise of authority is not a heavy and responsible job which strains their mental capacity and industry to the utmost, but a delightful sport to be indulged for its own sake, and asserted and reasserted by cruelty and monstrosity.

PREFACE

DEMOCRACY MISUNDERSTOOD

Democracy and equality, without which no State can achieve the maximum of beneficence and stability, are still frightfully misunderstood and confused. Popular logic about them is, like most human logic, mere association of ideas, or, to call it by the new name invented by its monstrous product Pavlov, conditional reflex. Government of the people for the people, which is democracy, is supposed to be achievable through government by the people in the form of adult suffrage, which is finally so destructive of democracy that it ends in a reaction into despot-idolatry. Equality is supposed to mean similarity of political talent, which varies as much as musical or mathematical or military capacity from individual to individual, from William Rufus to Charles II, from Nero to Marcus Aurelius, from Monmouth and Prince Charlie to Alexander and Napoleon. Genuine democracy requires that the people shall choose their rulers, and, if they will, change them at sufficient intervals; but the choice must be limited to the public spirited and politically talented, of whom Nature always provides not only the necessary percentage, but superfluity enough to give the people a choice. Equality, which in practice means intermarriageability, is based on the hard facts that the greatest genius costs no more to feed and clothe and lodge than the narrowest minded duffer, and at a pinch can do with less, and that the most limited craftsman or laborer who can do nothing without direction from a thinker, is, if worth employing at all, as necessary and important socially as the ablest director. Equality between them is either equality of income and of income only or an obvious lie.

Equality of income is practicable enough: any sporting peer with his mind bounded by the racecourse can dine on equal terms with an astronomer whose mental domain is the universe. Their children are intermarriageable without misalliance. But when we face the democratic task of forming panels of the persons eligible for choice as qualified rulers we find first that none of our tests are trustworthy or sufficient, and finally that we have no qualified

23

rulers at all, only bosses. The rule of vast commonwealths is beyond the political capacity of mankind at its ablest. Our Solons, Cæsars and Washingtons, Lenins, Stalins and Nightingales, may be better than their best competitors; but they die in their childhood as far as statesmanship is concerned, playing golf and tennis and bridge, smoking tobacco and drinking alcohol as part of their daily diet, hunting, shooting, coursing, reading tales of murder and adultery and police news, wearing fantastic collars and cuffs, with the women on high heels staining their nails, daubing their lips, painting their faces: in short, doing all sorts of things that are child's play and not the exercises or recreations of statesmen and senators. Even when they have read Plato, the Gospels, and Karl Marx, and to that extent know what they have to do, they do not know how to do it, and stick in the old grooves for want of the new political technique which is evolving under pressure of circumstances in Russia. Their attempts at education and schooling end generally in boy farms and concentration camps with flogging blocks, from which the prisoners when they adolesce emerge as trained and prejudiced barbarians with a hatred of learning and discipline, and a dense ignorance of what life is to nine tenths of their compatriots.

"GREAT MEN"

Here and there, however, cases of extraordinary faculty shew what mankind is capable of within its existing framework. In mathematics we have not only Newtons and Einsteins, but obscure illiterate "lightning calculators," to whom the answers to arithmetical and chronological problems that would cost me a long process of cyphering (if I could solve them at all) are instantly obvious. In grammar and scripture I am practically never at a loss; but I have never invented a machine, though I am built like engineers who, though they are never at a loss with machinery, are yet so unable to put descriptions of their inventions into words that they have to be helped out by patent agents of no more than common literary ability. Mozart, able in his infancy to do anything he pleased in music, from the simplest sonata to the most elaborate symphony or from the subtlest comic or tragic opera to fugal settings of the Mass, resembled millions of Austrians who could not to save their lives hum a line of *Deutschland über Alles* nor compose a bar of music playable by one finger, much less concerted for 30 different orchestral instruments. In philosophy we spot Descartes and Kant, Swift and Schopenhauer, Butler and Bergson, Richard Wagner and Karl Marx, Blake and Shelley, Ruskin and Morris, with dozens of uncrucified Jesuses and saintly women in every generation, look like vindictive retaliators, pugnacious sportsmen, and devout believers in ancient tribal idols. The geniuses themselves are steeped in vulgar superstitions and prejudices: Bunyan and Newton astound us not only by their specific talents but by their credulity and Bible fetichism. We prate gravely of their achievements and faculties as attainments of mankind, as if every Italian were Michael Angelo and Raphael and Dante and Galileo rolled into one, every German a Goethe, and every Englishman a compound of Shakespear and Eddington. Of this folly we have had more than enough. The apparent freaks of nature called Great Men mark not human attainment but human possibility and hope. They prove that though we in the mass are only child Yahoos it is possible for creatures built exactly like us, bred from our unions and developed from our seeds, to reach the heights of these towering heads. For the moment, however, when we are not violently persecuting them we are like Goldsmith's villagers, wondering how their little heads can carry all they know and ranking them as passing rich on four hundred pounds a year when they are lucky enough to get paid for their work instead of persecuted.

We Can and Must Live Longer

Considering now that I have lived fourteen years longer than twice as long as Mozart or Mendelssohn, and that within my experience men and women, especially women, are younger at fifty than they were at thirty in the middle of the nineteenth century, it is impossible to resist at least a strong suspicion that the term of human life cannot be fixed at seventy years or indeed fixed at all. If we master the art of living instead of digging our graves with our teeth as we do at present we may conceivably reach a point at which the sole cause of death will be the fatal accident which is statistically inevitable if we live long enough. In short, it is not proved that there is such a thing as natural death: it is life that is natural and infinite.

How long, then, would it take us to mature into competent rulers of great modern States instead of, as at present, trying vainly to govern empires with the capacity of village headmen. In my Methuselah cycle I put it at three hundred years: a century of childhood and adolescence, a century of administration, and a century of oracular senatorism.

But nobody can foresee what periods my imaginary senators will represent. The pace of evolutionary development is not constant: the baby in the womb recapitulates within a few months an evolution which our biologists assure us took millions of years to acquire. The old axiom that Nature never jumps has given way to a doubt whether Nature is not an incorrigible kangaroo. What is certain is that new faculties, however long they may be dreamt of and desired, come at last suddenly and miraculously like the balancing of the bicyclist, the skater, and the acrobat. The development of homo sapiens into a competent political animal may occur in the same way.

The Next Discovery

Meanwhile here we are, with our incompetence armed with atomic bombs. Now power civilizes and develops mankind, though not without having first been abused to the point of wiping out entire civilizations. If the atomic bomb wipes out ours we shall just have to begin again. We may agree on paper not to use it as it is too dangerous and destructive; but tomorrow may see the discovery of that poisonous gas lighter than air and capable before it evaporates through the stratosphere of killing

PREFACE

all the inhabitants of a city without damaging its buildings or
sewers or water supplies or railways or electric plants. Victory
might then win cities if it could repopulate them soon enough,
whereas atomic bombing leaves nothing for anyone, victor or
vanquished. It is conceivable even that the next great invention
may create an overwhelming interest in pacific civilization and
wipe out war. You never can tell.

Ayot Saint Lawrence
1945

GENEVA

ACT I

*A May morning in Geneva, in a meagrely equipped office with
secondhand furniture, much the worse for wear, consisting of a dingy
writing table with an old typewriter on it in the middle of the room,
a revolving chair for the typist, an old press which has not been
painted or varnished for many years, and three chairs for visitors
against the wall near the door. The stove, an undecorated iron one of
the plainest sort, designed rather for central heating in a cellar than
for an inhabited apartment, is to the typist's right, the press facing it
at the opposite side on the typist's left. The door is beside the press.
The window is behind the typist.*

*A young Englishwoman is seated in the revolving chair. From the
state of the table she seems to have been working at the compilation
of a card index, as there are cards scattered about, and an open case
to put them in, also a pile of foolscap from which she has been copying
the card inscriptions. But at present she is not at work. She is smoking and reading an illustrated magazine with her heels on the table.
A thermos flask, a cup and saucer, and a packet of cigarettes are
beside her on a sliding shelf drawn out from the table. She is a self-
satisfied young person, fairly attractive and well aware of it. Her
dress, though smartly cut, is factory made; and her speech and
manners are London suburban.*

*Somebody knocks at the door. She hastily takes her heels off the
table; jumps up; throws her cigarette into the stove; snatches the
things off the sliding shelf and hides them in the press; finally resumes
her seat and looks as busy as possible.*

THE TYPIST [*calling*]. Entrez, s'il vous plaît.

*A middle-aged gentleman of distinguished appearance, with a
blond beard and moustache, top hatted, frock coated, and gloved,
comes in. He contemplates the room and the young woman with
evident surprise.*

HE. Pardon, mademoiselle: I seek the office of the International

29

Committee for Intellectual Co-operation.

SHE. Yes: thats quite all right. Take a seat, please.

HE [*hesitating*] Thank you; but my business is of great importance: I must see your chief. This is not the head office, is it?

SHE. No: the head office is in Paris. This is all there is here. Not much of a place, is it?

HE. Well, I must confess that after visiting the magnificent palace of the International Labor Office and the new quarters of the Secretariat, I expected to find the Committee for Intellectual Co-operation lodged in some imposingly monumental structure.

SHE. Oh, isnt it scandalous? I wish youd write to the papers about it. Do please sit down.

HE. Thank you. [*He is about to take one of the chairs from the wall*].

SHE. No, not that one: one of its legs isnt safe: it's there only for show. Will you please take the other?

HE. Can the Committee not afford you a new chair?

SHE. It cant afford anything. The intellectual budget is the interest on two million paper francs that one is glad to get three-pence for: they used to be tuppence. So here I am in one rotten little room on the third floor of a tumbledown old house full of rats. And as to my salary I should be ashamed to name it. A Church charity would be ashamed to pay it.

HE. I am utterly astounded. [*He takes a sound chair from the wall; places it near the office table; and sits down*]. The intellectual co-operation of sixty nations must be a very extensive business. How can it possibly be conducted in this bare little place?

SHE. Oh, I conduct it all right. It's never in a hurry, you know.

HE. But really—pardon me if I am taking too much of your time—

SHE. Oh, thats quite all right. I'm only too glad to have a bit of chat with somebody. Nobody ever comes in here: people dont seem to know that the Committee exists.

HE. Do you mean that you have nothing to do?

SHE. Oh no. I tell you I have to do all the intellectual co-operation. I have to do it singlehanded too: I havnt even an office boy to help me. And theres no end to the work. If it werent, as I say, that theres no hurry about it, I should never get through it. Just look here at this nice little job theyve given me! A card index of all the universities with the names and addresses of their bursars and their vice chancellors. And there is a correspondence about the protection of professional titles that takes up half my time.

HE. And do they call that intellectual co-operation?

SHE. Well, what else would you call it?

HE. It is mere compilation. How are the intellectual giants who form your committee bringing the enormous dynamic force of their brains, their prestige, their authority, to bear on the destinies of the nations? What are they doing to correct the mistakes of our ignorant politicians?

SHE. Well, we have their names on our notepaper, you know. What more can they do? You cant expect them to sit in this little hole talking to people. I have never seen one of them.

HE. So they leave it all to you?

SHE. Oh, I wouldnt say all. Theres the head office in Paris, you know, and some offices in other countries. I suppose they do their bit; and anyhow we all do a lot of writing to oneanother. But I must say it's as dull as ditchwater. When I took the job I thought it was going to be interesting, and that I'd see all the great men. I am ambitious, you know: I won a London County Council scholarship. I wanted a job that would draw out my faculties, if you understand me. But theres nothing to do here that any common typist couldnt do. And nobody ever comes near the place. Oh, it is dull.

HE. Shall I give you an interesting job, mademoiselle? One that would get you appreciated and perhaps a little talked about?

SHE. I'll just jump at it—if it is all right.

HE. How all right?

SHE. Morally, you know. No hanky panky. I am respectable; and I mean to keep respectable.

HE. I pledge you my word that my intentions are completely honorable.

SHE. Well, what about the pay? And how long will the job

31

last? The work here may be dull; and the pay is just short of starvation; but I have the appointment for 25 years certain; and I darent give it up for anything chancy. You dont know what it is to be out of a job.

HE. I shall not ask you to give up your post here. On the contrary, it is essential that you should keep it. But I think I can make it more interesting for you. And I should of course make you a suitable present if at any time you found that your emoluments here were insufficient.

SHE. They are. But I mustnt take bribes, you know.

HE. You need not. Any friendly service I may be able to render will be entirely independent of your official work here.

SHE. Look here: I dont half like this. Whats the game?

THE JEW. I must begin by explaining that I am a Jew.

SHE. I dont believe you. You dont look like one.

THE JEW. I am not a primitive Hittite. You cannot draw my nose in profile by simply writing down the number six. My hair is not black, nor do I wear it in excessively oiled ringlets. I have all the marks of a German blond. German is my native language: in fact I am in every sense a German. But I worship in the synagogue; and when I worship I put my hat on, whereas a German takes it off. On this ground they class me as a non-Aryan, which is nonsense, as there is no such thing as an Aryan.

SHE. I'm so glad to hear you say that. The Germans here say that I am an Aryan; but I tell them I am nothing of the kind: I'm an Englishwoman. Not a common Englishwoman, of course: I'm a Camberwell woman; and though the west end may turn up its nose at Camberwell, Camberwell is better than Peckham any day in the week.

THE JEW. No doubt. I have not been there.

SHE. I never could abide Peckham people. They are disliked everywhere. It's instinctive, somehow. Havnt you noticed it?

THE JEW. All peoples are disliked in the lump. The English are disliked: the Germans are disliked: the French are disliked. The Protestants are disliked; and all their hundreds of sects dislike one-another. So are the Catholics, the Jesuits, the Freemasons. You tell me that the inhabitants of Peckham are disliked: no doubt they deserve it.

SHE. They do.

THE JEW. Some of the greatest men have disliked the human race. But for Noah, its Creator would have drowned it. Can we deny that He had good reasons for disliking it? Can I deny that there are good reasons for disliking Jews? On the contrary, I dislike most of them myself.

SHE. Oh, dont say that. Ive known lots of quite nice Jews. What I say is why pick on the Jews, as if they were any worse than other people?

THE JEW. That is precisely my business here today. I find you most intelligent—most sympathetic.

SHE. Come now! none of that. Whats the game?

THE JEW. I have been assaulted, plundered, and driven from my native soil by its responsible ruler. I, as a ruined individual, can do nothing. But the League of Nations can act through its Committee for Intellectual Co-operation. The Committee can act through the permanent court of International Justice at the Hague, which is also an organ of the League. My business here is to ask the Committee to apply to the court for a warrant against the responsible ruler. I charge him with assault and battery, burglary—

SHE. Burglary! Did they break into your house?

THE JEW. I cannot speak of it. Everything I treasured. Wrecked! Smashed! Defiled! Never will I forgive: never can I forget.

SHE. But why didnt you call the police?

THE JEW. Mademoiselle: the police did it. The Government did it. The Dictator who controls the police is responsible before Europe! before civilization! I look to the League of Nations for redress. It alone can call unrighteous rulers to account. The initiative must be taken by its Committee for Intellectual Co-operation: that is, for the moment, by you, mademoiselle.

SHE. But what can I do? I cant go out and collar your unrighteous ruler.

THE JEW. No, mademoiselle. What you must do is to write to

33

the International Court, calling on it to issue a warrant for the arrest of my oppressor on a charge of attempting to exterminate a section of the human race.

SHE. Well, it seems like taking a lot on myself, doesnt it?

THE JEW. Not at all. You will be acting, not for yourself, but for the intellect of Europe. I assure you it is the correct course.

SHE. But I'm not sure that I know how to write a letter with all those police court things in it.

THE JEW. It is quite simple. But if you will allow me I will draft the letter for you.

SHE. Oh I say, Mister Jew, I dont like this.

THE JEW. Then write the letter yourself. I am sure you will do it perfectly. It will be an opportunity for you to shew the Committee what you are made of.

SHE. Well, look here. I have a particular friend, an American journalist. Would you mind if I shewed him your draft before I send it off?

THE JEW. An American journalist! Excellent, excellent. By all means submit my draft to him and ask him to correct it if necessary. My English is German English, and may leave something to be desired.

SHE. Yes: thatll be splendid. Thank you ever so much.

THE JEW. Not at all. [*Rising*] I will bring the draft in the course of the afternoon. Au revoir, then.

SHE. Au revoir.

They shake hands cordially. Meanwhile the door is opened by an obstinate-looking middle-aged man of respectable but not aristocratic appearance, speaking English like a shopkeeper from the provinces, or perhaps, by emigration, the dominions.

NEWCOMER. Can I see the boss, miss?

SHE [*with haughty nonchalance in a would-be distinguished accent startlingly unlike her unaffected deference to the gentlemanlike Jew*] I am sorry. Our chiefs are scattered over Europe, very eminent persons, you know. Can I do anything?

NEWCOMER [*looking at the Jewish gentleman*] I'm afraid I'm interrupting.

THE JEW. Not at all: my business is finished. [*Clicking his heels and bowing*] Until the afternoon, mademoiselle. Monsieur— [*He bows to the newcomer, and goes out*].

SHE. You can sit down.

NEWCOMER. I will keep you only a minute, miss. [*He sits and takes out some notes he has made*].

SHE. Be as quick as you can, please. I am busy this morning.

NEWCOMER. Yes: you have the brainwork of the world on your shoulders here. When any of the nations goes off the rails, this is the place to have it put back. Thats so, isnt it?

SHE [*with aplomb*] Undoubtedly.

NEWCOMER. Well, it's like this. In my country weve had an election. We thought it lay between our usual people: the National Party and the Labor Party; but it was won by an upstart kind of chap who called himself a Business Democrat. He got a clear majority over the Nationals and the Labor Party; so it was up to him to form a Government. And what do you suppose the fellow did when he became Prime Minister?

SHE [*bored*] Cant imagine, I'm sure.

NEWCOMER. He said he had been returned to power as a business democrat, and that the business part of it meant that he was not to waste time, but to get the nation's work done as quickly as possible.

SHE. Quite, quite. Nothing to complain of in that, is there?

NEWCOMER. Wait. I'm going to astonish you. He said the country had decided by its democratic vote that it should be governed by him and his party for the next five years, and that no opposition could be tolerated. He said the defeated minority must step down and out instead of staying there to obstruct and delay and annoy him. Of course the Opposition werent going to stand that: they refused to leave the Chamber. So he adjourned the House until next day; and when the Opposition turned up the police wouldnt let them in. Most of them couldnt get as far as the doors, because the Prime Minister had organized a body of young men called the Clean Shirts, to help the police.

SHE. Well?

35

NEWCOMER. Well!!! Is that all you have to say to me?

SHE. What do you expect me to say? It seems all right to me. It's what any man of business would do. Wouldnt you?

NEWCOMER. Of course I should do it in business; but this is politics.

SHE. Well! arnt politics business?

NEWCOMER. Of course theyre not. Just the opposite. You know that, dont you?

SHE. Oh, quite, quite.

NEWCOMER. What I say is, business methods are business methods; and parliamentary methods are parliamentary methods.

SHE [*brightly*] "And never the twain shall meet," as Kipling puts it.

NEWCOMER. No: I dont hold with Kipling. Too imperialist for me. I'm a democrat.

SHE. But not a business democrat, if I follow you.

NEWCOMER. No, no: not a business democrat. A proper democrat. I'm all for the rights of minorities.

SHE. But I always thought that democracy meant the right of the majority to have its way.

NEWCOMER. Oh no: that would be the end of all liberty. You have nothing to say against liberty, I hope.

SHE. I have nothing to say against anything. I am not here to discuss politics with everyone who walks into my office. What do you want?

NEWCOMER. Well, heres a Prime Minister committing high treason and rebellion and breach of privilege; levying armed forces against the Crown; violating the constitution; setting up a dictatorship and obstructing the lawful ingress of duly elected members to the legislative Chamber. Whats to be done with him?

SHE. Quite simple. I shall apply to the International Court at the Hague for a warrant for his arrest on all those charges. You can look in at the end of the week, when the answer from the Hague will have arrived. You will supply me with the man's name and the particulars—

NEWCOMER [*putting his notes on the table before her*] Here they are, miss. By Gosh, thats a splendid idea.

SHE. Thank you. That is all. Good morning.

NEWCOMER [*rising and going to the door*] Well, you know how to do business here: theres no mistake about that. Good morning, miss.

As he is going out the door opens in his face; and a widow comes in: a Creole lady of about forty, with the remains of a gorgeous and opulent southern beauty. Her imposing style and dress at once reduce the young lady of the office to nervous abjection.

THE WIDOW. Are you the president of the Intellectual Cooperation Committee of the League of Nations?

NEWCOMER. No, maam. This lady will do all you require [*he goes out*].

THE WIDOW. Am I to take that seriously? My business is important. I came here to place it before a body of persons of European distinction. I am not prepared to discuss it with an irresponsible young woman.

SHE. I am afraid I dont look the part, do I? I am only the staff, so to speak. Still, anything I can do I shall be most happy.

THE WIDOW. But where are your chiefs?

SHE. Ah, there you have me. They live all over the world, as you might say.

THE WIDOW. But do they not come here to attend to their business?

SHE. Well, you see, there is really nothing for them to attend to. It's only intellectual business, you know.

THE WIDOW. But do they not take part in the Assembly of the League?

SHE. Some of them have been, once. Nobody ever goes to the Assembly twice if they can help it.

THE WIDOW. But I must see somebody—somebody of importance.

SHE. Well, I'm sorry. Theres nobody but me. I can do whatever is necessary. Did you by any chance want a warrant from the International Court at the Hague?

THE WIDOW. Yes: that is exactly what I do want. A death warrant.

SHE. A what?!!

THE WIDOW. A death warrant. I will sit down, if you will allow me.

SHE. Oh please—

THE WIDOW [*sitting down*] Do you see that? [*She takes an automatic pistol from her bag, and throws it on the table*].

SHE. Oh, thats not allowed in Geneva. Put it up quick. Somebody might come in.

THE WIDOW [*replacing the pistol in her bag*] This is the most absurd place. In my country everybody carries a gun.

SHE. What country, may I ask?

THE WIDOW. The Republic of the Earthly Paradise.

SHE. My mother has a school prize called The Earthly Paradise. What a coincidence!

THE WIDOW. Then you know that the Earthly Paradise is one of the leading States in the world in culture and purity of race, and that its capital contained more than two thousand white inhabitants before the last revolution. There must be still at least fifteen hundred left.

SHE. But is it a member of the League?

THE WIDOW. Of course it is. And allow me to remind you that by its veto it can put a stop to all action by the League until its affairs are properly attended to.

SHE. Can it? I didnt know that. Of course I shall be only too pleased to apply for a warrant; but I'd rather not call it a death warrant. Death warrant sounds a bit thick, if you understand me. All you need do is to give me a list of the charges you make against—well, against whoever it is.

THE WIDOW. Simply one charge of the wilful murder of my late husband by the President of the Earthly Paradise.

SHE. Surely if a president kills anyone it's an execution; but if anyone kills a president it's an assassination.

THE WIDOW. And is not that just the state of things the League of Nations is here to put a stop to?

SHE. Oh, dont ask me. All I know about the League is that it pays my salary. Just give me the gentleman's name and who he murdered. Murder stories are thrillingly interesting.

THE WIDOW. You would not think so if you lived in a country where there is at least one murder in every family.

SHE. What an awful place! Is it as barbarous as that?

THE WIDOW. Barbarous! Certainly not. The Earthly Paradise is the most civilized country in the world. Its constitution is absolutely democratic: every president must swear to observe it in every particular. The Church is abolished: no moral authority is recognized except that of the people's will. The president and parliament are elected by adult suffrage every two years. So are all the judges and all the officials, even the road sweepers. All these reforms, which have made The Earthly Paradise the most advanced member of the League of Nations, were introduced by my late husband the sixth president. He observed the constitution strictly. The elections were conducted with absolute integrity. The ballot was secret. The people felt free for the first time in their lives. Immediately after the elections the budget was passed providing for two years. My husband then prorogued the Parliament until the end of that period, and governed the country according to his own ideas whilst the people enjoyed themselves and made money in their own ways without any political disturbances or arguments. He was re-elected three times, and is now known in the Paradise as the father of his country.

SHE. But you said he was murdered, and that the president murdered him. How could that be if he was the president? He couldnt murder himself.

THE WIDOW. Unhappily he had certain weaknesses. He was an affectionate husband: I may even say an uxorious one; but he was very far from being faithful to me. When he abolished the Church he would have abolished marriage also if public opinion would have stood for it. And he was much too indulgent to his enemies. Naturally, whenever he won an election his opponent raised an army and attempted a revolution; for we are a high spirited race and do not submit to the insult of defeat at the polls. But my husband was a military genius. He had no difficulty in putting down these revolutions; but instead of having his opponent shot in the proper and customary way, he pardoned him and challenged him to try again as often as he pleased. I urged him again and again not to trifle with his own safety in this way. Useless: he would not listen to me. At last I found out the reason. He was carrying on an intrigue with his opponent's wife, my best friend. I had to shoot her—shoot her dead—my dearest friend [*she is overcome with emotion*].

SHE. Oh, you shouldnt have done that. That was going a little too far, wasnt it?

THE WIDOW. Public opinion obliged me to do it as a self-respecting wife and mother. God knows I did not want to do it: I loved her: I would have let her have ten husbands if I had had them to give. But what can you do against the etiquette of your class? My brothers had to fight duels and kill their best friends because it was etiquette.

SHE. But where were the police? Werent you tried for it?

THE WIDOW. Of course I was tried for it; but I pleaded the unwritten law and was acquitted. Unfortunately the scandal destroyed my husband's popularity. He was defeated at the next election by the man he had so foolishly spared. Instead of raising an army to avenge this outrage, my husband, crushed by the loss of his mistress, just moped at home until they came and shot him. They had come to shoot me; and [*with a fresh burst of tears*] I wish to Heaven they had; but I was out at the time; so they thought they might as well shoot my husband as there was nobody else to shoot.

SHE. What a dreadful thing for you!

THE WIDOW. Not at all. It served him right, absolutely. He never spoke to me after I had to kill the woman we both loved more than we loved oneanother. I believe he would have been only too glad if they had shot me; and I dont blame him. What is the use of the League of Nations if it cannot put a stop to such horrors?

SHE. Well, it's not the League's business, is it?

GENEVA

THE WIDOW. Not the League's business! Do you realize, young woman, that if the League does not bring the murderer of my husband to justice my son will be obliged to take up a blood feud and shoot the murderer with his own hands, though they were at the same school and are devoted to oneanother? It is against Nature, against God: if your committee does not stop it I will shoot every member of it, and you too. [*She rises*]. Excuse me. I can bear no more of this: I shall faint unless I get into the fresh air. [*She takes papers and a card from her bag and throws them on the table*]. There are the particulars. This is my card. Good morning. [*She goes as abruptly as she came in*].

SHE [*rising*] Good—

But the widow has gone and the young office lady, greatly upset, drops back into her seat with a prolonged Well!!!!!

A smart young American gentleman looks in.

THE GENTLEMAN. Say, baby: who is the old girl in the mantilla? Carmen's grandmother, eh? [*He sits on the table edge, facing her, on her right*].

SHE. A murderess. Her dearest friend. She had to. Horrible. Theyve shot her husband. She says she will shoot me unless the League stops it.

HE. Grand! Fine!

SHE. Is that all you care? Well, look at my morning's work! Persecutions, revolutions, murders, all sorts. The office has been full of people all the morning. We shant have it all to ourselves any more.

HE. No, baby; but I shall have some dough to spend. I have been kicking my heels here for months faking news for my people when there was no news. And here you hand me a mouthful. What a scoop for me, honey! You are a peach. [*He kisses her*].

Someone knocks at the door.

SHE. Shsh! Someone knocking.

They separate hastily, he going to the stove and she composing herself in her chair.

HE. Come in! Entrez! Herein!

A gaitered English bishop enters. He is old, soft, gentle and rather infirm.

THE BISHOP. Excuse me; but does anyone here speak English?

HE [*putting on all the style he is capable of*] My native language, my lord. Also this lady's. [*Exchange of bows*]. Will you take a pew, my lord?

BISHOP [*sitting*] Thank you. Your stairs are somewhat trying to me: I am not so young as I was; and they tell me I must be careful not to overstrain my heart. The journey to Geneva is a terrible one for a man of my years. Nothing but the gravest emergency could have forced me to undertake it.

HE. Is the emergency one in which we can have the honor of assisting you, my lord?

BISHOP. Your advice would be invaluable to me; for I really dont know what to do or where to go here. I am met with indifference—with apathy—when I reveal a state of things that threatens the very existence of civilized society, of religion, of the family, of the purity of womanhood, and even, they tell me, of our commercial prosperity. Are people mad? Dont they know? Dont they care?

HE. My! my! my! [*He takes a chair to the end of the table nearest the stove*] Pray be seated, my lord. What has happened?

BISHOP [*sinking into the chair*] Sir: they are actually preaching Communism in my diocese. Communism!!! My butler, who has been in the palace for forty years, a most devoted and respectable man, tells me that my footman—I am the only bishop in England who can afford to keep a footman now—that my footman is a cell.

HE. A sell? You mean that he has disappointed you?

BISHOP. No: not that sort of cell. C.E. double L. A communist cell. Like a bee in a hive. Planted on me by the Communists to make their dreadful propaganda in my household! And my grandson at Oxford has joined a Communist club. The Union—the Oxford Union—has raised the red flag. It is dreadful. And my granddaughter a nudist! I was graciously allowed to introduce my daughters to good Queen Victoria. If she could see my

42

granddaughter she would call the police. Is it any wonder that I have a weak heart? Shock after shock. My own footman, son of the most respectable parents, and actually an Anglo-Catholic!

HE. I can hardly believe it, my lord. What times we are living in!

SHE [*with her most official air*] Surely this is a case for the International Court at the Hague, my lord.

BISHOP. Yes, yes. An invaluable suggestion. The Court must stop the Bolshies from disseminating their horrible doctrines in England. It is in the treaties.

He is interrupted by the entrance of a very smart Russian gentleman, whom he receives with pleased recognition.

BISHOP [*rising*] Ah, my dear sir, we meet again. [*To the others*] I had the pleasure of making this gentleman's acquaintance last night at my hotel. His interest in the Church of England kept us up talking long after my usual hour for retirement. [*Shaking his hand warmly*] How do you do, my dear friend? how do you do?

RUSSIAN. Quite well, thank you, my lord. Am I interrupting your business?

BISHOP. No no no no: I beg you to remain. You will help: you will sympathize.

RUSSIAN. You are very kind, my lord: I am quite at your service.

BISHOP [*murmuring gratefully as he resumes his seat*] Thank you. Thank you.

RUSSIAN. Let me introduce myself. I am Commissar Posky of the Sovnarkom and Politbureau, Soviet delegate to the League Council.

BISHOP [*aghast, staggering to his feet*] You are a Bolshevik!
COMMISSAR. Assuredly.
The Bishop faints. General concern. The men rush to him.
COMMISSAR. Do not lift him yet. He will recover best as he is.
SHE. I have some iced lemonade in my thermos. Shall I give him some?
BISHOP [*supine*] Where am I? Has anything happened?
HE. You are in the office of the Intellectual Co-operation

Committee in Geneva. You have had a slight heart attack.

COMMISSAR. Lie still, comrade. You will be quite yourself presently.

BISHOP [*sitting up*] It is not my heart. [*To the Commissar*] It is moral shock. You presented yourself to me yesterday as a cultivated and humane gentleman, interested in the Church of England. And now it turns out that you are a Bolshie. What right had you to practise such a cruel imposture on me? [*He rises: the Commissar helps him*] No: I can rise without assistance, thank you. [*He attempts to do so, but collapses into the arms of the Commissar*].

COMMISSAR. Steady, comrade.

BISHOP [*regaining his seat with the Commissar's assistance*] Again I must thank you. But I shudder at the touch of your bloodstained hands.

COMMISSAR. My hands are not bloodstained, comrade. I have not imposed on you. You have not quite recovered yet, I think. I am your friend of last night. Dont you recognize me?

BISHOP. A Bolshie! If I had known, sir, I should have repudiated your advances with abhorrence.

HE [*again posting himself at the stove*] Russia is a member of the League, my lord. This gentleman's standing here is the same as that of the British Foreign Secretary.

BISHOP [*intensely*] Never. Never.

SHE [*airily*] And what can we do for you, Mr Posky? I'm sorry I cant offer you a chair. That one isnt safe.

COMMISSAR. Pray dont mention it. My business will take only a moment. As you know, the Soviet Government has gone as far as possible in agreeing not to countenance or subsidize any propaganda of Communism which takes the form of a political conspiracy to overthrow the British National Government.

BISHOP. And in violation of that agreement you have corrupted my footman and changed him from an honest and respectable young Englishman into a Cell.

COMMISSAR. Have we? I know nothing of your footman. If he is intelligent enough to become a Communist, as so many famous Englishmen did long before the Russian revolution, we cannot prevent him. But we do not employ him as our agent nor support him financially in any way.

HE. But what, then, is your difficulty, Comrade Posky?

COMMISSAR. We have just discovered that there is a most dangerous organization at work in Russia, financed from the British Isles, having for its object the overthrow of the Soviet system and the substitution of the Church of England and the British Constitution.

BISHOP. And why not, sir? Why not? Could any object be more desirable, more natural? Would you in your blind hatred of British institutions and of all liberty of thought and speech, make it a crime to advocate a system which is universally admitted to be the best and freest in the world?

COMMISSAR. We do not think so. And as the obligation to refrain from this sort of propaganda is reciprocal, you are bound by it just as we are.

HE. But what is this seditious organization you have just discovered?

COMMISSAR. It is called the Society for the Propagation of the Gospel in Foreign Parts. It has agents everywhere. They call themselves missionaries.

BISHOP. I cannot bear this: the man is insane. I subscribe to the Society almost beyond my means. It is a body of the highest respectability and piety.

COMMISSAR. You are misinformed: its doctrines are of the most subversive kind. They have penetrated to my own household. My wife is a busy professional woman, and my time is taken up altogether by public work. We are absolutely dependent for our domestic work on our housekeeper Feodorovna Ballyboushka. We were ideally happy with this excellent woman for years. In her youth she was a udarnik, what you call a shock worker.

BISHOP. You are all shock workers in Russia now. You have seen the effect on me?

COMMISSAR. That was in the early days of the revolution, when she was young and ardent. Now she is elderly; and her retirement into domestic service suits her years and her helpful and affectionate temperament. Two months ago an extraordinary change came over her. She refused to do any work that was not immediately necessary, on the ground that the end of the world is at hand. She declared that she was in a condition which she described as "saved," and interrupted my work continually with attempts to save me. She had long fits of crying because she could not bear the thought of my wife spending eternity in hell. She accused the Soviets of being the hornets prophesied in the Book of Revelation. We were about to have her certified as insane—most reluctantly; for we loved our dear Ballyboushka—when we discovered that she had been hypnotized by this illegal Society. I warned our Secret Police, formerly known to you as the Gay Pay Ooh. They followed up the clue and arrested four missionaries.

BISHOP. And shot them. Christian martyrs! All who fall into the hands of the terrible Gay Pay Ooh are shot at once, without trial, without the ministrations of the Church. But I will have a memorial service said for them. To that extent at last I can defeat your Godless tyranny.

COMMISSAR. You are quite mistaken: they have not been shot. They will be sent back to England: that is all.

BISHOP [passionately] What right had you to arrest them? How dare you arrest Englishmen? How dare you persecute religion?

COMMISSAR. They have been very patiently examined by our official psychologists, who report that they can discover nothing that could reasonably be called religion in their minds. They are obsessed with tribal superstitions of the most barbarous kind. They believe in human sacrifices, in what they call the remission of sins by the shedding of blood. No man's life would be safe in Russia if such doctrines were propagated there.

BISHOP. But you dont understand. Oh, what dreadful ignorance!

COMMISSAR. Let us pass on to another point. Our police have found a secret document of your State Church, called the Thirty-nine Articles.

BISHOP. Secret! It is in the Prayer Book!

COMMISSAR. It is not read in church. That fact speaks for

itself. Our police have found most of the articles incomprehensible; but there is one, the eighteenth, which declares that all Russians are to be held accursed. How would you like it if our chief cultural institution, endowed by our government, the Komintern, were to send its agents into England to teach that every Englishman is to be held accursed?

BISHOP. But surely, surely, you would not compare the Komintern to the Church of England!!

COMMISSAR. Comrade Bishop: the Komintern is the State Church in Russia exactly as the Church of England is the State Church in Britain.

The Bishop slides to the floor in another faint.

SHE. Oh! He's gone off again. Shall I get my thermos?

HE. I should break things to him more gently, Mr Posky. People die of shock. He maynt recover next time. In fact, he maynt recover this time.

COMMISSAR. What am I to do? I have said nothing that could possibly shock any educated reasonable person; but this man does not seem to know what sort of world he is living in.

SHE. He's an English bishop, you know.

COMMISSAR. Well? Is he not a rational human being?

SHE. Oh no: nothing as common as that. I tell you he's a bishop.

BISHOP. Where am I? Why am I lying on the floor? What has happened?

HE. You are in the Intellectual Co-operation Bureau in Geneva; and you have just been told that the Russian Komintern is analogous to the Church of England.

BISHOP [*springing to his feet unaided, his eyes blazing*] I still have life enough left in me to deny it. Karl Marx—Antichrist—said that the sweet and ennobling consolations of our faith are opium given to the poor to enable them to endure the hardships of that state of life to which it has pleased God to call them. Does your Komintern teach that blasphemy or does it not?

COMMISSAR. Impossible. There are no poor in Russia.

BISHOP. Oh! [*he drops dead*].

HE [*feeling his pulse*] I am afraid you have shocked him once too often, Comrade. His pulse has stopped. He is dead.

POSKY. Was he ever alive? To me he was incredible.

SHE. I suppose my thermos is of no use now. Shall I ring up a doctor?

HE. I think you had better ring up the police. But I say, Mr Posky, what a scoop!

COMMISSAR. A scoop? I do not understand. What is a scoop?

HE. Read all the European papers tomorrow and youll see.

ACT II

Office of the secretary of the League of Nations. Except for the small writing table at which the secretary is seated there is no office furniture. The walls are covered with engraved prints or enlarged photographs of kings, presidents, and dictators, mostly in military uniforms. Above these bellicose pictures the cornice is decorated with a row of plaster doves in low relief. There is one large picture in oils, representing a lifesize Peace, with tiny figures, also in military uniforms, kneeling round her feet and bowing their heads piously beneath the wreath which she offers them. This picture faces the secretary from the other side of the room as he sits at his table with his back to the window presenting his left profile to anyone entering from the door, which is in the middle of the wall between them. A suite of half a dozen chairs is ranged round the walls, except one, which stands near the writing table for the convenience of people interviewing the secretary.

He is a disillusioned official with a habit of dogged patience acquired in the course of interviews with distinguished statesmen of different nations, all in a condition of invincible ignorance as to the spirit of Geneva and the constitution of the League of Nations, and each with a national axe to grind. On this occasion he is rather exceptionally careworn. One pities him, as he is of a refined type, and, one guesses, began as a Genevan idealist. Age fifty or thereabouts.

There is a telephone on the table which he is at present using.

THE SECRETARY. Yes: send her up instantly. Remind me of her name. What?! . . . Ammonia? Nonsense! that cant be her name. Spell it . . . V E? . . . Oh, *B* E. Do you mean to say that her name is Begonia? Begonia Brown? . . . Farcical.

He replaces the receiver as Begonia enters. She is the Intellectual Co-operation typist. She is in walking dress, cheap, but very smart.

THE SECRETARY. Miss Brown?

BEGONIA [*with her best smile*] Yes.

THE SECRETARY. Sit down.

BEGONIA [*complying*] Kew [*short for Thank you*].

49

THE SECRETARY [*gravely*] You have heard the news, no doubt?

BEGONIA. Oh yes. Jack Palamedes has won the dancing tournament. I had ten francs on him; and I have won a hundred. Had you anything on?

THE SECRETARY [*still more gravely*] I am afraid you will think me very ignorant, Miss Brown; but I have never heard of Mr Palamedes.

BEGONIA. Fancy that! He's the talk of Geneva, I assure you.

THE SECRETARY. There are other items of news, Miss Brown. Germany has withdrawn from the League.

BEGONIA. And a good riddance, if you ask me. My father lost a lot of money through the war. Otherwise—you wont mind my telling you—youd never have got me slaving at a typewriter here for my living.

THE SECRETARY. No doubt. A further item is that the British Empire has declared war on Russia.

BEGONIA. Well, what could you expect us to do with those awful Bolshies? We should have done it long ago. But thank goodness we're safe in Geneva, you and I.

THE SECRETARY. We are safe enough everywhere, so far. The war is one of sanctions only.

BEGONIA. More shame for us, say I. I should give those Bolshies the bayonet: thats the way to talk to scum of that sort. I cant contain myself when I think of all the murder and slavery of them Soviets—[*correcting herself*] those Soviets.

THE SECRETARY. In consequence Japan has declared war on Russia and is therefore in military alliance with Britain. And the result of that is that Australia, New Zealand and Canada have repudiated the war and formed an anti-Japanese alliance with the United States under the title of the New British Federation. South Africa may join them at any moment.

BEGONIA [*flushing with indignation*] Do you mean that theyve broken up our dear Empire?

THE SECRETARY. They have said nothing about that.

BEGONIA. Oh, then thats quite all right. You know, when I was at school I was chosen five times to recite on Empire Day; and in my very first year, when I was the smallest child there, I presented the bouquet to King George's sister, who came to our prize giving. Say a word against the Empire, and you have finished with Begonia Brown.

THE SECRETARY. Then you went to school, did you?

BEGONIA. Well, of course: what do you take me for? I went to school for seven years and never missed a single day. I got fourteen prizes for regular attendance.

THE SECRETARY. Good God!

BEGONIA. What did you say?

THE SECRETARY. Nothing. I was about to tell you what has happened in Quetzalcopolis, the chief seaport of the Earthly Paradise.

BEGONIA. I know. In Central America, isnt it?

THE SECRETARY. Yes. The mob there has attacked the British Consulate, and torn down the British flag.

BEGONIA [*rising in a fury*] Insulted the British flag!!!

THE SECRETARY. They have also burnt down three convents and two churches.

BEGONIA. Thats nothing: theyre only Catholic churches. But do you mean to say that they have dared to touch the British flag?

THE SECRETARY. They have. Fortunately it was after hours and the staff had gone home. Otherwise they would assuredly have been massacred.

BEGONIA. Dirty swine! I hope the British fleet will not leave a stone standing or a nigger alive in their beastly seaport. Thatll teach them.

THE SECRETARY. There is only one other trifle of news. The little Dominion of Jacksonsland has declared itself an independent republic.

BEGONIA. It ought to be ashamed of itself. Republics are a low lot. But dont you be anxious about that: the republicans will soon be kicked out. The people may be misled for a while; but they always come back to king and country.

THE SECRETARY. And now, Miss Brown, I must ask you

whether you fully realize that all this is your doing?

BEGONIA. Mine!

THE SECRETARY. Yours and nobody else's. In every one of these cases, it was your hand that started the series of political convulsions which may end in the destruction of civilization.

BEGONIA [*flattered*] Really? How?

THE SECRETARY. Those letters that you sent to the Court of International Justice at the Hague—

BEGONIA. Oh, of course. Yes. Fancy that!

THE SECRETARY. But did you not know what you were doing? You conducted the correspondence with very remarkable ability —more, I confess, than I should have given you credit for. Do you mean to tell me that you did not foresee the consequences of your action? That you did not even read the newspapers to see what was happening?

BEGONIA. I dont read political news: it's so dry. However, I seem to be having a big success; and I wont pretend I am not gratified.

THE SECRETARY. Unfortunately the Powers do not consider it a success. They are blaming me for it.

BEGONIA. Oh, if there is any blame I am ready to take it all on myself.

THE SECRETARY. That is very magnanimous of you, Miss Brown.

BEGONIA. Not so magnanimous either: thank you all the same. I tell you I back the Empire; and the Empire will back me. So dont be uneasy.

THE SECRETARY. You are very possibly right. And now may I ask you a personal question? How did you become interested in the League of Nations? How did you get this post of yours, which has placed the world's destiny so unexpectedly in your hands?

BEGONIA. Was I interested in the League? Let me see. You know that there is a Society called the League of Nations Union, dont you?

THE SECRETARY. I do. I shudder whenever I think of it.

BEGONIA. Oh, theres nc harm in it. I'd never heard of it until

52

last year, when they opened a branch in Camberwell with a whist drive. A friend gave me a ticket for it. It was opened by the Conservative candidate: an innocent young lad rolling in money. He saw that I was a cut above the other girls there, and picked me for his partner when he had to dance. I told him I'd won a County Council scholarship and was educated and knew shorthand and a bit of French and all that, and that I was looking out for a job. His people fixed me up for Geneva all right. A perfect gentleman I must say: never asked so much as a kiss. I was disappointed.

THE SECRETARY. Disappointed at his not kissing you?

BEGONIA. Oh no: there were plenty of kisses going from better looking chaps. But he was a bit of a sucker; and I thought he had intentions; and of course he would have been a jolly good catch for me. But when his people got wind of it they packed him off for a tour round the Empire, and got me this job here—to keep me out of his way, I suppose. Anyhow here I am, you see.

THE SECRETARY. Were you examined as to your knowledge and understanding of the Covenant of the League, and its constitution?

BEGONIA. No. They didnt need to examine me to find out that I was educated. I had lots of prizes and certificates; and there was my L.C.C. scholarship. You see, I have such a good memory: examinations are no trouble to me. Theres a book in the office about the League. I tried to read it; but it was such dry stuff I went to sleep over it.

THE SECRETARY [rising] Well, Miss Brown, I am glad to have made your acquaintance, and delighted to learn that though you have produced a first class political crisis, including what promises to be a world war, and made an amazing change in the constitution of the British Empire all in the course of a single morning's work, you are still in high spirits and in fact rather proud of yourself.

BEGONIA [she has also risen] Oh, I am not a bit proud; and I'm quite used to being a success. You know, although I was always at the top of my class at school, I never pretended to be clever. Silly clever, I call it. At first I was frightened of the girls that went in for being clever and having original ideas and all that sort of crankiness. But I beat them easily in the examinations; and they never got anywhere. That gave me confidence. Wherever I go I always find that lots of people think as I do. The best sort of people always do: the real ladies and gentlemen, you know. The others are oddities and outsiders. If you want to know what real English public opinion is, keep your eye on me. I'm not a bit afraid of war: remember that England has never lost a battle, and that it does no harm to remind the foreigners of it when they get out of hand. Good morning. So pleased to have met you.

They shake hands; and he goes to the door and opens it for her. She goes out much pleased with herself.

THE SECRETARY [*ruminating dazedly*] And thats England! [*The telephone rings. He returns to the table to attend to it*]. Yes? . . . Which Foreign Secretary? Every hole and corner in the Empire has its own Foreign Secretary now. Do you mean the British Foreign Secretary, Sir Orpheus Midlander? . . . Well, why didnt you say so? Shew him up at once.

Sir Orpheus comes in. He is a very welldressed gentleman of fifty or thereabouts, genial in manner, quickwitted in conversation, altogether a pleasant and popular personality.

THE SECRETARY. Do sit down. I cant say how I feel about your being dragged here all the way from London in Derby week.

SIR O. [*sitting*] Well, my friend, it's you who have dragged me. And I hope you wont mind my asking you what on earth you think you have been doing? What induced you to do it?

THE SECRETARY. I didnt do it. It was done by the Committee for Intellectual Co-operation.

SIR O. The what??! I never heard of such a body.

THE SECRETARY. Neither did I until this business was sprung on me. Nobody ever heard of it. But I find now that it is part of the League, and that its members are tremendous swells with European reputations. Theyve all published translations from the Greek or discovered new planets or something of that sort.

SIR O. Ah yes: outside politics: I see. But we cant have literary people interfering in foreign affairs. And they must have held meetings before taking such an outrageous step as this. Why were we not told? We'd have squashed them at once.

THE SECRETARY. They are quite innocent: they know no more about it than I did. The whole thing was done by a young woman named Begonia Brown.

SIR O. Begonia Brown! But this is appalling. I shall be personally compromised.

THE SECRETARY. You! How?

SIR O. This woman—it must be the same woman; for there cant be another female with such a name in the world—she's engaged to my nephew.

THE SECRETARY. She told me about it. But I had no idea the man was your nephew. I see how awkward it is for you. Did you ever talk to her about it?

SIR O. I! I never set eyes on her in my life. I remember her ridiculous name: thats all.

THE SECRETARY. Were you in the habit of discussing foreign affairs with your nephew?

SIR O. With Benjy! You might as well discuss Einstein's general theory of relativity with a blue behinded ape. I havnt exchanged twenty words with the boy since I tipped him when he was going from Eton to Oxford.

THE SECRETARY. Then I cant understand it. Her correspondence with the Hague Court has been conducted with remarkable ability and in first-rate style. The woman herself is quite incapable of it. There must be somebody behind her. Can it be your nephew?

SIR O. If, as you say, the work shews political ability and presentable style, you may accept my assurance that Sue's boy has nothing to do with it. Besides, he is at present in Singapore, where the native dancing girls are irresistible.

The telephone rings.

THE SECRETARY. Excuse me. Yes? . . . Hold on a moment. [*To Sir O.*] The Senior Judge of the Court of International Justice at the Hague is downstairs. Hadnt you better see him?

SIR O. By all means. Most opportune.

THE SECRETARY [*into the telephone*] Send him up.

SIR O. Have you had any correspondence about this business?

THE SECRETARY. Correspondence!!! I havnt read one tenth
of it. The Abyssinian war was a holiday job in comparison. Weve
never had anything like it before.

*The Senior Judge enters. He is a Dutchman, much younger than a
British judge: under forty, in fact, but very grave and every inch a
judge.*

THE SECRETARY. I am desolate at having brought your honor
all the way from the Hague. A word from you would have
brought me there and saved you the trouble. Have you met the
British Foreign Secretary, Sir Orpheus Midlander?

JUDGE. I have not had that pleasure. How do you do, Sir
Midlander?

SIR O. How do you do?

*They shake hands whilst the Secretary places a chair for the
judge in the middle of the room, between his table and Sir Orpheus.
They all sit down.*

JUDGE. I thought it best to come. The extraordinary feature
of this affair is that I have communicated with all the members
of the Intellectual Committee; and every one of them denies any
knowledge of it. Most of them did not know that they are
members.

SIR O. Do you mean to say that it is all a hoax?

JUDGE. It may be that someone was hoaxing the Court. But
now that the applications for warrants have been made public,
the Court must take them seriously. Otherwise it would cut a
ridiculous figure in the eyes of Europe.

SIR O. But surely such a procedure was never contemplated
when the Powers joined the League?

JUDGE. I do not think anything was contemplated when the
Powers joined the League. They signed the Covenant without
reading it, to oblige President Wilson. The United States then
refused to sign it to disoblige President Wilson, also without
reading it. Since then the Powers have behaved in every respect
as if the League did not exist, except when they could use it for

their own purposes.

SIR O. [*naïvely*] But how else could they use it?

JUDGE. They could use it to maintain justice and order between the nations.

SIR O. There is nothing we desire more. The British Empire stands for justice and order. But I must tell you that the British Foreign Office would take a very grave view of any attempt on the part of the Court to do anything without consulting us. I need not remind you that without us you have no powers. You have no police to execute your warrants. You cant put the Powers in the dock: you havnt got a dock.

JUDGE. We have a court room at the Hague which can easily be provided with a dock if you consider such a construction necessary, which I do not. We have employees to whom we can assign police duties to any necessary extent.

SIR O. Pooh! You cant be serious. You have no jurisdiction.

JUDGE. You mean that our jurisdiction is undefined. That means that our jurisdiction is what we choose to make it. You are familiar with what you call judgemade law in England. Well, Sir Midlander, the judges of the Court of International Justice are not nonentities. We have waited a long time for a case to set us in motion. You have provided us with four cases; and you may depend on us to make the most of them. They will affirm our existence, which is hardly known yet. They will exercise our power, which is hardly felt yet. All we needed was a *cause célèbre*; and Miss Begonia Brown has found several for us very opportunely.

SIR O. My dear sir: Miss Brown is a nobody.

JUDGE. Unless the highest court can be set in motion by the humblest individual justice is a mockery.

SIR O. Of course I agree with that—in principle. Still, you know, there are people you can take into court and people you cant. Your experience at the bar—

JUDGE [*interrupting him sharply*] I have had no experience at the bar. Please remember that you are not now in England, where judges are only worn-out barristers, most of whom have forgotten any sense of law they may ever have acquired.

SIR O. How very odd! I own I was surprised to find the judicial bench represented by so young a man; and I am afraid I must add that I prefer our British system. We should have had no trouble with a British judge.

JUDGE. Why should you have any trouble with me? I am simply a Judge, first and last. To me it is a continual trouble and scandal that modern statesmen are slipping back, one after another, from the reign of law based on the eternal principle of justice, to the maintenance of governments set up by successful demagogues or victorious soldiers, each of whom has his proscription list of enemies whom he imprisons, exiles, or murders at his pleasure until he is himself overcome by an abler rival and duly proscribed, imprisoned, exiled or assassinated in his turn. Such a state of things is abhorrent to me. I have spent years in trying to devise some judicial procedure by which these lawbreakers can be brought to justice. Well, the Intellectual Co-operation Committee—of the existence of which I must confess I was entirely ignorant—has found the procedure; and the Court will back it up to the utmost of its powers.

SIR O. I am afraid you are a bit of an idealist.

JUDGE. Necessarily. Justice is an ideal; and I am a judge. What, may I ask, are you?

SIR O. I! Oh, only a much harassed Foreign Secretary. You see, my young friend—if you will allow me to call you so—justice, as you say, is an ideal, and a very fine ideal too; but what I have to deal with is Power; and Power is often a devilishly ugly thing. If any of these demagogue dictators issues a warrant for your arrest or even an order for your execution, you will be arrested and shot the moment you set foot in their country. You may even be kidnapped and carried there: remember Napoleon and the Duc d'Enghien. But if you issue a warrant or pronounce a sentence against one of them Europe will just laugh at you, because you have no power. It will be as futile as a decree of excommunication.

JUDGE. Would you like to be excommunicated?

SIR O. Hardly a serious question, is it?

JUDGE. Very serious.

SIR O. My dear sir, it couldnt happen.

JUDGE. Pardon me: it could.

SIR O. [*obstinately*] Pardon me: it couldnt. Look at the thing practically. To begin with I am not a Roman Catholic. I am a member of the Church of England; and down at my place in the country the Church living is in my gift. Without my subscription the churchwardens could not make both ends meet. The rector has no society except what he gets in my house.

JUDGE. The rector is a freeholder. If you are a notoriously evil liver, he can refuse to admit you to Communion.

SIR O. But I am not a notoriously evil liver. If the rector suggested such a thing I should have him out of his rectory and in a lunatic asylum before the end of the week.

JUDGE. Suppose the rector were prepared to risk that! Suppose the war of 1914 were renewed, and you were responsible for sending the young men of your country to drop bombs on the capital cities of Europe! Suppose your rector, as a Christian priest, took the view that you were in a condition of mortal sin and refused you Communion! Suppose, if you wish, that you had him locked up as a lunatic! Would you like it?

SIR O. Suppose the villagers burnt down his rectory and ducked him in the horse pond to teach him a little British patriotism! How would he like it?

JUDGE. Martyrdom has its attractions for some natures. But my question was not whether he would like it, but whether you would like it.

SIR O. I should treat it with contempt.

JUDGE. No doubt; but would you like it?

SIR O. Oh, come! Really! Really!

JUDGE. Believe me, Sir Midlander, you would not like it. And if the International Court, moved by the Committee for Intellectual Co-operation, were to deliver an adverse judgment on you, you would not like it. The man whom the Hague condemns will be an uncomfortable man. The State which it finds to be in the wrong will be an uncomfortable State.

SIR O. But you cant enforce anything. You have no sanctions.

JUDGE. What, exactly, do you mean by sanctions, Sir Midlander?

SIR O. I mean what everybody means. Sanctions, you know. That is plain English. Oil, for instance.

JUDGE. Castor oil?

SIR O. No no: motor oil. The stuff you run your aeroplanes on.

JUDGE. Motor oil is a sanction when you withhold it. Castor oil is a sanction when you administer it. Is there any other difference?

SIR O. [smiling] Well, that has never occurred to me before; but now you mention it there is certainly an analogy. But in England the castor oil business is just one of those things that are not done. Castor oil is indecent. Motor oil is all right.

JUDGE. Well, you need not fear that the Hague will resort to any other sanction than the sacredness of justice. It will affirm this sacredness and make the necessary applications. It is the business of a judge to see that there is no wrong without a remedy. Your Committee for Intellectual Co-operation has been appealed to by four persons who have suffered grievous wrongs. It has very properly referred them to the International Court. As president of that court it is my business to find a remedy for their wrongs; and I shall do so to the best of my ability even if my decisions should form the beginning of a new code of international law and be quite unprecedented.

SIR O. But, my dear sir, what practical steps do you propose to take? What steps can you take?

JUDGE. I have already taken them. I have fixed a day for the trial of the cases, and summoned the plaintiffs and defendants to attend the court.

THE SECRETARY. But the defendants are the responsible heads of sovereign States. Do you suppose for a moment that they will obey your summons?

JUDGE. We shall see. That, in fact, is the object of my experiment. We shall see. [He rises] And now I must ask you to excuse me. Sir Midlander: our interview has been most instructive to me as to the attitude of your country. Mr Secretary: you are very good to have spared me so much of your valuable time. Good afternoon, gentlemen. [*He goes out*].

SIR O. What are we to do with men like that?

THE SECRETARY. What are they going to do with us? That is the question we have to face now.

SIR O. Pooh! They cant do anything, you know, except make speeches and write articles. They are free to do that in England. British liberty is a most useful safety valve.

THE SECRETARY. I was on his honor's side myself once, until my official experience here taught me how hopeless it is to knock supernationalism—

SIR O. Super what? Did you say supernaturalism?

THE SECRETARY. No. Supernationalism.

SIR O. Oh, I see. Internationalism.

THE SECRETARY. No. Internationalism is nonsense. Pushing all the nations into Geneva is like throwing all the fishes into the same pond: they just begin eating oneanother. We need something higher than nationalism: a genuine political and social catholicism. How are you to get that from these patriots, with their national anthems and flags and dreams of war and conquest rubbed into them from their childhood? The organization of nations is the organization of world war. If two men want to fight how do you prevent them? By keeping them apart, not by bringing them together. When the nations kept apart war was an occasional and exceptional thing: now the League hangs over Europe like a perpetual warcloud.

SIR O. Well, dont throw it at my head as if I disagreed with you.

THE SECRETARY. I beg your pardon. I am worried by this crisis. Let us talk business. What are we to do with Begonia Brown?

SIR O. Do with her! Squash her, impudent little slut. She is nobody: she doesnt matter.

The conversation is abruptly broken by the irruption of Begonia herself in a state of ungovernable excitement.

BEGONIA. Have you heard the news? [*Seeing Sir Orpheus*] Oh,

I beg your pardon: I didnt know you were engaged.

THE SECRETARY. This is Sir Orpheus Midlander, the British Foreign Secretary, Miss Brown.

BEGONIA. Oh, most pleased to meet you, Sir Orpheus. I know your nephew. We are quite dear friends [*she shakes Sir O.'s hand effusively*]. Have you heard the news? Lord Middlesex is dead.

SIR O. Indeed? Let me see. Middlesex? I dont attach any significance to the news. He must have been a backwoodsman. Remind me about him.

BEGONIA. His son is Lord Newcross.

SIR O. Oh! Then Newcross goes to the Lords to succeed his father. That means a by-election in Camberwell.

BEGONIA. Yes; and the Conservatives want me to stand.

BOTH GENTLEMEN. What!!!

BEGONIA. Dont you think I ought to? I have been a lot in the papers lately. It's six hundred a year for me if I get in. I shall be the patriotic candidate; and the Labor vote will be a split vote; for the Communists are putting up a candidate against the Labor man; and the Liberals are contesting the seat as well. It will be just a walk-over for me.

SIR O. But my nephew is the Government candidate. Has he not told you so?

BEGONIA. Oh, thats quite all right. He has withdrawn and proposed me. He'll pay my election expenses.

SIR O. I thought he was in Singapore.

BEGONIA. So he is. It's all been done by cable. Ive just this minute heard it. You see, dear Billikins is not very bright; and he'd better not be here to muddle everything up. [*She sits*].

SIR O. But will his committee accept you?

BEGONIA. Only too glad to get a candidate that will do them credit. You see, no matter how carefully they coached Bill for the public meetings he made the most awful exhibition of himself. And he knew it, poor lamb, and would never have gone in for it if his mother hadnt made him.

SIR O. And do you think you will be able to make a better impression at the meetings? You are not a politician, are you?

GENEVA

BEGONIA. The same as anybody else, I suppose. I shall pick up all the politics I need when I get into the House; and I shall get into the House because there are lots of people in Camberwell who think as I do. You bet I shall romp in at the head of the poll. I am quite excited about it. [*To the Secretary*] You were so kind to me just now that I thought you had a right to know before anyone else. [*To Sir O.*] And it's splendid news for the Government, isnt it, Sir Orpheus?

SIR O. Thrilling, Miss Brown.

BEGONIA. Oh, do call me Begonia. We're as good as related, arnt we?

SIR O. I am afraid so.

BEGONIA. I am sure to get in, arnt I?

SIR O. If your three opponents are foolish enough to go to the poll, it's a cert.

BEGONIA. Yes: isnt it? I wonder would you mind lending me my fare to London. I dont like taking money off Billikins. I will pay you when my ship comes home: the six hundred a year, you know.

SIR O. Will a five pound note be any use [*he produces one*]?

BEGONIA [*taking it*] Thanks ever so much: itll just see me through. And now I must toddle off to my little constituency. I have barely time to pack for the night train. Goodbye, Mr Secretary [*They shake hands*]; and [*to Sir O. effusively*] thanks ever so much, and au revoir. [*She goes out*].

THE SECRETARY. What an amazing young woman! You really think she will get in?

SIR O. Of course she will. She has courage, sincerity, good looks, and big publicity as the Geneva heroine. Everything that our voters love.

THE SECRETARY. But she hasnt a political idea in her head.

SIR O. She need not have. The Whips will pilot her through the division lobby until she knows the way. She need not know anything else.

THE SECRETARY. But she is a complete ignoramus. She will give herself away every time she opens her mouth.

63

SIR O. Not at all. She will say pluckily and sincerely just what she feels and thinks. You heard her say that there are lots of people in Camberwell who feel and think as she does. Well, the House of Commons is exactly like Camberwell in that respect.

THE SECRETARY. But can you contemplate such a state of things without dismay?

SIR O. Of course I can. I contemplated my nephew's candidature without dismay.

THE SECRETARY. The world is mad. Quite mad.

SIR O. Pooh! you need a cup of tea. Nothing wrong with the world: nothing whatever.

THE SECRETARY [*resignedly sitting down and speaking into the telephone*] Tea for two, please.

ACT III

Afternoon in the lounge of a fashionable restaurant overlooking the Lake of Geneva. Three tea tables, with two chairs at each, are in view. There is a writing table against the wall. The Secretary is seated at the centre table, reading a magazine. The American journalist comes in flourishing a cablegram.

THE JOURNALIST. Heard the news, boss?

THE SECRETARY. What news? Anything fresh from the Hague?

THE JOURNALIST. Yes. The International Court has abolished Intellectual Co-operation [*he seats himself at the next table on the Secretary's left*].

THE SECRETARY. What!

THE JOURNALIST. They have had enough of it. The Court also finds the big Powers guilty of flagrant contempt of the League Covenant.

THE SECRETARY. So they are, of course. But the League was doing as well as could be expected until Dame Begonia took a hand in it. By the way, have you heard the latest about her?

THE JOURNALIST. No. She has dropped me completely since she became a Dame of the British Empire.

THE SECRETARY. Well, at a fashion demonstration in the Albert Hall, some blackshirt thought it would be a good joke to pretend to forget her name and call her Mongolia Muggins. Sixteen newspapers quoted this; and Begonia took an action against every one of them. They settled with her for three hundred apiece. Begonia must have netted at least four thousand.

THE JOURNALIST. And to think I might have married that girl if only I had had the foresight to push myself on her!

THE SECRETARY. Ah! A great opportunity missed: she would have made a most comfortable wife. Pleasant-looking, good-natured, able to see everything within six inches of her nose and nothing beyond. A domestic paragon: a political idiot. In short, an ideal wife.

GENEVA

The widow enters on the arm of Sir Orpheus Midlander. She still carries her handbag, heavy with the weight of her pistol.

SIR O. I assure you, señora, this is the only place in Geneva where you can be perfectly happy after a perfect tea.

THE WIDOW. It is easy for you to be happy. But think of this weight continually hanging on my arm, and reminding me at every moment of my tragic destiny.

SIR O. Oh, you must allow me to carry it for you. I had no idea it was heavy. Do you keep all your money in it?

THE WIDOW. Money! No: it is this [*she takes the weapon from it and throws it on the nearest table on the Secretary's right. The pair seat themselves there*].

SIR O. Good gracious! What do you carry that for? It is against the law in Geneva.

THE WIDOW. There is no longer any law in Geneva. The Hague has abolished the Intellectual Committee, leaving my husband's murder still unexpiated. That throws me back on the blood feud. Properly this is the business of my son. I cabled him to shoot the usurping president at once. But the boy is a shameless dastard.

SIR O. A bastard!

THE WIDOW. No: I wish he were: he has disgraced me. A dastard, a coward. He has become a Communist, and pretends that the blood feud is a bourgeois tradition, contrary to the teachings of Karl Marx.

SIR O. Well, so much the better. I can hardly believe that Marx taught anything so entirely reasonable and proper as that it is wrong to shoot a president; but if he did I must say I agree with him.

THE WIDOW. But public opinion in the Earthly Paradise would never tolerate such a monstrous violation of natural justice as leaving the murder of a father unavenged. If our relatives could be murdered with impunity we should have people shooting them all over the place. Even cousins five times removed have to be avenged if they have no nearer relative to take on that duty.

SIR O. Dear me! But if your son wont, he wont; and there is an end to it. A very happy end, if I may say so.

THE WIDOW. An end of it! Nothing of the sort. If my son will not shoot the president, I shall have to do it myself. The president has two brothers who will shoot me unless I stay in this ghastly Europe instead of returning to my beloved Earthly Paradise.

SIR O. To me as an Englishman, all this seems ridiculous. You really need not shoot him.

THE WIDOW. You dont know how strong public opinion is in the Earthly Paradise. You couldnt live there if you defied it. And then there is my own sense of right and wrong. You mustnt think I have no conscience.

SIR O. People have such extraordinary consciences when they have not been educated at an English public school! [*To the secretary*] Talking of that, have you read the Prime Minister's speech in the debate on the League last night?

THE SECRETARY [*illhumoredly*] Yes. Half about Harrow as a nursery for statesmen, and the other half about the sacredness of treaties. He might have shewn some consideration for me.

SIR O. But, my dear fellow, in what way could his speech have possibly hurt you? He has made that speech over and over again. You know very well that after a certain age a man has only one speech. And you have never complained before.

THE SECRETARY. Well, he had better get a new speech, and stop talking about the sacredness of treaties. Will you fellows in London never take the trouble to read the Covenant of the League? It entirely abolishes the sacredness of treaties. Article 26 expressly provides for the revision and amendment both of the treaties and the League itself.

SIR O. But how can that be? Surely the League was created to see the Treaty of Versailles carried out. With what other object would we have joined it?

THE SECRETARY [*desperately*] Oh, there is no use talking to you. You all come here to push your own countries without the faintest notion of what the League is for; and I have to sit here listening to foreign ministers explaining to me that their countries are the greatest countries in the world and their people God's

GENEVA

chosen race. You are supposed to be international statesmen; but none of you could keep a coffee stall at Limehouse because you would have to be equally civil to sailors of all nations.

SIR O. Nerves, my dear boy, nerves. I sometimes feel like that myself. I tell my wife I am sick of the whole business, and am going to resign; but the mood passes.

The Jew enters, in animated conversation with the quondam newcomer. The rest become discreetly silent, but keep their ears open.

THE JEW. My good sir, what is your grievance compared to mine? Have you been robbed? Have you been battered with clubs? gassed? massacred? Have you been commercially and socially ruined? Have you been imprisoned in concentration camps commanded by hooligans? Have you been driven out of your country to starve in exile?

THE NEWCOMER. No; but if the people vote for it there is no violation of democratic principle in it. Your people voted ten to one for getting rid of the Jews. Hadnt they the right to choose the sort of people they would allow to live in their own country? Look at the British! Will they allow a yellow man into Australia? Look at the Americans! Will they let a Jap into California? See what happened to the British Government in 1906 when it wanted to let Chinese labor into Lancashire!

THE JEW. Your own country! Who made you a present of a piece of God's earth?

THE NEWCOMER. I was born on it, wasnt I?

THE JEW. And was not I born in the country from which I have been cast out?

THE NEWCOMER. You oughtnt to have been born there. You ought to have been born in Jerusalem.

THE JEW. And you, my friend, ought never to have been born at all. You claim a right to shut me out of the world; but you burn with indignation because you yourself have been shut out of your trumpery little parliament.

THE NEWCOMER. Easy! easy! dont lose your temper. I dont want to shut you out of the world: all I say is that you are not in the world on democratic principles; but I ought to be in parliament on democratic principles. If I shoot a Jew, thats murder; and I ought to be hanged for it. But if I vote for a Jew, as I often have, and he is elected and then not let into Parliament, what becomes of democracy?

THE JEW. The question is not what becomes of democracy but what becomes of you? You are not less rich, less happy, less secure, less well or badly governed because you are making speeches outside your Parliament House instead of inside it. But to me the persecution is a matter of life and death.

THE NEWCOMER. It's a bit hard on you, I admit. But it's not a matter of principle.

THE WIDOW [to the Jew] Do you know what I would do if I were a president?

THE JEW. No, madam. But it would interest me to hear it.

THE WIDOW. I would shoot every Jew in the country: that is what I would do.

THE JEW. Pray why?

THE WIDOW. Because they crucified my Savior: that is why. I am a religious woman; and when I meet a God murderer I can hardly keep my hands off my gun.

THE JEW. After all, madam, your Savior was a Jew.

THE WIDOW. Oh, what a horrible blasphemy! [she reaches for her pistol].

Sir Orpheus seizes her wrist. The Secretary secures her left arm.

THE WIDOW [struggling] Let me go. How dare you touch me? If you were Christians you would help me to kill this dirty Jew. Did you hear what he said?

SIR O. Yes, yes, señora: I heard. I assure you he did not mean to blaspheme. Ethnologically, you know, he was right. Only ethnologically, of course.

THE WIDOW. I do not understand that long word. Our Savior and his Virgin Mother were good Catholics, were they not?

SIR O. No doubt, señora, no doubt. We are all good Catholics, I hope, in a sense. You will remember that our Savior was of the house of King David.

THE WIDOW. You will be telling me next that King David was

a Jew, I suppose.

SIR O. Well, ethnologically—

THE WIDOW. Eth no fiddlesticks. Give me my gun.

SIR O. I think you had better let me carry it for you, señora. You shall have it when this gentleman has gone.

THE NEWCOMER. Give it to the police. That woman is not safe.

THE WIDOW. I spit upon you.

SIR O. The police would arrest her for carrying arms.

THE WIDOW. Three men and a Jew against one disarmed woman!   Cowards.

THE JEW. Fortunate for you, madam, and for me.   But for these three gentlemen you would soon be awaiting death at the hands of the public executioner; and I should be a corpse.

THE JOURNALIST. A cadaver. Put it nicely. A cadaver.

THE WIDOW. Do you believe that any jury would find me guilty for ridding the world of a Jew?

THE JEW. One can never be quite certain, madam. If there were women on the jury, or some Jews, your good looks might not save you.

THE WIDOW. Women on juries are an abomination. Only a Jew could mention such a thing to a lady [*she gives up the struggle and resumes her seat*].

The Commissar comes in with Begonia and the Judge, of whom she has evidently made a conquest.

BEGONIA [*to the Secretary*] Good evening, boss. Cheerio, Sir Orpheus. You remember me, señora. You know the judge, boss.

THE SECRETARY. Do me the honor to share my table, your honor.

THE JUDGE. Thank you.   May I introduce Commissar Posky. [*He seats himself on the Secretary's left*].

THE SECRETARY. We have met. Pray be seated.

THE JOURNALIST. Take my place, Commissar. I must get on with my work. [*He retires to the writing table, where he sits and sets to work writing his press messages, withdrawing from the conversation, but keeping his ears open*].

70

THE COMMISSAR [*taking the vacated seat beside the Newcomer*] I thank you.

THE SECRETARY. There is room for you here, Dame Begonia [*indicating chair on his right*].

BEGONIA [*taking it*] There is always room at the top.

THE COMMISSAR. I represent the Soviet.

THE WIDOW [*exploding again*] Another Jew!!!

THE SECRETARY. No, no. You have Jews on the brain.

THE WIDOW. He is a Bolshevist. All Bolshevists are Jews. Do you realize that if I lived under the horrible tyranny of the Soviet I should be shot?

THE JEW. I take that to be a very striking proof of the superior civilization of Russia.

THE COMMISSAR. Why should we shoot her, comrade?

THE JEW. She has just tried to shoot me.

THE COMMISSAR. We do not shoot Jews as such: we civilize them. You see, a Communist State is only possible for highly civilized people, trained to Communism from their childhood. The people we shoot are gangsters and speculators and exploiters and scoundrels of all sorts who are encouraged in other countries in the name of liberty and democracy.

THE NEWCOMER [*starting up*] Not a word against liberty and democracy in my presence! Do you hear?

THE COMMISSAR. And not a word against Communism in mine. Agreed?

THE NEWCOMER [*sits down sulkily*] Oh, all right.

THE COMMISSAR [*continuing*] I find it very difficult to accustom myself to the exaggerated importance you all attach to sex in these western countries. This handsome lady, it seems, has some lover's quarrel with this handsome gentleman.

THE WIDOW. A lover's quarrel!!!

THE COMMISSAR. In the U.S.S.R. that would be a triviality. At the very worst it would end in a divorce. But here she tries to shoot him.

THE WIDOW. You are mad. And divorce is a deadly sin: only Bolsheviks and Protestants would allow such an infamy. They will all go to hell for it. As to my loving this man, I hate, loathe, and abhor him. He would steal my child and cut it in pieces and sprinkle its blood on his threshold. He is a Jew.

THE COMMISSAR. Come to Russia. Jews do not do such things there. No doubt they are capable of anything when they are corrupted by Capitalism.

THE JEW. Lies! lies! Excuses for robbing and murdering us.

THE COMMISSAR. For that, comrade, one excuse is as good as another. I am not a Jew; but the lady may shoot me because I am a Communist.

THE WIDOW. How can I shoot you? They have stolen my gun. Besides, shooting Communists is not a religious duty but a political one; and in my country women do not meddle in politics.

THE COMMISSAR. Then I am safe.

BEGONIA [*recovering from her astonishment at the shooting conversation*] But dont you know, señora, that you mustnt go about shooting people here? It may be all right in your country; but here it isnt done.

THE WIDOW. Where I am is my country. What is right in my country cannot be wrong in yours.

SIR O. Ah, if you were a Foreign Secretary—

THE SECRETARY. If you were the secretary of the League of Nations—

SIR O. You would make the curious discovery that one nation's right is another nation's wrong. There is only one way of reconciling all the nations in a real league, and that is to convert them all to English ideas.

THE COMMISSAR. But all the world is in revolt against English ideas, especially the English themselves. The future is for Russian ideas.

THE NEWCOMER. Where did Russia get her ideas? From England. In Russia Karl Marx would have been sent to Siberia and flogged to death. In England he was kept in the British Museum at the public expense and let write what he liked. England is the country where, as the poet says, "A man may say the thing he wills—"

THE JUDGE. Pardon me: that is an illusion. I have gone into that question; and I can assure you that when the British Government is alarmed there are quite as many prosecutions for sedition, blasphemy and obscenity as in any other country. The British Government has just passed a new law under which any person obnoxious to the Government can be imprisoned for opening his mouth or dipping his pen in the ink.

SIR O. Yes; but whose fault is that? Your Russian propaganda. Freedom of thought and speech is the special glory of Britain; but surely you dont expect us to allow your missionaries to preach Bolshevism, do you?

THE COMMISSAR [laughing] I dont expect any government to tolerate any doctrine that threatens its existence or the incomes of its rulers. The only difference is that in Russia we dont pretend to tolerate such doctrines; and in England you do. Why do you give yourselves that unnecessary and dangerous trouble?

THE NEWCOMER. Karl Marx was tolerated in England: he wouldnt have been tolerated in Russia.

THE COMMISSAR. That was a weakness in the British system, not a virtue. If the British Government had known and understood what Marx was doing, and what its effect was going to be on the mind of the world, it would have sent him to prison and destroyed every scrap of his handwriting and every copy of his books. But they did not know where to strike. They persecuted poor men for making profane jokes; they suppressed newspapers in England as well as in Ireland; they dismissed editors who were too independent and outspoken; they burnt the books of novelists who had gone a little too far in dealing with sex; they imprisoned street corner speakers on charges of obstructing traffic; and all the time they were providing Karl Marx with the finest reading room in the world whilst he was writing their death warrants.

SIR O. Those warrants have not yet been executed in England. They never will be. The world may be jolted out of its tracks for a moment by the shock of a war as a railway train may be thrown off the rails; but it soon settles into its old grooves. You are a Bolshevik; but nobody would know it. You have the appearance, the dress, the culture of a gentleman: your clothes might have been made within half a mile of Hanover Square.

THE COMMISSAR. As a matter of fact they were: I buy them in London.

SIR O. [*triumphant*] You see! You have given up all this Marxian nonsense and gone back to the capitalist system. I always said you would.

THE COMMISSAR. If it pleases you to think so, Sir Orpheus, I shall do nothing to disturb your happiness. Will you be so good as to convey to your Government my great regret and that of the Soviet Cabinet that your bishop should have died of his personal contact with Russian ideas. I blame myself for not having been more considerate. But I had never met that kind of man before. The only other British Bishop I had met was nearly seven feet high, an athlete, and a most revolutionary preacher.

SIR O. That is what makes the Church of England so easy to deal with. No types. Just English gentlemen. Not like Catholic priests.

THE WIDOW. Oh, Sir Orpheus! You, of all men, to insult my faith!

SIR O. Not at all, not at all, I assure you. I have the greatest respect for the Catholic faith. But you cannot deny that your priests have a professional air. They are not like other men. Our English clergy are not like that. You would not know that they were clergy at all if it were not for their collars.

THE WIDOW. I call that wicked. A priest should not be like other men.

THE COMMISSAR. Have you ever tried to seduce a priest, madam?

THE WIDOW. Give me my gun. This is monstrous. Have Bolsheviks no decency?

THE NEWCOMER. I knew a priest once who—

THE SECRETARY. No, please. The subject is a dangerous one.

THE COMMISSAR. All subjects are dangerous in Geneva, are they not?

THE JUDGE. Pardon me. It is not the subjects that are dangerous in Geneva, but the people.

THE WIDOW. Jews! Bolsheviks! Gunmen!

THE JEW. What about gunwomen? Gunmolls they are called in America. Pardon my reminding you.

THE WIDOW. You remind me of nothing that I can decently mention.

THE NEWCOMER. Hullo, maam! You know, ladies dont say things like that in my country.

THE WIDOW. They do in mine. What I have said I have said.

THE JUDGE. When the International Court was moved to action by the enterprise of my friend Dame Begonia, it found that the moment the League of Nations does anything on its own initiative and on principle, it produces, not peace, but threats of war or secession or both which oblige it to stop hastily and do nothing until the Great Powers have decided among themselves to make use of it as an instrument of their oldfashioned diplomacy. That is true, Mr. Secretary, is it not?

THE SECRETARY. It is too true. Yet it is not altogether true. Those who think the League futile dont know what goes on here. They dont know what Geneva means to us. The Powers think we are nothing but their catspaw. They flout us openly by ignoring the Covenant and making unilateral treaties that should be made by us. They have driven us underground as if we were a criminal conspiracy. But in little ways of which the public knows nothing we sidetrack them. We sabotage them. We shame them. We make things difficult or impossible that used to be easy. You dont know what the atmosphere of Geneva is. When I came here I was a patriot, a Nationalist, regarding my appointment as a win for my own country in the diplomatic game. But the atmosphere of Geneva changed me. I am now an Internationalist. I am the ruthless enemy of every nation, my own included. Let me be frank. I hate the lot of you.

ALL THE OTHERS. Oh!

THE SECRETARY. Yes I do. You the Jew there: I hate you because you are a Jew.

THE JEW. A German Jew.

THE SECRETARY. Worse and worse. Two nationalities are worse than one. This gunwoman here: I hate her because she is heaven knows what mixture of Spaniard and Indian and savage.

THE WIDOW. Men with red blood in them do not hate me.

THE SECRETARY. You, Sir Orpheus, are an amiable and honest man. Well, I never hear you talking politics without wanting to shoot you.

SIR O. Dear me! Fortunately I have the lady's gun in my pocket. But of course I dont believe you.

THE SECRETARY. If you had the Geneva spirit you would believe me. This Russian here: I hate him because his Government has declared for Socialism in a single country.

THE COMMISSAR. You are a Trotskyite then?

THE SECRETARY. Trotsky is nothing to me; but I hate all frontiers; and you have shut yourself into frontiers.

THE COMMISSAR. Only because infinite space is too much for us to manage. Be reasonable.

THE SECRETARY. On this subject I am not reasonable. I am sick of reasonable people: they see all the reasons for being lazy and doing nothing.

THE NEWCOMER. And what price me? Come on. Dont leave me out.

THE SECRETARY. You! You are some sort of half-Americanized colonist. You are a lower middle-class politician. Your pose is that of the rugged individualist, the isolationist, at bottom an Anarchist.

THE NEWCOMER. Anarchist yourself. Anyhow I have more common sense than you: I dont hate all my fellow creatures.

THE SECRETARY. You are all enemies of the human race. You are all armed to the teeth and full of patriotism. Your national heroes are all brigands and pirates. When it comes to the point you are all cut-throats. But Geneva will beat you yet. Not in my time, perhaps. But the Geneva spirit is a fact; and a spirit is a fact that cannot be killed.

ALL THE REST. But—

THE SECRETARY [*shouting them down*] I am not going to argue with you: you are all too damnably stupid.

SIR O. Are you sure you are quite well this afternoon? I have always believed in you and supported you as England's truest friend at Geneva.

THE SECRETARY. You were quite right. I am the truest friend England has here. I am the truest friend of all the Powers if they only knew it. That is the strength of my position here. Each of you thinks I am on his side. If you hint that I am mad or drunk I shall hint that you are going gaga and that it is time for the British Empire to find a younger Foreign Secretary.

SIR O. Gaga!!!

THE SECRETARY. I cannot afford to lose my job here. Do not force me to fight you with your own weapons in defence of my hardearned salary.

THE WIDOW [*to Sir O.*] The best weapon is in your hands. You stole it from me. In my country he would now be dead at your feet with as many holes drilled through him as there are bullets in the clip.

THE SECRETARY. In your country, señora, I might have fired first.

THE WIDOW. What matter! In either case honor would be satisfied.

THE SECRETARY. Honor! The stock excuse for making a corpse.

THE JOURNALIST. A cadaver.

THE WIDOW. Thank you.

THE SECRETARY. A slovenly unhandsome corse. I am quoting Shakespear.

THE WIDOW. Then Shakespear, whoever he may be, is no gentleman.

THE SECRETARY. Judge: you hear what we have to contend with here. Stupidity upon stupidity. Geneva is expected to make a league of nations out of political blockheads.

77

GENEVA

THE JUDGE. I must rule this point against you. These people are not stupid. Stupid people have nothing to say for themselves: these people have plenty to say for themselves. Take Sir Midlander here for example. If you tell me he is stupid the word has no meaning.

SIR O. Thank you, my dear Judge, thank you. But for Heaven's sake dont call me clever or I shall be defeated at the next election. I have the greatest respect for poetry and the fine arts and all that sort of thing; but please understand that I am not an intellectual. A plain Englishman doing my duty to my country according to my poor lights.

THE JUDGE. Still, doing it with ability enough to have attained Cabinet rank in competition with hundreds of other successful and ambitious competitors.

SIR O. I assure you I am not ambitious. I am not competitive. I happen to be fairly well off; but the money was made by my grandfather. Upon my honor I dont know how I got landed where I am. I am quite an ordinary chap really.

THE JUDGE. Then you have risen by sheer natural ordinary superiority. However, do not be alarmed: all I claim for the purposes of my argument is that you are not a born fool.

SIR O. Very good of you to say so. Well, I will let it go at that.

THE JUDGE. At the other extreme, take the case of this passionate and attractive lady, whose name I have not the pleasure of knowing.

THE JEW. Try Dolores.

THE WIDOW. I suppose you think you are insulting me. You are simply making a fool of yourself. My name is Dolores.

SIR O. I guessed it, Señora. In my undergraduate days I used to quote Oscar Wilde's famous poem

"We are fain of thee still, we are fain.
O sanguine and subtle Dolores
Our Lady of pain."

THE JOURNALIST. Swinburne, Sir Orpheus.

SIR O. Was it Swinburne? Well, it does not matter: it was one

78

of the literary set.

THE WIDOW. It sounds well; but English is not my native language. I do not understand the first line. "We are fain of thee still: we are fain." What does fain mean?

SIR O. Ah well, never mind, Señora, never mind. We are interrupting his honor the Judge. [*To the Judge*] You were about to say—?

THE JUDGE. I was about to point out that whatever is the matter with this lady it is not stupidity. She speaks several languages. Her intelligence is remarkable: she takes a point like lightning. She has in her veins the learning of the Arabs, the courage and enterprise of the Spanish conquistadores, the skyward aspiration of the Aztecs, the selfless devotion to divine purposes of the Jesuit missionaries, and the readiness of them all to face death in what she conceives to be her social duty. If we have been actually obliged to disarm her to prevent her from sacrificing this harmless Jewish gentleman as her ancestors would have sacrificed him to the God Quetzalcoatl on the stepped altars of Mexico, it is not because she is stupid.

THE WIDOW. I hardly follow you, however intelligent you may think me. But I am proud of having Aztec blood in my veins, though I should never dream of insulting Quetzalcoatl by sacrificing a Jew to him.

THE JUDGE. As to the Jewish gentleman himself, I need not dwell on his case, as he has been driven out of his native country solely because he is so thoughtful and industrious that his fellow-countrymen are hopelessly beaten by him in the competition for the conduct of business and for official positions. I come to our democratic friend here. I do not know what his business is—

THE NEWCOMER. I'm a retired builder, if you want to know.

THE JUDGE. He has had ability enough to conduct a builder's business with such success that he has been able to retire at his present age, which cannot be far above fifty.

THE NEWCOMER. I am no millionaire, mind you. I have just enough to do my bit on the Borough Council, and fight the enemies of democracy.

THE JUDGE. Precisely. That is the spirit of Geneva. What you lack is not mind but knowledge.

THE NEWCOMER. My wife says I'm pigheaded. How is that for a testimonial?

THE JUDGE. A first rate one, sir. Pigs never waver in their convictions, never give in to bribes, arguments, nor persuasions. At all events you are wise enough to be dissatisfied with the existing world order, and as anxious to change it as anybody in Geneva.

THE NEWCOMER. The world's good enough for me. Democracy is what I want. We were all for democracy when only the privileged few had votes. But now that everybody has a vote, women and all, where's democracy? Dictators all over the place! and me, an elected representative, kept out of parliament by the police!

THE JUDGE. I come to our Russian friend. He must be a man of ability, or he could not be a Commissar in a country where nothing but ability counts. He has no fears for the future, whereas we are distracted by the continual dread of war, of bankruptcy, of poverty. But there is no evidence that he is a superman. Twenty years ago he would have been talking as great nonsense as any of you.

THE REST [*except the Russian and Begonia*] Nonsense!

THE JUDGE. Perhaps I should have said folly; for folly is not nonsensical: in fact the more foolish it is, the more logical, the more subtle, the more eloquent, the more brilliant.

SIR O. True. True. I have known men who could hold the House of Commons spellbound for hours; but most unsafe. Mere entertainers.

BEGONIA. My turn now. I suppose. I see you are looking at me. Well, all politics are the same to me: I never could make head or tail of them. But I draw the line at Communism and atheism and nationalization of women and doing away with marriage and the family and everybody stealing everybody's property and having to work like slaves and being shot if you breathe a word against it all.

THE JUDGE. You are intelligent enough, well-meaning enough,

to be against such a state of things, Dame Begonia, are you?

BEGONIA. Well, of course I am. Wouldnt anybody?

THE JUDGE. It does you the greatest credit.

THE COMMISSAR. But allow me to remark—

THE JUDGE. Not now, Mr. Posky, or you will spoil my point, which is that Dame Begonia's sympathies and intentions are just the same as yours.

BEGONIA. Oh! I never said so. I hate his opinions.

THE COMMISSAR. I must protest. The lady is a bourgeoise: I am a Communist. How can there be the smallest sympathy between us? She upholds the dictatorship of the capitalist, I the dictatorship of the proletariat.

THE JUDGE. Never mind your opinions: I am dealing with the facts. It is evident that the lady is wrong as to the facts, because the inhabitants of a country conducted as she supposes Russia to be conducted would all be dead in a fortnight. It is evident also that her ignorance of how her own country is conducted is as complete as her ignorance of Russia. None of you seem to have any idea of the sort of world you are living in. Into the void created by this ignorance has been heaped a groundwork of savage superstitions: human sacrifices, vengeance, wars of conquest and religion, falsehoods called history, and a glorification of vulgar erotics and pugnacity called romance which transforms people who are naturally as amiable, as teachable, as companionable as dogs, into the most ferocious and cruel of all the beasts. And this, they say, is human nature! But it is not natural at all: real human nature is in continual conflict with it; for amid all the clamor for more slaughter and the erection of monuments to the great slaughterers the cry for justice, for mercy, for fellowship, for peace, has never been completely silenced: even the worst villainies must pretend to be committed for its sake.

SIR O. Too true: oh, too true. But we must take the world as we find it.

THE JUDGE. Wait a bit. How do you find the world? You find it sophisticated to the verge of suicidal insanity. This makes trouble for you as Foreign Secretary. Why not cut out the sophistication? Why not bring your economics, your religion, your history, your political philosophy up to date? Russia has made a gigantic effort to do this; and now her politicians are only about fifty years behind her philosophers and saints whilst the rest of the civilized world is from five hundred to five thousand behind it. In the west the vested interests in ignorance and superstition are so overwhelming that no teacher can tell his young pupils the truth without finding himself starving in the street. The result is that here we despair of human nature, whereas Russia has hopes that have carried her through the most appalling sufferings to the forefront of civilization. Then why despair of human nature when it costs us so much trouble to corrupt it? Why not stop telling it lies? Are we not as capable of that heroic feat as the Russians?

THE COMMISSAR. Apparently not. There are qualities which are produced on the Russian soil alone. There may be a future for the western world if it accepts the guidance of Moscow; but left to its childish self it will decline and fall like as all the old capitalist civilizations.

SIR O. Let me tell you, Mr. Posky, that if ever England takes to Communism, which heaven forbid, it will make a first-rate job of it. Downing Street will not take its orders from Moscow. Moscow took all its ideas from England, as this gentleman has told you. My grandfather bought sherry from John Ruskin's father; and very good sherry it was. And John Ruskin's gospel compared with Karl Marx's was like boiling brandy compared with milk and water.

THE JEW. Yes; but as the British would not listen to Ruskin he produced nothing. The race whose brains will guide the world to the new Jerusalem is the race that produced Karl Marx, who produced Soviet Russia.

THE JUDGE. Race! Nonsense! You are all hopeless mongrels pretending to be thoroughbreds. Why not give up pretending?

SIR O. I am not pretending. I am an Englishman: an Englishman from the heart of England.

THE JUDGE. You mean a British islander from Birmingham, the choicest breed of mongrels in the world. You should be proud of your cross-fertilization.

SIR O. At least I am not a Frenchman nor a negro.

THE JUDGE. At least you are not a Scot, nor an Irishman, nor a man of Kent, nor a man of Devon, nor a Welshman—

SIR O. One of my grandmothers was a Welsh girl. Birmingham is nearer the Welsh border than a Cockney concentration camp like London.

THE JUDGE. In short, you are a mongrel.

THE WIDOW. What is a mongrel? I thought it was a cheap kind of dog.

THE JUDGE. So it is, madam. I applied the word figuratively to a cheap kind of man: that is, to an enormous majority of the human race. It simply indicates mixed ancestry.

THE WIDOW. Ah, that is the secret of the unique distinction of the upper class in the Earthly Paradise. My blood is a blend of all that is noblest in history: the Maya, the Aztec, the Spaniard, the Mexican, the—

THE SECRETARY [*flinging away his pen, with which he has been making notes of the discussion*].You see, Judge. If you knock all this nonsense of belonging to superior races out of them, they only begin to brag of being choice blends of mongrel. Talk till you are black in the face: you get no good of them. In China the Manchus have given up binding the women's feet and making them cripples for life; but we still go on binding our heads and making fools of ourselves for life.

THE JUDGE. Yes; but do not forget that as lately as the nineteenth century the world believed that the Chinese could never change. Now they are the most revolutionary of all the revolutionists.

THE JEW [*to the Widow*] May I ask have you any engagement for dinner this evening?

THE WIDOW. What is that to you, pray?

THE JEW. Well, would you care to dine with me?

THE WIDOW. Dine with you! Dine with a Jew!

THE JEW. Only a Jew can appreciate your magnificent type of beauty, señora. These Nordics, as they ridiculously call themselves, adore girls who are dolls and women who are cows. But wherever the Jew dominates the theatre and the picture gallery— and he still dominates them in all the great capitals in spite of persecution—your type of beauty is supreme.

THE WIDOW. It is true. You have taste, you Jews. You have appetites. You are vital, in your oriental fashion. And you have boundless ambition and indefatigable pertinacity: you never stop asking for what you want until you possess it. But let me tell you that if you think you can possess me for the price of a dinner, you know neither your own place nor mine.

THE JEW. I ask nothing but the pleasure of your company, the luxury of admiring your beauty and experiencing your sex appeal, and the distinction of being seen in public with you as my guest.

THE WIDOW. You shall not get them. I will not accept your dinner.

THE JEW. Not even if I allow you to pay for it?

THE WIDOW. Is there any end to your impudence? I have never dined with a Jew in my life.

THE JEW. Then you do not know what a good dinner is. Come! Try dining with a Jew for the first time in your life.

THE WIDOW [considering it] It is true that I have nothing else to do this evening. But I must have my gun.

SIR O. [taking the pistol from his pocket] Well, as we seem to have got over the Anti-Semite difficulty I have no further excuse for retaining your property. [He hands her the pistol].

THE WIDOW [replacing it in her handbag] But remember. If you take the smallest liberty—if you hint at the possibility of a more intimate relation, you are a dead man.

THE JEW. You need have no fear. If there are any further advances they must come from yourself.

THE WIDOW. I could never have believed this.

BEGONIA. Geneva is like that. You find yourself dining with all sorts.

SIR O. By the way, Mr. Posky, have you anything particular to do this evening? If not, I should be glad if you would join me at dinner. I want to talk to you about this funny Russian business. You need not dress.

THE COMMISSAR. I will dress if you will allow me. They are rather particular about it now in Moscow.

BEGONIA. Well I never! Fancy a Bolshie dressing!

THE JUDGE. May I suggest, gracious Dame, that you and I dine together?

BEGONIA. Oh, I feel I am imposing on you: I have dined with you three times already. You know, I am a little afraid of you, you are so deep and learned and what I call mental. I may be a Dame of the British Empire and all that; but I am not the least bit mental; and what attraction you can find in my conversation I cant imagine.

THE SECRETARY. Geneva is so full of mental people that it is an inexpressible relief to meet some cheerful person with absolutely no mind at all. The Judge can have his pick of a hundred clever women in Geneva; but what he needs to give his brain a rest is a soft-bosomed goose without a political idea in her pretty head.

BEGONIA. Go on: I am used to it. I know your opinion of me: I am the only perfect idiot in Geneva. But I got a move on the League; and thats more than you ever could do, you old stick-in-the-mud.

THE WIDOW. Take care, señorita! A woman should not wear her brains on her sleeve as men do. She should keep them up it. Men like to be listened to.

BEGONIA. I have listened here until I am nearly dead. Still, when men start talking you can always think of something else. They are so taken up with themselves that they dont notice it.

THE WIDOW. Do not give away the secrets of our sex, child. Be thankful, as I am, that you have made sure of your next dinner.

THE JOURNALIST. What about my dinner?

THE SECRETARY. You had better dine with me. You can tell me the latest news.

THE JUDGE. I can tell you that. The trial of the dictators by the Permanent Court of International Justice has been fixed for this day fortnight.

THE REST. Where?

THE JUDGE. At the Hague, in the old palace.

THE SECRETARY. But the trial will be a farce. The dictators wont come.

THE JUDGE. I think they will. You, Sir Orpheus, will, I presume, be present with a watching brief from the British Foreign Office.

SIR O. I shall certainly be present. Whether officially or not I cannot say.

THE JUDGE. You will all be present, I hope. May I suggest that you telephone at once to secure rooms at the Hague. If you wait until the news becomes public you may find yourselves crowded out.

All except the Judge and the Secretary rise hastily and disappear in the direction of the hotel bureau.

THE SECRETARY. You really think the dictators will walk into the dock for you?

THE JUDGE. We shall see. There will be no dock. I shall ask you to act as Clerk to the Court.

THE SECRETARY. Impossible.

THE JUDGE. It seems so now; but I think you will.

THE SECRETARY. Well, as Midlander is coming I shall certainly be there to hear what he may say. But the dictators? Bombardone? Battler? How can you make them come? You have not a single soldier. Not even a policeman.

THE JUDGE. All the soldiers and police on earth could not move them except by the neck and heels. But if the Hague becomes the centre of the European stage all the soldiers and police in the world will not keep them away from it.

THE SECRETARY [*musing*] Hm! Well— [*he shakes his head and gives it up*].

THE JUDGE [*smiles*] They will come. Where the spotlight is, there will the despots be gathered.

86

ACT IV

A salon in the old palace of the Hague. On a spacious dais a chair of State, which is in fact an old throne, is at the head of a table furnished with chairs, writing materials, and buttons connected with telephonic apparatus. The table occupies the centre of the dais. On the floor at both sides chairs are arranged in rows for the accommodation of spectators, litigants, witnesses, etc. The tall windows admit abundance of sunlight and shew up all the gilding and grandeur of the immovables. The door is at the side, on the right of the occupant of the chair of state, at present empty. The formal arrangement of the furniture suggests a sitting or hearing or meeting of some kind. A waste paper basket is available.

The secretary of the League of Nations has a little central table to himself in front of the other. His profile points towards the door. Behind him, in the front row of chairs are the Jew, the Commissar and the Widow. In the opposite front row are Begonia and a cheerful young gentleman, powerfully built, with an uproarious voice which he subdues to conversational pitch with some difficulty. Next him is the quondam Newcomer. They are all reading newspapers. Begonia and her young man have one excessively illustrated newspaper between them. He has his arm round her waist and is shamelessly enjoying their physical contact. The two are evidently betrothed.

THE JEW. Do you think anything is really going to happen, Mr Secretary?

THE SECRETARY. Possibly not. I am here to be able to report from personal knowledge whether any notice has been taken of the summonses issued by the court.

THE BETROTHED. The judge himself hasnt turned up.

THE SECRETARY (*looking at his watch*). He is not due yet: you have all come too early.

THE BETROTHED. We came early to make sure of getting seats. And theres not a soul in the bally place except ourselves.

Sir Orpheus comes in.

SIR ORPHEUS. What! Nobody but ourselves! Dont they admit the public?

THE SECRETARY. The public is not interested, it seems.

BEGONIA. One free lance journalist looked in; but she went away when she found there was nothing doing.

THE BETROTHED. The doors are open all right. All are affectionately invited.

SIR ORPHEUS (*seating himself next Begonia*). But what a dreadful fiasco for our friend the judge! I warned him that this might happen. I told him to send special invitations to the press, and cards to all the leading people and foreign visitors. And here! not a soul except ourselves! All Europe will laugh at him.

THE SECRETARY. Yes; but if the affair is going to be a fiasco the fewer people there are to witness it the better.

BEGONIA. After all, theres more than half a dozen of us. Quite a distinguished audience I call it. Remember, you are the Foreign Secretary, Nunky. You are an honorable, Billikins. And I'm not exactly a nobody.

THE BETROTHED (*kissing her hand*) My ownest and bestest, you are a Dame of the British Empire. The Camberwell Times has celebrated your birthday by a poem hailing you as the Lily of Geneva; but on this occasion only, you are not the centre of European interest. The stupendous and colossal joke of the present proceedings is that this court has summoned all the dictators to appear before it and answer charges brought against them by the Toms, Dicks, Harriets, Susans and Elizas of all nations.

THE WIDOW. Pardon me, young Señor. I am neither Susan nor Eliza.

THE BETROTHED. Present company excepted, of course, Señora. But the point—the staggering, paralyzing, jolly bally breath-bereaving point of our assembly today is that the dictators have been summoned and that they wont come. Young Johnny Judge has no more authority over them than his cat.

THE NEWCOMER. But if they wont come, gentlemen, what are we here for?

THE BETROTHED. To see the fun when Johnny Judge comes and finds nothing doing, I suppose.

THE WIDOW. Is he not late? We seem to have been waiting here for ages.

THE SECRETARY [*looking at his watch*] He is due now. It is on the stroke of ten.

The Judge, in his judicial robe, enters. They all rise. He is in high spirits and very genial.

THE JUDGE [*shaking hands with Sir Orpheus*] Good morning, Sir Midlander. [*He passes on to the judicial chair, greeting them as he goes*] Good morning, ladies and gentlemen. Good morning, mademoiselle. Good morning, Señora. Good morning. Good morning. [*Takes his seat*] Pray be seated.

They all sit, having bowed speechlessly to his salutations.

THE JUDGE. Any defendants yet, Mr Secretary?

THE SECRETARY. None, your Honor. The parties on your left are all plaintiffs. On your right, Sir Orpheus Midlander has a watching brief for the British Foreign Office. The lady, Dame Begonia Brown, represents the Committee for Intellectual Co-operation. The young gentleman is the public.

THE JUDGE. An impartial spectator, eh?

THE BETROTHED. No, my lord. Very partial to the girl. Engaged, in fact.

THE JUDGE. My best congratulations. May I warn you all that the instruments on the table are microphones and televisors? I have arranged so as to avoid a crowd and make our proceedings as unconstrained and comfortable as possible; but our apparent privacy is quite imaginary.

General consternation. They all sit up as in church.

BEGONIA. But they should have told us this when we came in. Billikins has been sitting with his arm round my waist, whispering all sorts of silly things. Theyll be in The Camberwell Times tomorrow.

THE JUDGE. I'm sorry. You should have been warned. In the International Court no walls can hide you, and no distance deaden your lightest whisper. We are all seen and heard in Rome, in Moscow, in London, wherever the latest type of receiver is installed.

BEGONIA. Heard! You mean overheard.

THE WIDOW. And overlooked. Our very clothes are transparent to the newest rays. It is scandalous.

THE JUDGE. Not at all, Señora. The knowledge that we all live in public, and that there are no longer any secret places where evil things can be done and wicked conspiracies discussed, may produce a great improvement in morals.

THE WIDOW. I protest. All things that are private are not evil; but they may be extremely indecent.

BEGONIA. We'd better change the subject, I think.

THE BETROTHED. What about the dictators, my lord? Do you really think any of them will come?

THE JUDGE. They are not under any physical compulsion to come. But every day of their lives they do things they are not physically compelled to do.

SIR ORPHEUS. That is a fact, certainly. But it is hardly a parliamentary fact.

A telephone rings on the Judge's desk. He holds down a button and listens.

THE JUDGE. You will not have to wait any longer, Sir Midlander. [*Into the telephone*] We are waiting for him. Shew him the way. [*He releases the button*]. The very first dictator to arrive is Signor Bombardone.

ALL THE REST. Bombardone!!!

The Dictator enters, dominant, brusque, every inch a man of destiny.

BOMBARDONE. Is this the so-called International Court?

THE JUDGE. It is.

BBDE. My name is Bombardone. [*He mounts the dais; takes the nearest chair with a powerful hand and places it on the Judge's left; then flings himself massively into it*] Do not let my presence embarrass you. Proceed.

THE JUDGE. I have to thank you, Signor Bombardone, for so promptly obeying the summons of the court.

BBDE. I obey nothing. I am here because it is my will to be

here. My will is part of the world's will. A large part, as it happens. The world moves towards internationalism. Without this movement to nerve you you would never have had the audacity to summon me. Your action is therefore a symptom of the movement of civilization. Wherever such a symptom can be detected I have a place: a leading place.

SIR ORPHEUS. But pardon me, Signor: I understand that you are a great nationalist. How can you be at once a nationalist and an internationalist?

BBDE. How can I be anything else? How do you build a house? By first making good sound bricks. You cant build it of mud. The nations are the bricks out of which the future world State must be built. I consolidated my country as a nation: a white nation. I then added a black nation to it and made it an empire. When the empires federate, its leaders will govern the world; and these leaders will have a superleader who will be the ablest man in the world: that is my vision. I leave you to imagine what I think of the mob of bagmen from fifty potty little foreign States that calls itself a League of Nations.

JUDGE. Your country is a member of that League, Signor.

BBDE. My country has to keep an eye on fools. The scripture tells us that it is better to meet a bear in our path than a fool. Fools are dangerous; and the so-called League of Nations is a League of Fools; therefore the wise must join it to watch them. That is why all the effective Powers are in the League, as well as the little toy republics we shall swallow up in due time.

THE ÇI-DEVANT NEWCOMER. Steady on, mister. I dont understand.

BBDE. [contemptuously to the Judge] Tell him that this is a court of people who understand, and that the place of those who do not understand is in the ranks of silent and blindly obedient labor.

NEWCOMER. Oh, thats your game, is it? Who are you that I should obey you? What about democracy?

BBDE. I am what I am: you are what you are; and in virtue of these two facts I am where I am and you are where you are.

Try to change places with me: you may as well try to change the path of the sun through the heavens.

THE NEWCOMER. You think a lot of yourself, dont you? I ask you again: what about democracy?

An unsmiling middle aged gentleman with slim figure, erect carriage, and resolutely dissatisfied expression, wanders in.

THE DISSATISFIED GENTLEMAN. Is this the sitting of the department of international justice?

BBDE. [*springing up*] Battler, by all thats unexpected!

BATTLER [*equally surprised*] Bombardone, by all thats underhand!

BBDE. You thought you could steal a march on me, eh?

BATTLER. You have ambushed me. Fox!

BBDE. [*sitting down*] Undignified, Ernest. Undignified.

BATTLER. True, Bardo. I apologize. [*He takes a chair from behind Sir Orpheus, and mounts the dais to the right of the Judge, who now has a dictator on each side of him*] By your leave, sir. [*He sits*].

JUDGE. I thank you, Mr Battler, for obeying the summons of the court.

BATTLER. Obedience is hardly the word, sir.

JUDGE. You have obeyed. You are here. Why?

BATTLER. That is just what I have come to find out. Why are you here, Bardo?

BBDE. I am everywhere.

THE BETROTHED [*boisterously*] Ha ha! Ha ha ha! Dam funny, that.

THE JUDGE. I must ask the public not to smile.

NEWCOMER [*who has no sense of humor*] Smile! He was not smiling: he laughed right out. With all respect to your worship we are wasting our time talking nonsense. How can a man be everywhere? The other gentleman says he came here to find out why he came here. It isnt sense. These two gents are balmy.

BBDE. Pardon me. What does balmy mean?

NEWCOMER. Balmy. Off your chumps. If you want it straight, mad.

BBDE. You belong to the lower orders, I see.

NEWCOMER. Who are you calling lower orders? Dont you know that democracy has put an end to all that?

BBDE. On the contrary, my friend, democracy has given a real meaning to it for the first time. Democracy has thrown us both into the same pair of scales. Your pan has gone up: mine has gone down; and nothing will bring down your pan while I am sitting in the other. Democracy has delivered you from the law of priest and king, of landlord and capitalist, only to bring you under the law of personal gravitation. Personal gravitation is a law of nature. You cannot cut its head off.

NEWCOMER. Democracy can cut your head off. British democracy has cut off thicker heads before.

BBDE. Never. Plutocracy has cut off the heads of kings and archbishops to make itself supreme and rob the people without interference from king or priest; but the people always follow their born leader. When there is no leader, no king, no priest, nor any body of law established by dead kings and priests, you have mob law, lynching law, gangster law: in short, American democracy. Thank your stars you have never known democracy in England. I have rescued my country from all that by my leadership. I am a democratic institution.

NEWCOMER. Gosh. You democratic! Youve abolished democracy, you have.

BBDE. Put my leadership to the vote. Take a plebiscite. If I poll less than 95 per cent of the adult nation I will resign. If that is not democracy what is democracy?

NEWCOMER. It isnt British democracy.

BATTLER. British democracy is a lie. I have said it.

NEWCOMER. Oh, dont talk nonsense, you ignorant foreigner. Plebiscites are unEnglish, thoroughly unEnglish.

BEGONIA. Hear hear!

SIR O. May I venture to make an observation?

BATTLER. Who are you?

SIR O. Only a humble Englishman, listening most respectfully to your clever and entertaining conversation. Officially, I am the British Foreign Secretary.

Both Leaders rise and give the Fascist salute. Sir Orpheus remains seated, but waves his hand graciously.

BBDE. I must explain to the court that England is no longer of any consequence apart from me. I have dictated her policy for years [*he sits*].

BATTLER. I have snapped my fingers in England's face on every issue that has risen between us. Europe looks to me, not to England. [*He also resumes his seat*].

SIR O. You attract attention, Mr Battler: you certainly do attract attention. And you, Signor Bombardone, are quite welcome to dictate our policy as long as it is favorable to us. But the fact is, we are mostly unconscious of these triumphs of yours in England. I listen to your account of them with perfect complacency and—I hope you will not mind my saying so—with some amusement. But I must warn you that if your triumphs ever lead you to any steps contrary to the interests of the British Empire we shall have to come down rather abruptly from triumphs to facts; and the facts may not work so smoothly as the triumphs.

BATTLER. What could you do, facts or no facts?

SIR O. I dont know.

BATTLER.
BBDE. } You dont know!!!

SIR O. I dont know. Nor do you, Mr Battler. Nor you, Signor.

BBDE. Do you mean that I do not know what you could do, or that I do not know what I should do.

SIR O. Both, Signor.

BBDE. What have you to say to that, Ernest?

BATTLER. I should know what to do: have no doubt about that.

SIR O. You mean that you would know what to do when you knew what England was going to do?

BATTLER. I know already what you could do. Nothing. I tore up your peace treaty and threw the pieces in your face. You did nothing. I took your last Locarno pact and marched 18,000 soldiers through it. I threw down a frontier and doubled the size and power of my realm in spite of your teeth. What did you do?

Nothing.

SIR O. Of course we did nothing. It did not suit us to do anything. A child of six could have foreseen that we should do nothing; so you shook your fist at us and cried "Do anything if you dare." Your countrymen thought you a hero. But as you knew you were quite safe, we were not impressed.

BBDE. You are quite right, Excellency. It was your folly and France's that blew Ernest up the greasy pole of political ambition. Still, he has a flair for power; and he has my example to encourage him. Do not despise Ernest.

BATTLER. I have never concealed my admiration for you, Bardo. But you have a failing that may ruin you unless you learn to keep it in check.

BBDE. And what is that, pray?

BATTLER. Selfconceit. You think yourself the only great man in the world.

BBDE. [calm] Can you name a greater?

BATTLER. There are rivals in Russia, Arabia, and Iran.

BBDE. And there is Ernest the Great. Why omit him?

BATTLER. We shall see. History, not I, must award the palm.

JUDGE. Let us omit all personalities, gentlemen. Allow me to recall you to the important point reached by Sir Midlander.

SIR O. What was that, my lord?

JUDGE. When you were challenged as to what your country would do in the event of a conflict of interest, you said frankly you did not know.

SIR O. Well, I dont.

BATTLER. And you call yourself a statesman!

SIR O. I assure you I do not. The word is hardly in use in England. I am a member of the Cabinet, and in my modest amateur way a diplomatist. When you ask me what will happen if British interests are seriously menaced you ask me to ford the stream before we come to it. We never do that in England. But when we come to the stream we ford it or bridge it or dry it up. And when we have done that it is too late to think about it. We have found that we can get on without thinking. You see, thinking is very little use unless you know the facts. And we never do know the political facts until twenty years after. Sometimes a hundred and fifty.

JUDGE. Still, Sir Midlander, you know that such an activity as thought exists.

SIR O. You alarm me, my lord. I am intensely reluctant to lose my grip of the realities of the moment and sit down to think. It is dangerous. It is unEnglish. It leads to theories, to speculative policies, to dreams and visions. If I may say so, I think my position is a more comfortable one than that of the two eminent leaders who are gracing these proceedings by their presence here today. Their remarks are most entertaining: every sentence is an epigram: I, who am only a stupid Englishman, feel quite abashed by my commonplaceness. But if you ask me what their intentions are I must frankly say that I dont know. Where do they stand with us? I dont know. But they know what England intends. They know what to expect from us. We have no speculative plans. We shall simply stick to our beloved British Empire, and undertake any larger cares that Providence may impose on us. Meanwhile we should feel very uneasy if any other Power or combinations of Powers were to place us in a position of military or naval inferiority, especially naval inferiority. I warn you—I beg you—do not frighten us. We are a simple wellmeaning folk, easily frightened. And when we are frightened we are capable of anything, even of things we hardly care to remember afterwards. Do not drive us in that direction. Take us as we are; and let be. Pardon my dull little speech. I must not take more of your time.

BATTLER. Machiavelli!

BBDE. A most astute speech. But it cannot impose on us.

JUDGE. It has imposed on both of you. It is a perfectly honest speech made to you by a perfectly honest gentleman; and you both take it as an outburst of British hypocrisy.

BEGONIA. A piece of damned cheek, I call it. I wont sit here and listen to my country being insulted.

THE BETROTHED. Hear hear! Up, Camberwell!

BATTLER. What does he mean by "Up, Camberwell!"? What is Camberwell?

BEGONIA. Oh! He doesnt know what Camberwell is!

THE SECRETARY. Camberwell, Mr Battler, is a part of London which is totally indistinguishable from any other part of London, except that it is on the south side of the Thames and not on the north.

BEGONIA. What do you mean—indistinguishable? It maynt be as distangay as Mayfair; but it's better than Peckham anyhow.

BBDE. Excuse my ignorance; but what is Peckham?

BEGONIA. Oh! He doesnt know what Peckham is. These people dont know anything.

THE SECRETARY. Peckham is another part of London, adjacent to Camberwell and equally and entirely indistinguishable from it.

BEGONIA. Dont you believe him, gentlemen. He is saying that just to get a rise out of me. The people in Camberwell are the pick of south London society. The Peckham people are lower middle class: the scum of the earth.

BATTLER. I applaud your local patriotism, young lady; but I press for an answer to my question. What does "Up, Camberwell!" mean?

JUDGE. I think it is the south London equivalent to "Heil, Battler!"

BBDE. Ha ha ha! Ha ha! Good.

BATTLER. Am I being trifled with?

JUDGE. You may depend on me to keep order, Mr Battler. Dame Begonia is making a most valuable contribution to our proceedings. She is shewing us what we really have to deal with. Peace between the Powers of Europe on a basis of irreconcilable hostility between Camberwell and Peckham: that is our problem.

SIR O. Do not deceive yourself, my lord. Fire a shot at England; and Camberwell and Peckham will stand shoulder to shoulder against you.

BATTLER. You hear, Bardo. This Englishman is threatening us.

SIR O. Not at all. I am only telling you what will happen in certain contingencies which we sincerely wish to avoid. I am doing my best to be friendly in manner, as I certainly am in spirit. I respectfully suggest that if an impartial stranger were present his impression would be that you two gentlemen are threatening me: I might almost say bullying me.

BBDE. But we are. We shall not be thought the worse of at home for that. How are we to keep up the selfrespect of our people unless we confront the rest of the world with a battle cry? And—will you excuse a personal criticism?

SIR O. Certainly. I shall value it.

BBDE. You are very kind: you almost disarm me. But may I say that your technique is out of date? It would seem amusingly quaint in a museum, say in the rooms devoted to the eighteenth century; but of what use is it for impressing a modern crowd? And your slogans are hopelessly obsolete.

SIR O. I do not quite follow. What, exactly, do you mean by my technique?

BBDE. Your style, your gestures, the modulations of your voice. Public oratory is a fine art. Like other fine arts, it cannot be practised effectively without a laboriously acquired technique.

SIR O. But I am an experienced public speaker. My elocution has never been complained of. Like other public speakers I have taken pains to acquire a distinct articulation; and I have had the best parliamentary models before me all through my public life. I suppose—now that you put it in that way—that this constitutes a technique; but I should be sorry to think that there is anything professional about it.

BATTLER. Yes; but what a technique! I contemplated it at first with amazement, then with a curiosity which obliged me to study it—to find out what it could possibly mean. To me the object of public speaking is to propagate a burning conviction of truth and importance, and thus produce immediate action and enthusiastic faith and obedience. My technique, like that of my forerunner opposite, was invented and perfected with that object. You must admit that it has been wonderfully successful: your parliaments have been swept away by the mere breath of it; and we ourselves exercise a personal authority unattainable by any king, president, or minister. That is simple, natural, reasonable. But what is your technique? What is its object? Apparently its object is to destroy conviction and to paralyze action. Out of the ragbag of stale journalism and Kikkeronian Latin—

SIR O. I protest. I beg. I ask the court to protect me.

THE JUDGE. What is the matter? Protect you from what?

SIR O. From these abominable modern mispronunciations. Kikkeronian is an insult to my old school. I insist on Sisseronian.

THE BETROTHED. Hear hear!

BBDE. Take care, Ernest. This is part of the British technique. You were talking of something really important. That is dangerous. He switches you off to something of no importance whatever.

SIR O. I did not intend that, I assure you. And I cannot admit that the modern corruption of our old English pronunciation of the classics is a matter of no importance. It is a matter of supreme importance.

JUDGE. We do not question its importance, Sir Midlander; but it is outside the jurisdiction of this court; and we must not allow it to divert us from our proper business. I recall you to a specific charge of a specific crime against a specific section of the community. It is a crime of the most horrible character to drop a bomb upon a crowded city. It is a crime only a shade less diabolical to strew the sea, the common highway of all mankind, with mines that will shatter and sink any ship that stumbles on them in the dark. These abominable crimes are being committed by young men—

SIR O. Under orders, my lord, and from patriotic motives.

JUDGE. No doubt. Suppose a young man picks your pocket, and, on being detected, alleges, first that somebody told him to do it, and second that he wanted your money to pay his income tax—a highly patriotic motive—would you accept that excuse?

SIR O. Ridiculous! Remember, sir, that if our young heroes are the killers, they are also the killed. They risk their own lives.

JUDGE. Let us then add a third plea to our pickpocket's defence. He runs the same risk of having his pocket picked as you. Would you accept that plea also?

SIR O. My lord: I abhor war as much as you do. But, damn it, if a fellow is coming at me to cut my throat, I must cut his if I can. Am I to allow him to kill me and ravish my wife and daughters?

JUDGE. I think that under such circumstances a plea of legitimate defence might be allowed. But what has a tussle with a murderer and a ravisher to do with laying a mine in the high seas to slaughter innocent travellers whose intentions towards yourself, your wife, and your daughters, if they have any intentions, are entirely friendly? What has it to do with dropping a bomb into the bed of a sleeping baby or a woman in childbirth?

SIR O. One feels that. It is terrible. But we cannot help its happening. We must take a practical view. It is like the London traffic. We know that so many children will be run over and killed every week. But we cannot stop the traffic because of that. Motor traffic is a part of civilized life. So is coalmining. So is railway transport. So is flying. The explosions in the mines, the collisions of the trains, the accidents in the shunting yards, the aeroplane crashes, are most dreadful; but we cannot give up flying and coalmining and railway travelling on that account. They are a part of civilized life. War is a part of civilized life. We cannot give it up because of its shocking casualties.

JUDGE. But the mine explosions and railway collisions and aeroplane crashes are not the objects of the industry. They are its accidents. They occur in spite of every possible precaution to prevent them. But war has no other object than to produce these casualties. The business and purpose of a coalminer is to hew the coal out of the earth to keep the home fires burning. But the soldier's business is to burn the homes and kill their inhabitants. That is not a part of civilization: it is a danger to it.

COMMISSAR. Come, Comrade Judge: have you never sentenced a criminal to death? Has the executioner never carried out your sentence? Is not that a very necessary part of civilization?

JUDGE. I sentence persons to death when they have committed some crime which has raised the question whether they are fit to live in human society, but not until that question has been decided against them by a careful trial at which they have every possible legal assistance and protection. This does not justify young men in slaughtering innocent persons at random. It would justify me in sentencing the young men to death if they were brought to trial. What we are here to investigate is why they are not brought to trial.

SIR O. But really, they only obey orders.

THE JUDGE. Why do you say "only"? The slaughter of human beings and the destruction of cities are not acts to be qualified by the word only. Why are the persons who give such atrocious orders not brought to trial?

SIR O. But before what court?

JUDGE. Before this court if necessary. There was a time when I might have answered "Before the judgment seat of God". But since people no longer believe that there is any such judgment seat, must we not create one before we are destroyed by the impunity and glorification of murder?

BBDE. Peace may destroy you more effectually. It is necessary for the cultivation of the human character that a field should be reserved for war. Men decay when they do not fight.

THE WIDOW. And when they fight they die.

BBDE. No no. Only a percentage, to give zest and reality to the conflict.

THE JUDGE. Would you describe a contest of a man against a machine gun, or a woman in childbirth against a cloud of mustard gas, as a fight?

BBDE. It is a peril: a deadly peril. And it is peril that educates us, not mere bayonet fencing and fisticuffs. Nations never do anything until they are in danger.

THE JEW. Is there not plenty of danger in the world without adding the danger of poison gas to it?

BBDE. Yes: there is the danger of getting your feet wet. But it has not the fighting quality that gives war its unique power over the imagination, and through the imagination over the characters and powers of mankind.

THE WIDOW. You have been a soldier. Are you the better for it? Were you not glad when your wounds took you out of the trenches and landed you in a hospital bed?

BBDE. Extremely glad. But that was part of the experience. War is not all glory and all bravery. You find out what a rotten coward you are as well as how brave you are. You learn what it is to be numbed with misery and terror as well as how to laugh at death. Ask my understudy here. He too has been a soldier. He knows.

BATTLER. We all begin as understudies, and end, perhaps, as great actors. The army was a school in which I learnt a good deal, because whoever has my capacity for learning can learn something even in the worst school. The army is the worst school, because fighting is not a whole-time-job, and in the army they pretend that it is. It ends in the discharged soldier being good for nothing until he recovers his civilian sense and the habit of thinking for himself. No, cousin: I am a man of peace; but it must be a voluntary peace, not an intimidated one. Not until I am armed to the teeth and ready to face all the world in arms is my Pacifism worth anything.

SIR O. Admirable! Precisely our British position.

NEWCOMER. I'm British. And what I say is that war is necessary to keep down the population.

BBDE. This man is a fool. War stimulates population. The soldier may go to his death; but he leaves behind him the pregnant woman who will replace him. Women cannot resist the soldier: they despise the coward. Death, the supreme danger, rouses life to its supreme ecstasy of love. When has a warlike race ever lacked children?

THE BETROTHED. Very romantic and all that, old man; but this notion of man on the battlefield and woman in the home wont wash nowadays. Home was a safe place when Waterloo was fought; but today the home is the bomber's favorite mark. The soldier is safe in his trench while the woman is being blown to smithereens by her baby's cot. Kill the women; and where will your population be? Egad, you wont have any population at all.

BATTLER. This man is not a fool. If the object of war is extermination, kill the women: the men do not matter.

BBDE. The object of war is not extermination: it is the preservation of man's noblest attribute, courage. The utmost safety for women, the utmost peril for men: that is the ideal.

THE BETROTHED. I say, Signor: do you take any precautions against assassination?

BBDE. I do not encourage it; but it is one of the risks of my position. I live dangerously. It is more intense than living safely.

NEWCOMER. Your worship: these gentlemen are talking nonsense.

JUDGE. All politicians talk nonsense. You mean, I presume, that it is not the sort of nonsense you are accustomed to.

NEWCOMER. No I dont. I am accustomed to hear statesmen talking proper politics. But this about living dangerously is not proper politics: it's nonsense to me. Am I to cross the street without looking to see whether there is a bus coming? Are there to be no red and green lights? Am I to sleep in a smallpox hospital? Am I to cross the river on a tight rope instead of on a bridge? Am I to behave like a fool or a man of sense?

BBDE. You would be a much more wonderful man if you could walk on a tight rope instead of requiring several feet of solid pavement, costing years of labor to construct.

SIR O. Do you seriously propose that we should be ruled by an aristocracy of acrobats?

BBDE. Is it more impossible than your British aristocracy of foxhunters?

SIR O. Signor: acrobats are not foxhunters.

BBDE. And gentlemen are not acrobats. But what a pity!

THE NEWCOMER. Oh, whats the use of talking to you people? Am I dreaming? Am I drunk?

BBDE. No: you are only out of your depth, my friend. And now to business. Strength. Silence. Order. I am here to meet my accusers, if any.

JUDGE. You are accused, it seems, of the murder and destruction of liberty and democracy in Europe.

BBDE. One cannot destroy what never existed. Besides, these

things are not my business. My business is government. I give
my people good government, as far as their folly and ignorance
permit. What more do they need?

THE NEWCOMER. Why am I locked out of the parliament of
Jacksonsland, to which I have been lawfully elected: tell me that.

BBDE. Presumably because you want to obstruct its work and
discredit its leaders. Half a dozen such obstructionists as you
could spin out to two years the work I do in ten minutes. The
world can endure you no longer. Your place is in the dustbin.

THE NEWCOMER. I give up. You are too much for me when it
comes to talking. But what do I care? I have my principles still.
Thats my last word. Now go on and talk yourself silly.

BBDE. It is your turn now, cousin.

BATTLER. Do I stand accused? Of what, pray?

THE JEW [*springing up*] Of murder. Of an attempt to exterminate the flower of the human race.

BATTLER. What do you mean?

THE JEW. I am a Jew.

BATTLER. Then what right have you in my country? I exclude
you as the British exclude the Chinese in Australia, as the Americans exclude the Japanese in California.

JEW. Why do the British exclude the Chinese? Because the
Chinaman is so industrious, so frugal, so trustworthy, that nobody will employ a white British workman or caretaker if there
is a yellow one within reach. Why do you exclude the Jew?
Because you cannot compete with his intelligence, his persist-
ence, his foresight, his grasp of finance. It is our talents, our
virtues, that you fear, not our vices.

BATTLER. And am I not excluded for my virtues? I may not
set foot in England until I declare that I will do no work there
and that I will return to my own country in a few weeks. In
every country the foreigner is a trespasser. On every coast he is
confronted by officers who say you shall not land without your
passport, your visa. If you are of a certain race or color you shall
not land at all. Sooner than let German soldiers march through
Belgium England plunged Europe into war. Every State chooses

its population and selects its blood. We say that ours shall be Nordic, not Hittite: that is all.

JEW. A Jew is a human being. Has he not a right of way and settlement everywhere upon the earth?

BATTLER. Nowhere without a passport. That is the law of nations.

JEW. I have been beaten and robbed. Is that the law of nations?

BATTLER. I am sorry. I cannot be everywhere; and all my agents are not angels.

THE JEW [*triumphantly*] Ah! Then you are NOT God Almighty, as you pretend to be. [*To the Judge*] Your honor: I am satisfied. He has admitted his guilt. [*He flings himself back into his seat*].

BATTLER. Liar. No Jew is ever satisfied. Enough. You have your warning. Keep away; and you will be neither beaten nor robbed. Keep away, I tell you. The world is wide enough for both of us. My country is not.

THE JEW. I leave myself in the hands of the court. For my race there are no frontiers. Let those who set them justify themselves.

BBDE. Mr President: if you allow Ernest to expatiate on the Jewish question we shall get no further before bed-time. He should have waited for a lead from me before meddling with it, and forcing me to banish the Jews lest my people should be swamped by the multitudes he has driven out. I say he should have waited. I must add that I have no use for leaders who do not follow me.

BATTLER. I am no follower of yours. When has a Nordic ever stooped to follow a Latin Southerner?

BBDE. You forget that my country has a north as well as a south, a north beside whose mountains your little provincial Alps are molehills. The snows, the crags, the avalanches, the bitter winds of those mountains make men, Ernest, MEN! The trippers' paradise from which you come breeds operatic tenors. You are too handsome, Ernest: you think yourself a blond beast. Ladies and gentlemen, look at him! Is he a blond beast? The blondest beast I know is the Calabrian bull. I have no desire to figure as a blond beast; but I think I could play the part more plausibly than Ernest if it were my cue to do so. I am everything that you mean by the word Nordic. He is a born Southerner; and the south is the south, whether it be the south of the Arctic circle or the south of the equator. Race is nothing: it is the number of metres above sealevel that puts steel into men. Our friend here was born at a very moderate elevation. He is an artist to his finger tips; but his favorite play as a boy was not defying avalanches. As to our races, they are so mixed that the whole human race must be descended from Abraham; for everybody who is alive now must be descended from everybody who was alive in Abraham's day. Ernest has his share in Abraham.

BATTLER. This is an intolerable insult. I demand satisfaction. I cannot punch your head because you are at least two stone heavier than I; but I will fight you with any weapon that will give me a fair chance against you.

THE JUDGE. Gentlemen: you are at the Hague, and in a Court of Justice. Duels are out of date. And your lives are too valuable to be risked in that way.

BBDE. True, your Excellency. I admit that Ernest's ancestors are totally unknown. I apologize.

BATTLER. I dont want an apology. I want satisfaction. You shall not rob me of it by apologizing. Are you a coward?

BBDE. We are both cowards, Ernest. Remember 1918. All men are cowards now.

BATTLER [*rising*] I shall go home.

WIDOW [*rising*] You shall not. Here at least we have come to the real business of this court; and you want to run away from it. If a man of you stirs I shall shoot. [*Panic*].

BBDE. Hands up, Ernest [*politely holding up his own*].

THE WIDOW. Listen to me. In my country men fight duels every day. If they refuse they become pariahs: no one will visit them or speak to them: their women folk are driven out of society as if they were criminals.

BATTLER. It was so in my country. But I have stopped it.

JUDGE. Yet you want to fight a duel yourself.

BATTLER. Not for etiquette. For satisfaction.

THE WIDOW. Yes: that is what men always want. Well, look at me. I am a murderess [*general consternation*]. My husband wanted satisfaction of another kind. He got it from my dearest friend; and etiquette obliged me to kill her. In my dreams night after night she comes to me and begs me to forgive her; and I have to kill her again. I long to go mad; but I cannot: each time I do this dreadful thing I wake up with my mind clearer and clearer, and the horror of it deeper and more agonizing.

BATTLER [*flinching*] Stop this. I cannot bear it.

BBDE. Who is this woman? What right has she to be here?

WIDOW. My name is Revenge. My name is Jealousy. My name is the unwritten law that is no law. Until you have dealt with me you have done nothing.

JUDGE. You have a specific case. State it.

WIDOW. My husband has been murdered by his successor. My son must murder him if there is to be no redress but the blood feud; and I shall dream and dream and kill and kill. I call on you to condemn him.

BBDE. And condemn you.

WIDOW. I shall condemn myself. Pass your sentence on me; and I shall execute it myself, here in this court if you will.

JUDGE. But do you not understand that the judgments of this court are followed by no executions? They are moral judgments only.

WIDOW. I understand perfectly. You can point the finger of the whole world at the slayer of my husband and say "You are guilty of murder." You can put the same brand on my forehead. That is all you need do, all you can do. Then my dreams will cease and I shall kill myself. As for him, let him bear the brand as best he can.

JUDGE. That is the justice of this court. I thank you, Señora, for your comprehension of it.

BATTLER [*distressed by the narrative*] I cannot bear this. Order that woman not to kill herself.

BBDE. No. If she has a Roman soul, who dares forbid her?

JUDGE. My authority does not go so far, Mr Battler.

BATTLER. Your authority goes as far as you dare push it and as far as it is obeyed. What authority have I? What authority has Bardo? What authority has any leader? We command and are obeyed: that is all.

BBDE. That is true, Signor judge. Authority is a sort of genius: either you have it or you have not. Either you are obeyed or torn to pieces. But in some souls and on some points there is an authority higher than any other. Of such is the Roman soul; and this is one of the points on which the Roman soul stands firm. The woman's life is in her own hands.

BATTLER. No: I tell you I cannot bear it. Forbid her to kill herself or I will leave the court.

JUDGE. Señora: I forbid you to kill yourself. But I will sentence the slayer of your husband when his offence is proved; and by that act I will deliver you from your dreams.

WIDOW. I thank your Honor [*she sits down*].

JUDGE. Are you satisfied, Mr Battler?

BATTLER. I also thank your Honor. I am satisfied [*he resumes his seat; but his emotion has not yet quite subsided*].

BBDE. No duel then?

BATTLER. Do not torment me. [*Impatiently*] Bardo: you are a damned fool.

BBDE. [*hugely amused*] Ha ha! [*To the Judge*] The incident is closed.

An attractive and very voluble middleaged English lady enters. She is dressed as a deaconess and carries a handbag full of tracts.

DEACONESS. May I address the court? [*She goes on without waiting for a reply*]. I feel strongly that it is my duty to do so. There is a movement in the world which is also a movement in my heart. It is a movement before which all war, all unkindness, all uncharitableness, all sin and suffering will disappear and make Geneva superfluous. I speak from personal experience. I can remember many witnesses whose experience has been like my own. I——

BBDE. [*thundering at her*] Madam: you have not yet received permission to address us.

DEACONESS [*without taking the slightest notice of the interruption*] It is so simple! and the happiness it brings is so wonderful! All you have to do is to open your heart to the Master.

BATTLER. What master? I am The Master.

BBDE. There are others, Ernest.

DEACONESS. If you knew what I was, and what I am, all that you are doing here would seem the idlest trifling.

BATTLER [*shouting*] Who is the Master? Name him.

DEACONESS. Not so loud, please. I am not deaf; but when one is listening to the inner voice it is not easy to catch external noises.

BATTLER. I am not an external noise. I am the leader of my people. I may become leader of many peoples. Who is this Master of whom you speak?

DEACONESS. His beloved name, sir, is Jesus. I am sure that when you were a child your mother taught you to say "All hail the power of Jesu's name."

THE BETROTHED. "Let angels prostrate fall."

BEGONIA. Now shut up, Billikins. I wont have you laughing at religion.

BBDE. In Ernest's country, madam, they say Heil Battler. He has abolished Jesus.

DEACONESS. How can you say that? Jesus is stronger than ever. Jesus is irresistible. You can perhaps unify your countrymen in love of yourself. But Jesus can unite the whole world in love of Him. He will live when you are dust and ashes. Can you find the way to my heart as Jesus has found it? Can you make better men and women of them as Jesus can? Can——

BATTLER. I have made better men and women of them. I live for nothing else. I found them defeated, humiliated, the doormats of Europe. They now hold up their heads with the proudest; and it is I, Battler, who have raised them to spit in the faces of their oppressors.

DEACONESS. Jesus does not spit in people's faces. If your people are really raised up, really saved, it is Jesus who has done it; and you, sir, are only the instrument.

NEWCOMER [*rising*] A point of order, Mister. Is this a court of justice or is it not? Are we to be interrupted by every dotty female who starts preaching at us? I protest.

DEACONESS. It is no use protesting, my friend. When He calls you must follow.

NEWCOMER. Rot. Where are the police?

THE JUDGE. The peculiarity of this court, sir, is that there are no police. The lady is raising a point of general importance: one we must settle before we can come to any fruitful conclusions here. I rule that Jesus is a party in this case.

NEWCOMER. You are as dotty as she is. I say no more. [*He resumes his seat sulkily*].

THE JEW. A party in what capacity, may I ask? I speak as a Jew, if Mr Battler will permit me.

THE JUDGE. In the capacity of a famous prophet who laid down the law in these words, "This commandment I give unto you, that ye love one another." Are you prepared to love one another?

ALL EXCEPT SIR O. [*vociferously*] No.

SIR O. Not indiscriminately.

THE BRITISH CONTINGENT. Hear hear!

SIR O. What about the Unlovables? Judas Iscariot, for instance?

DEACONESS. If he had loved the Master he would not have betrayed Him. What a proof of the truth of my message!

BBDE. Do you love Ernest here?

DEACONESS. Why of course I do, most tenderly.

BATTLER. Woman: do not presume.

BBDE. Ha! ha! ha!

DEACONESS. Why should I not love you? I am your sister in Christ. What is there to offend you in that? Is not this touchiness a great trouble to you? You can easily get rid of it. Bring it to Jesus. It will fall from you like a heavy burden; and your heart will be light, oh, so light! You have never been happy. I can see it in your face.

BBDE. He practises that terrible expression for hours every day before the looking glass; but it is not a bit natural to him. Look at my face: there you have the real thing.

DEACONESS. You have neither of you the light in your eyes of the love of the Master. There is no happiness in these expressions that you maintain so industriously. Do you not find it very tiresome to have to be making faces all day? [*Much laughter in the British section*].

BATTLER. Is this to be allowed? The woman is making fun of us.

DEACONESS. I cannot make fun. But God has ordained that when men are childish enough to fancy that they are gods they become what you call funny. We cannot help laughing at them.

BBDE. Woman: if you had ever had God's work to do you would know that He never does it Himself. We are here to do it for Him. If we neglect it the world falls into the chaos called Liberty and Democracy, in which nothing is done except talk while the people perish. Well, what you call God's work, His hardest work, His political work, cannot be done by everybody: they have neither the time nor the brains nor the divine call for it. God has sent to certain persons this call. They are not chosen by the people: they must choose themselves: that is part of their inspiration. When they have dared to do this, what happens? Out of the Liberal democratic chaos comes form, purpose, order and rapid execution.

NEWCOMER. Yes, the executions come along all right. We know what dictators are.

BBDE. Yes: the triflers and twaddlers are swept away. This trifler and twaddler here can see nothing but his own danger, which raises his twaddle to a squeak of mortal terror. He does not matter. His selfchosen ruler takes him by the scruff of the neck and flings him into some island or camp where he and his like can trifle and twaddle without obstructing God's effectives. Then comes this pious lady to bid me turn to God. There is no need: God has turned to me; and to the best of my ability I shall not fail Him, in spite of all the Democratic Liberal gabblers. I have spoken. Now it is your turn, Ernest, if you have anything left to say.

BATTLER. You have said it all in your oldfashioned way, perhaps more clearly than I could have said it. But this woman's old fairy tales do not explain me, Ernest Battler, born a nobody, and now in command above all kings and kaisers. For my support is no dead Jew, but a mighty movement in the history of the world. Impelled by it I have stretched out my hand and lifted my country from the gutter into which you and your allies were trampling it, and made it once more the terror of Europe, though the danger is in your own guilty souls and not in any malice of mine. And mark you, the vision does not stop at my frontiers, nor at any frontier. Do not mistake me: I am no soldier dreaming of military conquests: I am what I am, and have done what I have done, without winning a single battle. Why is this? Because I have snapped my fingers in the face of all your Jewish beliefs and Roman traditions, your futile treaties and halfhearted threats, and the vulgar abuse you have spat at me from your platforms and newspapers like the frightened geese you are. You must all come my way, because I march with the times, and march as pioneer, not as camp follower. As pioneer I know that the real obstacle to human progress is the sort of mind that has been formed in its infancy by the Jewish Scriptures. That obstacle I must smash through at all costs; and so must you, Bardo, if you mean to be yourself and not the tool of that accursed race.

COMMISSAR. I must intervene. Are we here to discuss the Jewish problem? If so, I have no business here: my country has solved it. And we did not solve it by badinage.

BBDE. Badinage! Are our proceedings to be described as badinage by a Bolshevist?

SECRETARY. You see how hopeless it is for us to get any further. You have only to say the word Jew to Herr Battler or the word Bolshevist to Signor Bombardone, and they cease to be reasonable men. You have only to say Peckham to the representative of the Intellectual Committee of the League of Nations to reveal her as an irreconcilable belligerent. You have—

BEGONIA. Whats that he called me? It sounded awful. What does it mean, Uncle O?

SIR O. I understood the secretary to imply that however large-minded your view of the brotherhood of mankind, you must make an exception in the case of Peckham.

BEGONIA. Okay. No Peckham for me. And mind: on that point I am a representative woman. Sorry I interrupted. Carry on, old man.

SECRETARY. I thank you, Dame Begonia. I must add, with great respect for the British Foreign Secretary, that you have only to say British Empire to discover that in his view the rest of the world exists only as a means of furthering the interests of that geographical expression.

SIR O. Surely the British Empire is something more than a geographical expression. But of course with me the British Empire comes first.

SECRETARY. Precisely. And as a common basis of agreement, this lady has proposed the policy of the Sermon on the Mount.

DEACONESS. Love oneanother. It is so simple.

SECRETARY. It turns out that we do not and cannot love one-another—that the problem before us is how to establish peace among people who heartily dislike oneanother, and have very good reasons for doing so: in short, that the human race does not at present consist exclusively or even largely of likeable persons.

DEACONESS. But I assure you, that does not matter. There is a technique you have not learnt.

SIR O. What! More techniques! Madam: before your arrival, I was accused of having a technique. Can we not keep on the plain track of commonsense?

DEACONESS. But this one is so simple. You have spites. You have hatreds. You have bad tempers. All you have to do is to bring them to Jesus. He will relieve you of them. He will shew you that they are all imaginary. He will fill your hearts with love of Himself; and in that love there is eternal peace. I know so many cases. I know by my own experience.

SECRETARY. You are an amiable lady; and no doubt there are, as you say, other cases—

DEACONESS. Oh, I was not an amiable lady. I was a perfect fiend, jealous, quarrelsome, full of imaginary ailments, as touchy as Mr Battler, as bumptious as Signor Bombardone—

BATTLER. Pardon. What does touchy mean?

BBDE. I am unacquainted with the word bumptious. What am I to understand by it?

DEACONESS. Look within, look within, and you will understand. I brought it all to Jesus; and now I am happy: I am what the gentleman is kind enough to describe as amiable. Oh, why will you not do as I have done? It is so simple.

BBDE. It is made much simpler by the fact that you are protected by an efficient body of policemen with bludgeons in their pockets, madam. You have never had to govern.

DEACONESS. I have had to govern myself, sir. And I am now governed by Jesus.

JUDGE. Allow the lady the last word, Mr Leader. Proceed, Mr Secretary.

SECRETARY. No: I have said enough. You know now what an impossible job I have here as secretary to the League of Nations. To me it is agony to have to listen to all this talk, knowing as I do that nothing can come of it. Have pity on me. Let us adjourn for lunch.

JUDGE. Oh, it is not lunch time yet, Mr Secretary. We have been here less than an hour.

SECRETARY. It seems to me twenty years.

JUDGE. I am sorry, Mr Secretary. But I am waiting for the arrival of a defendant who has not yet appeared, General Flanco de Fortinbras, who is accused of having slaughtered many thousands of his fellow countrymen on grounds that have never been clearly stated.

BBDE. But he has not yet been elected Leader. He is a mere soldier.

COMMISSAR. Half Europe describes him as your valet.

BBDE. I do not keep valets. But in so far as Flanco is striving to save his country from the horrors of Communism he has my sympathy.

COMMISSAR. Which includes the help of your guns and soldiers.

BBDE. I cannot prevent honest men from joining in a crusade, as volunteers, against scoundrels and assassins.

JUDGE. You also, Mr Battler, sympathize with General Flanco?

BATTLER. I do. He has accepted my definite offer to Europe to rid it of Bolshevism if the western states will co-operate.

JUDGE. And you, Sir Midlander, can of course assure General Flanco of British support?

SIR O. [*rising*] Oh, no, no, no. I am amazed at such a misunderstanding. The British Empire has maintained the strictest neutrality. It has merely recognized General Flanco as a belligerent.

BBDE. Flanco will not come. I have not authorized him to come.

General Flanco de Fortinbras enters at the door. He is a middle aged officer, very smart, and quite conventional.

FLANCO. Pardon. Is this the International Court?

JUDGE. It is.

FLANCO. My name is Flanco de Fortinbras—General Flanco de Fortinbras. I have received a summons.

JUDGE. Quite so, General. We were expecting you. You are very welcome. Pray be seated.

The secretary places a chair between the judge and Bombardone. Flanco crosses to it.

JUDGE [*before Flanco sits down*] You know these gentlemen, I think.

FLANCO [*sitting down carelessly*] No. But I have seen many caricatures of them. No introduction is necessary.

THE JUDGE. You recognize also the British Foreign Secretary, Sir Orpheus Midlander.

Flanco immediately rises; clicks his heels; and salutes Sir Orpheus with a distinguished consideration that contrasts very significantly with his contemptuous indifference to the two leaders. Sir Orpheus, as before, waves a gracious acknowledgment of the salute. Flanco resumes his seat.

FLANCO. I have come here because it seemed the correct thing to do. I am relieved to find that His Excellency the British Foreign Secretary agrees with me.

BBDE. In what capacity are you here, may I ask?

FLANCO. Do I seem out of place between you and your fellow talker opposite? A man of action always is out of place among talkers.

BBDE. Inconceivable nothingness that you are, do you dare to class me as a talker and not a man of action?

FLANCO. Have you done anything?

BBDE. I have created an empire.

FLANCO. You mean that you have policed a place infested by savages. A child could have done it with a modern mechanized army.

BBDE. Your little military successes have gone to your head. Do not forget that they were won with my troops.

FLANCO. Your troops do fairly well under my command. We have yet to see them doing anything under yours.

BBDE. Ernest: our valet has gone stark mad.

FLANCO. Mr. Battler may be a useful civilian. I am informed that he is popular with the lower middle class. But the fate of Europe will not be decided by your scraps of Socialism.

JUDGE. May I recall you to the business of the court, gentlemen. General: you are charged with an extraordinary devastation of your own country and an indiscriminate massacre of its inhabitants.

FLANCO. That is my profession. I am a soldier; and my business is to devastate the strongholds of the enemies of my country, and slaughter their inhabitants.

NEWCOMER. Do you call the lawfully constituted democratic government of your country its enemies?

FLANCO. I do, sir. That government is a government of cads. I stand for a great cause; and I have not talked about it, as these two adventurers talk: I have fought for it: fought and won.

JUDGE. And what, may we ask, is the great cause?

FLANCO. I stand simply for government by gentlemen against

116

government by cads. I stand for the religion of gentlemen against the irreligion of cads. For me there are only two classes, gentlemen and cads: only two faiths: Catholics and heretics. The horrible vulgarity called democracy has given political power to the cads and the heretics. I am determined that the world shall not be ruled by cads nor its children brought up as heretics. I maintain that all spare money should be devoted to the breeding of gentlemen. In that I have the great body of public opinion behind me. Take a plebiscite of the whole civilized world; and not a vote will be cast against me. The natural men, the farmers and peasants, will support me to a man, and to a woman. Even the peasants whom you have crowded into your towns and demoralized by street life and trade unionism, will know in their souls that I am the salvation of the world.

BBDE. A Saviour, no less! Eh?

FLANCO. Do not be profane. I am a Catholic officer and gentleman, with the beliefs, traditions, and duties of my class and my faith. I could not sit idly reading and talking whilst the civilization established by that faith and that order was being destroyed by the mob. Nobody else would do anything but read seditious pamphlets and talk, talk, talk. It was necessary to fight, fight, fight to restore order in the world. I undertook that responsibility and here I am. Everybody understands my position: nobody understands the pamphlets, the three volumes of Karl Marx, the theories of the idealists, the ranting of the demagogues: in short, the caddishness of the cads. Do I make myself clear?

BBDE. Am I a cad? Is Ernest here a cad?

FLANCO. You had better not force me to be personal.

BBDE. Come! Face the question. Are we cads or gentlemen? Out with it.

FLANCO. You are certainly not gentlemen. You are freaks.

BATTLER. Freaks!

BBDE. What is a freak?

JUDGE. An organism so extraordinary as to defy classification.

BBDE. Good. I accept that.

BATTLER. So do I. I claim it.

JUDGE. Then, as time is getting on, gentlemen, had we not better come to judgment?

BATTLER. Judgment!

BBDE. Judgment!

BATTLER. What do you mean? Do you presume to judge me?

BBDE. Judge me if you dare.

FLANCO. Give judgment against me and you pass out of history as a cad.

BATTLER. You have already passed out of history as a Catholic: that is, nine tenths a Jew.

BBDE. The bee in your bonnet buzzes too much, Ernest. [*To the Judge*] What is the law?

JUDGE. Unfortunately there is no law as between nations. I shall have to create it as I go along, by judicial precedents.

BATTLER. In my country I create the precedents.

BBDE. Well said, Ernest. Same here.

JUDGE. As you are not judges your precedents have no authority outside the operations of your police. You, Mr Battler, are here to answer an accusation made against you by a Jewish gentleman of unlawful arrest and imprisonment, assault, robbery, and denial of his right to live in the country of his birth. What is your defence?

BATTLER. I do not condescend to defend myself.

JEW. You mean that you have no defence. You cannot even find a Jewish lawyer to defend you, because you have driven them all from your country and left it with no better brains than your own. You have employed physical force to suppress intellect. That is the sin against the Holy Ghost. I accuse you of it.

JUDGE. What have you to say to that, Mr Battler?

BATTLER. Nothing. Men such as I am are not to be stopped by academic twaddle about intellect. But I will condescend to tell this fellow from the Ghetto that to every superior race that is faithful to itself a Messiah is sent.

DEACONESS. Oh, how true! If only you would accept him!

JUDGE. I understand you to plead divine inspiration, Mr Battler.

BATTLER. I say that my power is mystical, not rational.

BBDE. Ernest: take care. You are walking on a razor's edge between inspiration and the madness of the beggar on horseback. We two are beggars on horseback. For the credit of leadership let us ride carefully. Leadership, we two know, is mystical. Then let us not pretend to understand it. God may choose his leaders; but he may also drop them with a crash if they get out of hand. Tell yourself that every night before you get into bed, my boy; and you may last a while yet.

Loud applause from the British section.

BATTLER. Physician, cure yourself. You need not prescribe for me.

JUDGE. This is very edifying, gentlemen; and I thank you both in the name of all present. May I ask whether this divine guidance of which you are conscious has any limits? Does it not imply a world State with Mr Battler or Signor Bombardone or the British Foreign Office at its head?

FLANCO. Certainly not in my country. A frontier is a frontier; and there must be no monkeying with it. Let these gentlemen manage their own countries and leave us to manage ours.

JUDGE. Is that your view, Mr Battler?

BATTLER. No. I believe that the most advanced race, if it breeds true, must eventually govern the world.

JUDGE. Do you agree, Sir Midlander?

SIR O. With certain reservations, yes. I do not like the term "advanced race." I greatly mistrust advanced people. In my experience they are very difficult to work with, and often most disreputable in their private lives. They seldom attend divine service. But if you will withdraw the rather unfortunate word "advanced" and substitute the race best fitted by its character—its normal, solid, everyday character—to govern justly and prosperously, then I think I agree.

JUDGE. Precisely. And now may we have your opinion, Signor Leader?

BBDE. In principle I agree. It is easy for me to do so, as my people, being a Mediterranean people, can never be subject to northern barbarians, though it can assimilate and civilize them in unlimited numbers.

JUDGE. Has the Russian gentleman anything to say?

COMMISSAR. Nothing. These gentlemen talk of their countries. But they do not own their countries. Their people do not own the land they starve in. Their countries are owned by a handful of landlords and capitalists who allow them to live in it on condition that they work like bees and keep barely enough of the honey to keep themselves miserably alive. Russia belongs to the Russians. We shall look on whilst you eat each other up. When you have done that, Russia—Holy Russia—will save the soul of the world by teaching it to feed its people instead of robbing them.

FLANCO. Did your landlords ever rob the people as your bureaucracy now robs them to build cities and factories in the desert and to teach children to be atheists? Your country is full of conspiracies to get the old order back again. You have to shoot the conspirators by the dozen every month.

COMMISSAR. That is not many out of two hundred million people, General. Think of all the rascals you ought to shoot!

JUDGE. Pray, gentlemen, no more recriminations. Let us keep to the point of the superior race and the divine leadership. What is to happen if you disagree as to which of you is the divinely chosen leader and the superior race?

BBDE. My answer is eight million bayonets.

BATTLER. My answer is twelve million bayonets.

JUDGE. And yours, Sir Midlander?

SIR O. This sort of talk is very dangerous. Besides, men do not fight with bayonets nowadays. In fact they do not fight at all in the old sense. Mr Battler can wipe out London, Portsmouth, and all our big provincial cities in a day. We should then be obliged to wipe out Hamburg and all the eastern cities from Munster to Salzburg. Signor Bombardone can wipe out Tunis, Nice, Algiers, Marseilles, Toulouse, Lyons, and every city south of the Loire, and oblige the French, headed by the British fleet, to wipe out Naples, Venice, Florence, Rome, and even Milan by return of post. The process can go on until the European stock of munitions and air pilots is exhausted. But it is a process by which none of us can win, and all of us must lose frightfully. Which of us dare take the responsibility of dropping the first bomb?

BATTLER. Our precautions against attack from the air are perfect.

SIR O. Ours are not, unfortunately. Nobody believes in them. I certainly do not. You must allow me to doubt the efficiency of yours.

JUDGE. And your precautions, Signor? Are they efficient?

BBDE. They do not exist. Our strength is in our willingness to die.

JUDGE. That seems to complicate murder with suicide. However, am I to take it that you are all provided with the means to effect this destruction, and to retaliate in kind if they are used against you?

SIR O. What else can we do, sir?

JUDGE. I find myself in a difficulty. I have listened to you all and watched you very attentively. You seem to me to be personally harmless human beings, capable of meeting one another and chatting on fairly pleasant terms. There is no reason why you should not be good neighbors. So far, my work of building up a body of international law by judicial precedent would seem to be simple enough. Unfortunately when any question of foreign policy arises you confront me with a black depth of scoundrelism which calls for nothing short of your immediate execution.

The Leaders and the British contingent, except the Newcomer, rise indignantly.

NEWCOMER. Hear hear! Hear hear! Hear hear! SIR O. Scoundrelism! BATTLER. Execution! BOMBARDONE. You are mad.

JUDGE. If you dislike the word execution I am willing to substitute liquidation. The word scoundrelism and its adjectives I cannot withdraw. Your objective is domination: your weapons fire and poison, starvation and ruin, extermination by every means known to science. You have reduced one another to such a condition of terror that no atrocity makes you recoil and say that you will die rather than commit it. You call this patriotism, courage, glory. There are a thousand good things to be done in your countries. They remain undone for hundreds of years; but the fire and the poison are always up to date. If this be not scoundrelism what is scoundrelism? I give you up as hopeless. Man is a failure as a political animal. The creative forces which produce him must produce something better. [*The telephone rings*]. Pardon me a moment. [*Changing countenance and holding up his hand for silence*] I am sorry to have to announce a very grave piece of news. Mr Battler's troops have invaded Ruritania.

General consternation. All rise to their feet except Battler, who preserves an iron calm.

JUDGE. Is this true, Mr Battler?

BATTLER. I am a man of action, not a dreamer. While you have been talking my army has been doing. Bardo: the war for the mastery of the world has begun. It is you and I, and, I presume, our friend Fortinbras, against the effete so-called democracies of which the people of Europe and America are tired.

BBDE. Ernest: you have done this without consulting me. I warned you a year ago, when you were negotiating with a relative of Sir Orpheus here, that I could not afford another war.

FLANCO. Neither can I.

All sit down gradually, greatly relieved, except Battler.

BATTLER [*rising in great agitation*] Bardo: are you going to betray me? Remember the axis. Dare you break it?

BBDE. Damn the axis! Do you suppose I am going to ruin my country to make you emperor of the universe? You should know me better [*He resumes his seat majestically*].

BATTLER. This is the most shameless betrayal in human history. General Flanco: you owe your victory to my aid. Will you be such a monster of ingratitude as to desert me now?

FLANCO. I owe my victory equally to the aid of Signor Bombardone and to the masterly non-intervention policy of Sir Orpheus Midlander. I cannot prove ungrateful to either of them.

BATTLER. Well, traitors as you are, I can do without you. I can conquer Ruritania single-handed, no thanks to either of you. But where should I be if the British were not afraid to fight. Fortunately for me they do not believe in what they call brute force. [*He sits*].

SIR O. [*rising*] Pardon me. It is true that we abhor brute force, and are willing to make any sacrifice for the sake of peace—or almost any sacrifice. We understood that this was your attitude also. But I had the honor of informing you explicitly—very explicitly, Mr Battler—that Ruritania is, so to speak, our little sister, and that if you laid a finger on her we should—pardon me if in my indignant surprise at your breach of the peace I am unable to adhere to the language of diplomacy—we should be obliged to knock the stuffing out of you. That is our British method of meeting brute force.

BATTLER. What! You will fight?

SIR O. Fight, Mr Battler! We shall wipe you off the face of the earth. [*He resumes his seat*].

BATTLER. Then I am alone; *contra mundum*. Well, I have never failed yet.

FLANCO. Because you have never fought yet.

BATTLER. We shall see. I shall sweep through Ruritania like a hurricane.

COMMISSAR. Do so by all means, Comrade Battler. When you have finished you will settle with me how much of it you may keep.

BATTLER. What! You too! So the encirclement is complete.

SIR ORPHEUS. No! I cannot permit that expression. Outflanked if you like. Hemmed in if you will have it so. I will even go so far as to say surrounded. But encircled, NO.

NEWCOMER. It puts the kybosh on Battlerism anyhow.

The telephone rings again.

ALL EXCEPT THE JUDGE. Hush. Let us hear the news. The news. The news. [*They listen with strained attention*]. Sh-sh-sh-sh-sh-.

JUDGE. What? Say that again: I must take it down: I do not understand. [*Writing as he listens*] "Astronomers report that the orbit of the earth is jumping to its next quantum. Message received at Greenwich from three American observatories. Humanity is doomed." Thank you. Goodbye. Can anyone

GENEVA

explain this? Why is humanity doomed?

SECRETARY. It is intelligible enough, and very serious indeed.

JUDGE. It is not intelligible to me. Will you kindly explain?

SECRETARY. The orbit of the earth is the path in which it travels round the sun. As the sun is 93 million miles distant it takes us a year to get round.

JUDGE. We all know that. But the message says that the orbit is jumping to its next quantum. What does quantum mean?

SECRETARY. When orbits change they dont change gradually. They suddenly jump by distances called quantums or quanta. Nobody knows why. If the earth is jumping to a wider orbit it is taking us millions of miles further away from the sun. That will take us into the awful cold of space. The icecaps that we have on the north and south poles will spread over the whole earth. Even the polar bears will be frozen stiff. Not a trace of any sort of life known to us will be possible on this earth.

THE JEW [rising and hurrying to the door] Excuse me.

SECRETARY. No use running away, my friend. The icecap will overtake you wherever you go.

SECRETARY. Let him alone. The shock has made him ill.

THE JEW. No: not that. I must telephone [he goes out].

JUDGE [rising] Fellow citizens: this is the end. The end of war, of law, of leaders and foreign secretaries, of judges and generals. A moment ago we were important persons: the fate of Europe seemed to depend on us. What are we now? Democracy, Fascism, Communism: how much do they matter? Your totalitarian Catholic Church: does it still seem so very totalitarian?

FLANCO. Do not blaspheme at such a moment, sir. You tell us that nothing matters. Ten minutes ago the judgment of God seemed far off: now we stand at the gates of purgatory. We have to organize absolution for millions of our people; and we have barely priests enough to do it, even if we have no converts to deal with; and we shall have many converts. We Catholics know what to do; and I have no more time to spend trifling here with men who know nothing and believe nothing. [He moves towards the door. He stops to hear Sir O.]

124

SIR O. One moment, I beg of you. This rumor must be contradicted at all costs.

COMMISSAR. How can you contradict a scientific fact?

SIR O. It must be contradicted—officially contradicted. Think of the consequences if it is believed! People will throw off all decency, all prudence. Only the Jews, with the business faculty peculiar to their race, will profit by our despair. Why has our Jewish friend just left us? To telephone, he said. Yes; but to whom is he telephoning? To his stockbroker, gentlemen. He is instructing his stockbroker to sell gilt-edged in any quantity, at any price, knowing that if this story gets about before settling day he will be able to buy it for the price of waste paper and be a millionaire until the icecap overtakes him. It must not be. I will take the necessary steps in England. The Astronomer Royal will deny this story this afternoon. You two gentlemen must see to it at once that it is officially denied in your countries.

COMMISSAR. Suppose your Astronomer Royal refuses to tell a lie. Remember: he is a man of science, not a politician.

SIR O. He is an Englishman, sir, and has some common sense. He will do his duty. Can I depend on the rest of you gentlemen?

BBDE. Can you depend on the icecap? I must go home at once. There will be a rush to the equator. My country stands right in the way of that rush. I must stop it at our frontier at any cost.

COMMISSAR. Why? Will it matter?

BBDE. I will not tolerate disorder. I will not tolerate fear. We shall die decently, stoically, steadfast at our posts, like Romans. Remember: we shall not decay: we shall stand to all eternity in cold storage. When we are discovered by some explorer from another star or another race that can live and breathe at absolute zero, he shall find my people erect at their posts like the Pompeian sentinel. You also, Ernest, must— What! Crying!! For shame, man! The world looks to us for leadership. Shall it find us in tears?

BATTLER. Let me alone. My dog Blonda will be frozen to death. My doggie! My little doggie! [*He breaks down, sobbing convulsively*].

NEWCOMER. Oh, come, old man. Dont take it so hard. I used to keep dogs myself; but I had to give it up: I couldnt bear the shortness of their lives. Youd have had to lose your little doggie some day.

Battler takes out his handkerchief and controls himself; but the Deaconess bursts into tears.

BEGONIA. Oh for God's sake, dont you start crying. You will set us all off. It's hard enough on us without that.

THE SECRETARY. Yes, maam. Take your trouble to Jesus; and set all the women a good example.

DEACONESS. But in heaven I shall lose my Jesus. There He will be a king; and there will be no more troubles and sorrows and sins to bring to Him. My life has been so happy since I found Him and came to Him a year ago! He made heaven for me on earth; and now that is all over. I cannot bear it. [*Her tears overcome her*].

NEWCOMER. Oh come come! This wont do, you know. All you people seem to think you were going to live for ever. Well, you werent. Our numbers are up; but so they were before, sooner or later. I dont complain: I havnt had such a bad time of it; and I am ready to depart, as the poet says, if it must be. In fact I must depart now and cheer up the missus. [*He rises to go*].

DEACONESS. Oh, sir, do you believe this? May it not be untrue?

NEWCOMER [*gravely*] No: it's true all right enough. If it were a priest's tale or a superstition out of the Bible I shouldnt give a snap of my fingers for it. But Science cannot be wrong. Weve got to face it. Good morning, gents.

The Newcomer goes out; and his departure breaks up the court. The Leaders and the General rise and come forward together.

DEACONESS [*to Flanco*] Oh, General, is Science always right?

FLANCO. Certainly not: it is always wrong. But I await the decision of the Church. Until that is delivered the story has no authority.

SIR O. May I suggest that you use all your influence at Rome to obtain an immediate decision from the Church against this story?

FLANCO. You shock me. The Church cannot be influenced. It knows the truth as God knows it, and will instruct us accordingly. Anyone who questions its decision will be shot. My business is to see to that. After absolution, of course. Good morning. [*He goes out*].

WIDOW. He at least has something to offer to men about to die.

COMMISSAR. Dope.

JUDGE. Why not, if they die comforted?

BATTLER. Men must learn to die undeluded.

BBDE. Flanco is dead; but he does not know it. History would have kicked him out were not History now on its deathbed.

BEGONIA. I must say I thought the general a perfect gentleman. I never wanted to kick him while he was speaking. I wanted to kick you two all the time.

THE BETROTHED. Steady, Gonny, steady! Mustnt be rude, you know.

BEGONIA. Oh, what does it matter now? As we shall all be frozen stiff presently we may as well have the satisfaction of speaking our minds until then.

THE BETROTHED. Take it easy, dear. Have a choc.

BEGONIA. No, thank you.

THE BETROTHED. I say, Uncle O: this is the first time she has ever refused a choc.

SIR O. Our valuations have changed, naturally.

THE BETROTHED. Mine havnt. You know, uncle, I think theres something in your notion of selling out and having a tremendous spree before the icecaps nip us. How does that strike you, Gonny?

BEGONIA. I dont pretend it might not have appealed to me before I represented Intellectual Co-operation. But I am a Dame of the British Empire now; and if I must die I will die like a Dame. [*She goes out*].

SIR O. Go with her, sir. And mind you behave yourself.

THE BETROTHED. Well, it does seem rather a pity. However— [*He shrugs resignedly and goes out*].

SIR O. [*to the Commissar*] Do you, sir, understand what is going to happen? My classical education did not include science.

COMMISSAR. I await instructions. The Marxian dialectic does not include the quantum theory. I must consult Moscow. [*He goes out*].

SIR O. Have these men no minds of their own? One of them must consult Rome: the other must consult Moscow. You two gentlemen fortunately have no one but yourselves to consult. Can I rely on you to do your utmost to stifle this appalling news while I return to London to consult the Cabinet?

BBDE. You can rely on nothing but this. The news has just been broadcast to all the world through the arrangements made for publicity in this court. According to you, the result will be that the people will throw off all decency and repudiate all leadership. I say that the people will want a leader as they have never wanted one before. I have taught them to order their lives: I shall teach them to order their deaths. The magnitude of the catastrophe is the measure of the leader's greatness.

SIR O. You always have a speech which sounds equal to the occasion. In England that gift would make you Prime Minister. But your very excitable countrymen may run wild.

BBDE. In that case I can do nothing but fall at the head of an attempt to stem the rush. At least one man shall stand for human courage and dignity when the race expires.

SIR O. Yes: that is a very fine attitude and quite a correct one. But have you nothing better to propose than an attitude?

BBDE. Has anyone anything better to propose than an attitude?

SIR O. I suppose not; but I feel strongly that a burst of sincerity would be a great relief.

BBDE. [*to Battler*] Give him his burst of sincerity, Ernest. Cry for your dog again. Good morning, gentlemen. [*He goes to the door*].

BATTLER [*calling after him*] You will have the honor of sharing my little dog's fate. But nobody will weep for you, Bardo.

BBDE. I hope not. I do not deal in tears. [*He strides out*].

BATTLER. What an actor!

SECRETARY. You should be a good judge of that. You have

done a good deal in that line yourself.

BATTLER. We all have. But I claim to have done a little good with my acting. I will not have my work undone. We shall not stand in statuesque attitudes in Bardo's manner: we shall work to the last, and set an example to the new race of iceproof men who will follow us.

SIR O. Still, you know, it's no use going on making motor cars that you know will never run.

BATTLER. Yes: when the alternative is to wring our hands in despair or get drunk. We cannot work for ourselves to the last moment; but we can all work for honor. [*He goes out*].

SIR O. Wonderful luck that man has! His dog will get him into all the headlines. [*He goes out*].

JUDGE [*to the Deaconess and the widow*] Ladies: I am afraid there is nothing more to be done here.

DEACONESS [*rising*] None of you understands what this means to me, because none of you has learnt how to live. You are souls in torment, as I was until six months ago. And now I must die when I have only just learnt to live. Excuse me: I cannot bear to speak of it [*she goes out distractedly*].

JUDGE. She, at least, values her life.

SECRETARY. Yes: she belongs to some movement or other.

WIDOW [*taking her pistol from her handbag and rising*] I killed my best friend with this. I kept it to kill myself. It is useless now: God will execute His own judgment on us all. [*She throws it into the waste paper basket*]. But He is merciful; for I shall never dream again. And [*to the Secretary*] I do not belong to any movement.

He bows; and she goes out.

SECRETARY. Can you switch off?

JUDGE [*going to the table and turning a masterswitch*] No one can hear us now. [*Returning*] Can this thing be true?

SECRETARY. No. It is utter nonsense. If the earth made a spring to a wider orbit half a minute would carry us to regions of space where we could not breathe and our blood would freeze in our veins.

JUDGE. Yet we all believed it for the moment.

SECRETARY. You have nothing to do but mention the quantum theory, and people will take your voice for the voice of Science and believe anything. It broke up this farce of a trial, at all events.

JUDGE. Not a farce, my friend. They came, these fellows. They blustered: they defied us. But they came. They came.

CYMBELINE REFINISHED:

A VARIATION ON SHAKESPEAR'S ENDING

XLVI

FOREWORD

THE practice of improving Shakespear's plays, more especially in the matter of supplying them with what are called happy endings, is an old established one which has always been accepted without protest by British audiences. When Mr Harley Granville-Barker, following up some desperate experiments by the late William Poel, introduced the startling innovation of performing the plays in the West End of London exactly as Shakespear wrote them, there was indeed some demur; but it was expressed outside the theatre and led to no rioting. And it set on foot a new theory of Shakespearean representation. Up to that time it had been assumed as a matter of course that everyone behind the scenes in a theatre must know much better than Shakespear how plays should be written, exactly as it is believed in the Hollywood studios today that everyone in a film studio knows better than any professional playwright how a play should be filmed. But the pleasure given by Mr Granville-Barker's productions shook that conviction in the theatre; and the superstition that Shakespear's plays as written by him are impossible on the stage, which had produced a happy ending to King Lear, Cibber's Richard III, a love scene in the tomb of the Capulets between Romeo and Juliet before the poison takes effect, and had culminated in the crude literary butcheries successfully imposed on the public and the critics as Shakespear's plays by Henry Irving and Augustin Daly at the end of the last century, is for the moment heavily discredited. It may be asked then why I, who always fought fiercely against that superstition in the days when I was a journalist-critic, should perpetrate a spurious fifth act to Cymbeline, and do it too, not wholly as a literary *jeu d'esprit*, but in response to an actual emergency in the theatre when it was proposed to revive Cymbeline at no less sacred a place than the Shakespear Memorial Theatre at Stratford-upon-Avon.

Cymbeline, though one of the finest of Shakespear's later plays now on the stage, goes to pieces in the last act. In fact

I mooted the point myself by thoughtlessly saying that the revival would be all right if I wrote a last act for it. To my surprise this blasphemy was received with acclamation; and as the applause, like the proposal, was not wholly jocular, the fancy began to haunt me, and persisted until I exorcised it by writing the pages which ensue.

I had a second surprise when I began by reading the authentic last act carefully through. I had not done so for many years, and had the common impression about it that it was a cobbled-up affair by several hands, including a vision in prison accompanied by scraps of quite ridiculous doggerel.

For this estimate I found absolutely no justification nor excuse. I must have got it from the last revival of the play at the old Lyceum theatre, when Irving, as Iachimo, a statue of romantic melancholy, stood dumb on the stage for hours (as it seemed) whilst the others toiled through a series of *dénouements* of crushing tedium, in which the characters lost all their vitality and individuality, and had nothing to do but identify themselves by moles on their necks, or explain why they were not dead. The vision and the verses were cut out as a matter of course; and I ignorantly thanked Heaven for it.

When I read the act as aforesaid I found that my notion that it is a cobbled-up *pasticcio* by other hands was an unpardonable stupidity. The act is genuine Shakespear to the last full stop, and late phase Shakespear in point of verbal workmanship.

The doggerel is not doggerel: it is a versified masque, in Shakespear's careless woodnotes wild, complete with Jupiter as *deus ex machina*, eagle and all, introduced, like the Ceres scene in The Tempest, to please King Jamie, or else because an irresistible fashion had set in, just as at all the great continental opera houses a ballet used to be *de rigueur*. Gounod had to introduce one into his Faust, and Wagner into his Tannhäuser, before they could be staged at the Grand Opera in Paris. So, I take it, had Shakespear to stick a masque into Cymbeline. Performed as such, with suitable music and enough pictorial splendor, it is not only entertaining on the stage, but, with the very Shakespearean feature of a comic jailor which precedes it, just the thing to save the last act.

Without it the act is a tedious string of unsurprising *dénouements* sugared with insincere sentimentality after a ludicrous stage battle. With one exception the characters have vanished and left nothing but dolls being moved about like the glass balls in the game of solitaire until they are all got rid of but one. The exception is the hero, or rather the husband of the heroine, Leonatus Posthumus. The late Charles Charrington, who with his wife Janet Achurch broke the ice for Ibsen in England, used to cite Posthumus as Shakespear's anticipation of his Norwegian rival. Certainly, after being theatrically conventional to the extent of ordering his wife to be murdered, he begins to criticize, quite on the lines of Mrs Alving in Ghosts, the slavery to an inhuman ideal of marital fidelity which led him to this villainous extremity. One may say that he is the only character left really alive in the last act; and as I cannot change him for the better I have left most of his part untouched. I make no apology for my attempt to bring the others back to dramatic activity and individuality.

I should like to have retained Cornelius as the exponent of Shakespear's sensible and scientific detestation of vivisection. But as he has nothing to say except that the Queen is dead, and nobody can possibly care a rap whether she is alive or dead, I have left him with her in the box of puppets that are done with.

I have ruthlessly cut out the surprises that no longer surprise anybody. I really could not keep my countenance over the identification of Guiderius by the mole on his neck. That device was killed by Maddison Morton, once a famous farce writer, now forgotten by everyone save Mr Gordon Craig and myself. In Morton's masterpiece, Box and Cox, Box asks Cox whether he has a strawberry mark on his left arm. "No" says Cox. "Then you are my long lost brother" says Box as they fall into one another's arms and end the farce happily. One could wish that Guiderius had anticipated Cox.

Plot has always been the curse of serious drama, and indeed of serious literature of any kind. It is so out-of-place there that

Shakespear never could invent one. Unfortunately, instead of taking Nature's hint and discarding plots, he borrowed them all over the place and got into trouble through having to unravel them in the last act, especially in The Two Gentlemen of Verona and Cymbeline. The more childish spectators may find some delight in the revelation that Polydore and Cadwal are Imogen's long lost brothers and Cymbeline's long lost sons; that Iachimo is now an occupant of the penitent form and very unlike his old self; and that Imogen is so dutiful that she accepts her husband's attempt to have her murdered with affectionate docility. I cannot share these infantile joys. Having become interested in Iachimo, in Imogen, and even in the two long lost princes, I wanted to know how their characters would react to the *éclaircissement* which follows the battle. The only way to satisfy this curiosity was to rewrite the act as Shakespear might have written it if he had been post-Ibsen and post-Shaw instead of post-Marlowe.

In doing so I had to follow the Shakespearean verse pattern to match the 89 lines of Shakespear's text which I retained. This came very easily to me. It happened when I was a child that one of the books I delighted in was an illustrated Shakespear, with a picture and two or three lines of text underneath it on every third or fourth page. Ever since, Shakespearean blank verse has been to me as natural a form of literary expression as the Augustan English to which I was brought up in Dublin, or the latest London fashion in dialogue. It is so easy that if it were possible to kill it it would have been burlesqued to death by Tom Thumb, Chrononhotonthologos, and Bombastes Furioso. But Shakespear will survive any possible extremity of caricature.

I shall not deprecate the most violent discussion as to the propriety of meddling with masterpieces. All I can say is that the temptation to do it, and sometimes the circumstances which demand it, are irresistible. The results are very various. When a mediocre artist tries to improve on a great artist's work the effect is ridiculous or merely contemptible. When the alteration damages the original, as when a bad painter repaints a Velasquez or a Rembrandt, he commits a crime. When the changed work is sold or exhibited as the original, the fraud is indictable. But when it comes to complete forgery, as in the case of Ireland's Vortigern, which was much admired and at last actually performed as a play by Shakespear, the affair passes beyond the sphere of crime and becomes an instructive joke.

But what of the many successful and avowed variations? What about the additions made by Mozart to the score of Handel's Messiah? Elgar, who adored Handel, and had an unbounded contempt for all the lesser meddlers, loved Mozart's variations, and dismissed all purist criticism of them by maintaining that Handel must have extemporized equivalents to them on the organ at his concerts. When Spontini found on his visit to Dresden that Wagner had added trombone parts to his choruses, he appropriated them very gratefully. Volumes of variations on the tunes of other composers were published as such by Mozart and Beethoven, to say nothing of Bach and Handel, who played Old Harry with any air that amused them. Would anyone now remember Diabelli's vulgar waltz but for Beethoven's amazing variations, one of which is also a variation on an air from Don Giovanni?

And now consider the practice of Shakespear himself. Tolstoy declared that the original Lear is superior to Shakespear's rehandling, which he abhorred as immoral. Nobody has ever agreed with him. Will it be contended that Shakespear had no right to refashion Hamlet? If he had spoiled both plays, that would be a reason for reviving them without Shakespear's transfigurations, but not for challenging Shakespear's right to remake them.

Accordingly, I feel no qualm of conscience and have no apology to make for indulging in a variation on the last act of Cymbeline. I stand in the same time relation to Shakespear as Mozart to Handel, or Wagner to Beethoven. Like Mozart, I have not confined myself to the journeyman's job of writing "additional accompaniments": I have luxuriated in variations. Like Wagner dealing with Gluck's overture to *Iphigenia in Aulis* I have made a new ending for its own sake. Beethoven's Ninth Symphony towers among the classic masterpieces; but if Wagner had been old enough in his Dresden days not only to rescore the first and greatest movement as he did, but to supply the whole work with a more singable ending I should not have discouraged him; for I must agree with Verdi that the present ending, from the change to six-four onward, though intensely Beethovenish, is in performance usually a screaming voice destroying orgy.

I may be asked why all my instances are musical instead of literary. Is it a plot to take the literary critics out of their depth? Well, it may have that good effect; but I am not aiming at it. It is, I suppose, because music has succeeded to the heroic rank taken by literature in the sixteenth century. I cannot pretend to care much about what Nat Lee did in his attempts to impart Restoration gentility to Shakespear, or about Thomas Corneille's bowdlerization of Molière's *Festin de Pierre*, or any of the other literary precedents, though I am a little ashamed of being found in the company of their perpetrators. But I do care a good deal about what Mozart did to Handel, and Wagner to Gluck; and it seems to me that to discuss the artistic morality of my alternative ending without reference to them would be waste of time. Anyhow, what I have done I have done; and at that I must leave it.

I shall not press my version on managers producing Cymbeline if they have the courage and good sense to present the original word-for-word as Shakespear left it, and the means to do justice to the masque. But if they are halfhearted about it, and inclined to compromise by leaving out the masque and the comic jailor and mutilating the rest, as their manner is, I unhesitatingly recommend my version. The audience will not know the difference; and the few critics who have read Cymbeline will be too grateful for my shortening of the last act to complain.   G. B. S.

Ayot Saint Lawrence
December 1945

CYMBELINE REFINISHED

ACT V

A rocky defile. A wild evening. Philario, in armor, stands on a tall rock, straining his eyes to see into the distance. In the foreground a Roman captain, sword in hand, his helmet badly battered, rushes in panting. Looking round before he sits down on a rock to recover his breath, he catches sight of Philario.

CAPTAIN. Ho there, signor! You are in danger there.
You can be seen a mile off.

PHILARIO [*hastening down*] Whats your news?
I am sent by Lucius to find out how fares
Our right wing led by General Iachimo.

CAPTAIN. He is outgeneralled. There's no right wing now.
Broken and routed, utterly defeated,
Our eagles taken and the few survivors
In full flight like myself. And you?

PHILARIO.   My news
Is even worse. Lucius, I fear, is taken.
Our centre could not stand the rain of arrows.

CAPTAIN. Someone has disciplined these savage archers.
They shoot together and advance in step:
Their horsemen trot in order to the charge
And then let loose th' entire mass full speed.
No single cavaliers but thirty score
As from a catapult four hundred tons
Of horse and man in one enormous shock
Hurled on our shaken legions. Then their chariots
With every axle furnished with a scythe
Do bloody work. They made us skip, I promise you. Their
        slingers! [*He points to his helmet*]
—Well: see their work! Two inches further down
I had been blind or dead. The crackbrained Welshmen
Raged like incarnate devils.

PHILARIO.   Yes: they thought

139

We were the Britons. So our prisoners tell us.

CAPTAIN. Where did these bumpkins get their discipline?

PHILARIO. Ay: thats the marvel. Where?

CAPTAIN. Our victors say
Cassivelaunus is alive again.
But thats impossible.

PHILARIO. Not so impossible
As that this witless savage Cymbeline,
Whose brains were ever in his consort's head,
Could thus defeat Roman-trained infantry.

CAPTAIN. 'Tis my belief that old Belarius,
Banned as a traitor, must have been recalled.
That fellow knew his job. These fat civilians
When we're at peace, rob us of our rewards
By falsely charging us with this or that;
But when the trumpet sounds theyre on their knees to us.

PHILARIO. Well, Captain, I must hasten back to Lucius
To blast his hopes of any help from you.
Where, think you, is Iachimo?

CAPTAIN. I know not.
And yet I think he cannot be far off.

PHILARIO. He lives then?

CAPTAIN. Perhaps. When all was lost he fought
Like any legionary, sword in hand.
His last reported word was "Save yourselves:
Bid all make for the rocks; for there
Their horsemen cannot come". I took his counsel;
And here I am.

PHILARIO. You were best come with me.
Failing Iachimo, Lucius will require
Your tale at first hand.

CAPTAIN. Good. But we shall get
No laurel crowns for what we've done today.

Exeunt together. Enter Posthumus dressed like a peasant, but wearing a Roman sword and a soldier's iron cap. He has in his hand a bloodstained handkerchief.

POSTHUMUS. Yea, bloody cloth, I'll keep thee; for I wish'd
Thou shouldst be colour'd thus. You married ones,
If each of you should take this course, how many
Must murder wives much better than themselves
For wrying but a little? O Pisanio!
Every good servant does not all commands:
No bond, but to do just ones. Gods, if you
Should have ta'en vengeance on my faults, I ne'er
Had liv'd to put on this: so had you sav'd
The noble Imogen to repent, and struck
Me (wretch) more worth your vengeance. But, alack,
You snatch some hence for little faults: that's love,
To have them fall no more. You some permit
To second ills with ills, each elder worse,
And make them dread it, to the doers' thrift;
But Imogen is your own: do your best wills,
And make me blest to obey! I am brought hither
Among the Italian gentry, and to fight
Against my lady's kingdom: 'tis enough
That, Britain, I have kill'd thy mistress. Peace!
I'll give no wound to thee. I have disrobed me
Of my Italian weeds, and drest myself
As does a Briton peasant; so I've fought
Against the part I came with; so I'll die
For thee, O Imogen, even for whom my life
Is every breath a death; and thus unknown,
Pitied nor hated, to the face of peril
Myself I'll dedicate. Let me make men know
More valour in me than my habits shew.
Gods, put the strength o' the Leonati in me!
To shame the guise o' the world, I'll begin
The fashion, less without and more within.

He is hurrying off when he is confronted with Iachimo, battle stained, hurrying in the opposite direction. Seeing a British enemy he draws his sword.

POSTHUMUS. Iachimo! Peace, man: 'tis I, Posthumus.

CYMBELINE REFINISHED

IACHIMO. Peace if you will. The battle's lost and won.
Pass on.

POSTHUMUS. Do you not know me?

IACHIMO.   No.

POSTHUMUS.   Look closer.
You have some reason to remember me
And I to hate you. Yet we're sworn friends.

IACHIMO. By all the gods, Leonatus!

POSTHUMUS.   At your service,
Seducer of my wife.

IACHIMO.   No more of that.
Your wife, Posthumus, is a noble creature.
I'll set your mind at rest upon that score.

POSTHUMUS. At rest! Can you then raise her from the grave?
Where she lies dead to expiate our crime?

IACHIMO. Dead! How? Why? When? And expiate! What
  mean you?

POSTHUMUS. This only: I have had her murdered, I.
And at my best am worser than her worst.

IACHIMO. We are damned for this. [*On guard*] Let's cut each
other's throats.

POSTHUMUS [*drawing*] Ay, let us.
*They fight furiously. Enter Cymbeline, Belarius, Guiderius,
Arviragus, Pisanio, with Lucius and Imogen as Fidele: both of them
prisoners guarded by British soldiers.*

BELARIUS [*taking command instinctively*] Part them there. Make
fast the Roman.

*Guiderius pounces on Iachimo and disarms him. Arviragus pulls
Posthumus back.*

ARVIRAGUS. In the King's presence sheath your sword, you lout.

IACHIMO. In the King's presence I must yield perforce;
But as a person of some quality
By rank a gentleman, I claim to be
Your royal highness's prisoner, not this lad's.

LUCIUS. His claim is valid, sir. His blood is princely.

POSTHUMUS. 'Tis so: he's noble.

142

CYMBELINE. What art thou?

POSTHUMUS. A murderer.

IMOGEN. His voice! His voice! Oh, let me see his face. [*She rushes to Posthumus and puts her hand on his face*].

POSTHUMUS. Shall's have a play with this? There lies thy part [*he knocks her down with a blow of his fist*].

GUIDERIUS. Accursed churl: take that. [*He strikes Posthumus and brings him down on one knee*].

ARVIRAGUS. You dog, how dare you [*threatening him*].

POSTHUMUS. Soft, soft, young sirs. One at a time, an 't please you. [*He springs up and stands on the defensive*].

PISANIO [*interposing*] Hands off my master! He is kin to the king.

POSTHUMUS [*to Cymbeline*] Call off your bulldogs, sir. Why all this coil
About a serving boy?

CYMBELINE. My son-in-law!

PISANIO. Oh, gentlemen, your help. My Lord Posthumus:
You ne'er killed Imogen till now. Help! help!

IMOGEN. Oh, let me die. I heard my husband's voice
Whom I thought dead; and in my ecstasy,
The wildest I shall ever feel again,
He met me with a blow.

POSTHUMUS. Her voice. 'Tis Imogen.
Oh, dearest heart, thou livest. Oh, you gods,
What sacrifice can pay you for this joy?

IMOGEN. You dare pretend you love me.

POSTHUMUS. Sweet, I dare
Anything, everything. Mountains of mortal guilt
That crushed me are now lifted from my breast.
I am in heaven that was but now in hell.
You may betray me twenty times again.

IMOGEN. Again! And pray, when have I e'er betrayed you?

POSTHUMUS. I had the proofs. There stands your paramour.
Shall's have him home? I care not, since thou liv'st.

IMOGEN. My paramour! [*To Iachimo*] Oh, as you are a gentle-man,

Give him the lie.

IACHIMO.   He knows no better, madam.

We made a wager, he and I, in Italy

That I should spend a night in your bedchamber.

IMOGEN [to Posthumus] You made this wager! And I'm
   married to you!

POSTHUMUS. I did. He won it.

IMOGEN.   How? He never came

Within my bedchamber.

IACHIMO.   I spent a night there.

It was the most uncomfortable night

I ever passed.

IMOGEN.   You must be mad, signor.

Or else the most audacious of all liars

That ever swore away a woman's honor.

IACHIMO. I think, madam, you do forget that chest.

IMOGEN. I forget nothing. At your earnest suit

Your chest was safely houséd in my chamber;

But where were you?

IACHIMO.   I? I was in the chest [Hilarious sensation].

And on one point I do confess a fault.

I stole your bracelet while you were asleep.

POSTHUMUS. And cheated me out of my diamond ring!

IACHIMO. Both ring and bracelet had some magic in them

That would not let me rest until I laid them

On Mercury's altar. He's the god of thieves.

But I can make amends. I'll pay for both

At your own price, and add one bracelet more

For the other arm.

POSTHUMUS.   With ten thousand ducats

Due to me for the wager you have lost.

IMOGEN. And this, you think, signors, makes good to me

All you have done, you and my husband there!

IACHIMO. It remedies what can be remedied.

As for the rest, it cannot be undone.

We are a pitiable pair. For all that

You may go further and fare worse; for men
Will do such things to women.

IMOGEN.   You at least
Have grace to know yourself for what you are.
My husband thinks that all is settled now
And this a happy ending!

POSTHUMUS.   Well, my dearest,
What could I think? The fellow did describe
The mole upon your breast.

IMOGEN.   And thereupon
You bade your servant kill me.

POSTHUMUS.   It seemed natural.

IMOGEN. Strike me again; but do not say such things.

GUIDERIUS. An if you do, by Thor's great hammer stroke
I'll kill you, were you fifty sons-in-law.

BELARIUS. Peace, boy: we're in the presence of the king.

IMOGEN. Oh, Cadwal, Cadwal, you and Polydore,
My newfound brothers, are my truest friends.
Would either of you, were I ten times faithless,
Have sent a slave to kill me?

GUIDERIUS [shuddering]   All the world
Should die first.

ARVIRAGUS.   Whiles we live, Fidele,
Nothing shall harm you.

POSTHUMUS.   Child: hear me out.
Have I not told you that my guilty conscience
Had almost driven me mad when heaven opened
And you appeared? But prithee, dearest wife,
How did you come to think that I was dead?

IMOGEN. I cannot speak of it: it is too dreadful.
I saw a headless man drest in your clothes.

GUIDERIUS. Pshaw! That was Cloten: son, he said, to the
    king.
I cut his head off.

CYMBELINE.   Marry, the gods forefend!
I would not thy good deeds should from my lips

Pluck a hard sentence: prithee, valiant youth,
Deny 't again.

GUIDERIUS. I have spoke it, and I did it.

CYMBELINE. He was a prince.

GUIDERIUS. A most incivil one: the wrongs he did me
Were nothing prince-like; for he did provoke me
With language that would make me spurn the sea
If it could so roar to me. I cut off 's head;
And am right glad he is not standing here
To tell this tale of mine.

CYMBELINE. I am sorry for thee:
By thine own tongue thou art condemn'd, and must
Endure our law: thou 'rt dead. Bind the offender,
And take him from our presence.

BELARIUS. Stay, sir king:
This man is better than the man he slew,
As well descended as thyself, and hath
More of thee merited than a band of Clotens
Had ever scar for. [*To the Guard*] Let his arms alone,
They were not born for bondage.

CYMBELINE. Why, old soldier,
Wilt thou undo the worth thou art unpaid for,
By tasting of our wrath? How of descent
As good as we?

GUIDERIUS. In that he spake too far.

CYMBELINE. And thou shalt die for 't.

BELARIUS. We will die all three:
But I will prove that two on 's are as good
As I have given out him.

CYMBELINE. Take him away.
The whole world shall not save him.

BELARIUS. Not so hot.
First pay me for the nursing of thy sons;
And let it be confiscate all so soon
As I've received it.

CYMBELINE. Nursing of my sons!

CYMBELINE REFINISHED

BELARIUS. I am too blunt and saucy: here's my knee.
Ere I arise I will prefer my sons.
Then spare not the old father. Mighty sir:
These two young gentlemen that call me father,
And think they are my sons, are none of mine.
They are the issue of your loins, my liege,
And blood of your begetting.

CYMBELINE.   How? my issue?

BELARIUS. So sure as you your father's. These your princes
(For such and so they are) these twenty years
Have I train'd up: those arts they have as I
Could put into them; my breeding was, sir, as
Your highness knows. Come hither, boys, and pay
Your loves and duties to your royal sire.

GUIDERIUS. We three are fullgrown men and perfect
        strangers.
Can I change fathers as I'd change my shirt?

CYMBELINE. Unnatural whelp! What doth thy brother say?

ARVIRAGUS. I, royal sir? Well, we have reached an age
When fathers' helps are felt as hindrances.
I am tired of being preached at.

CYMBELINE [to Belarius]   So, sir, this
Is how you have bred my puppies.

GUIDERIUS.   He has bred us
To tell the truth and face it.

BELARIUS.   Royal sir:
I know not what to say: not you nor I
Can tell our children's minds. But pardon him.
If he be overbold the fault is mine.

GUIDERIUS. The fault, if fault there be, is in my Maker.
I am of no man's making. I am I:
Take me or leave me.

IACHIMO [to Lucius] Mark well, Lucius, mark.
There spake the future king of this rude island.

GUIDERIUS. With you, Sir Thief, to tutor me? No, no:
This kingly business has no charm for me.

When I lived in a cave methought a palace
Must be a glorious place, peopled with men
Renowned as councillors, mighty as soldiers,
As saints a pattern of holy living,
And all at my command were I a prince.
This was my dream. I am awake today.
I am to be, forsooth, another Cloten,
Plagued by the chatter of his train of flatterers,
Compelled to worship priest invented gods,
Not free to wed the woman of my choice,
Being stopped at every turn by some old fool
Crying "You must not", or, still worse, "You must".
Oh no, sir: give me back the dear old cave
And my unflattering four footed friends.
I abdicate, and pass the throne to Polydore.

    ARVIRAGUS. Do you, by heavens? Thank you for nothing,
       brother.

    CYMBELINE. I'm glad you're not ambitious. Seated monarchs
Do rarely love their heirs. Wisely, it seems.

    ARVIRAGUS. Fear not, great sir: we two have never learnt
To wait for dead men's shoes, much less their crowns.

    GUIDERIUS. Enough of this. Fidele: is it true
Thou art a woman, and this man thy husband?

    IMOGEN. I am a woman, and this man my husband.
He would have slain me.

    POSTHUMUS.   Do not harp on that.

    CYMBELINE. God's patience, man, take your wife home to
       bed.
You're man and wife: nothing can alter that.
Are there more plots to unravel? Each one here,
It seems, is someone else. [*To Imogen*] Go change your dress
For one becoming to your sex and rank.
Have you no shame?

    IMOGEN.   None.

    CYMBELINE.   How? None!

    IMOGEN.   All is lost.

Shame, husband, happiness, and faith in Man.
He is not even sorry.

POSTHUMUS.   I'm too happy.

IACHIMO. Lady: a word. When you arrived just now
I, as you saw, was hot on killing him.
Let him bear witness that I drew on him
To avenge your death.

IMOGEN.   Oh, do not make me laugh.
Laughter dissolves too many just resentments,
Pardons too many sins.

IACHIMO.   And saves the world
A many thousand murders. Let me plead for him.
He has his faults; but he must suffer yours.
You are, I swear, a very worthy lady;
But still, not quite an angel.

IMOGEN.   No, not quite,
Nor yet a worm. Subtle Italian villain!
I would that chest had smothered you.

IACHIMO.   Dear lady
It very nearly did.

IMOGEN.   I will not laugh.
I must go home and make the best of it
As other women must.

POSTHUMUS.   Thats all I ask. [*He clasps her*].

BELARIUS. The fingers of the powers above do tune
The harmony of this peace.

LUCIUS.   Peace be it then.
For by this gentleman's report and mine
I hope imperial Cæsar will reknit
His favour with the radiant Cymbeline,
Which shines here in the west.

CYMBELINE.   Laud we the gods,
And let our crooked smokes climb to their nostrils
From our blest altars. Publish we this peace
To all our subjects. Set we forward: let
A Roman and a British ensign wave

149

Friendly together: so through Lud's town march,
And in the temple of great Jupiter
Our peace we'll ratify; seal it with feasts.
Set on there! Never was a war did cease,
Ere bloody hands were wash'd, with such a peace.

[*Curtain*

THE END

"IN GOOD KING CHARLES'S GOLDEN DAYS"

A TRUE HISTORY THAT NEVER HAPPENED

XLVII

1939

PREFACE

In providing a historical play for the Malvern Festival of 1939 I departed from the established practice sufficiently to require a word of explanation. The "histories" of Shakespear are chronicles dramatized; and my own chief historical plays, Cæsar and Cleopatra and St Joan, are fully documented chronicle plays of this type. Familiarity with them would get a student safely through examination papers on their periods.

STAGE CHAPTERS OF HISTORY

A much commoner theatrical product is the historical romance, mostly fiction with historical names attached to the stock characters of the stage. Many of these plays have introduced their heroines as Nell Gwynn, and Nell's principal lover as Charles II. As Nell was a lively and lovable actress, it was easy to reproduce her by casting a lively and lovable actress for the part; but the stage Charles, though his costume and wig were always unmistakeable, never had any other resemblance to the real Charles, nor to anything else on earth except what he was not: a stage walking gentleman with nothing particular to say for himself.

Now the facts of Charles's reign have been chronicled so often by modern historians of all parties, from the Whig Macaulay to the Jacobite Hilaire Belloc, that there is no novelty left for the chronicler to put on the stage. As to the romance, it is intolerably stale: the spectacle of a Charles sitting with his arm round Nell Gwynn's waist, or with Moll Davis seated on his knee, with the voluptuous termagant Castlemaine raging in the background, has no interest for me, if it ever had for any grown-up person.

But when we turn from the sordid facts of Charles's reign, and from his Solomonic polygamy, to what might have happened to him but did not, the situation becomes interesting and fresh. For instance, Charles might have met that human prodigy Isaac Newton. And Newton might have met that prodigy of another sort, George Fox, the founder of the morally mighty Society of

153   L

Friends, vulgarly called the Quakers. Better again, all three might have met. Now anyone who considers a hundred and fiftieth edition of Sweet Nell of Old Drury more attractive than Isaac Newton had better avoid my plays: they are not meant for such. And anyone who is more interested in Lady Castlemaine's hips than in Fox's foundation of the great Cult of Friendship should keep away from theatres and frequent worse places. Still, though the interest of my play lies mainly in the clash of Charles, George, and Isaac, there is some fun in the clash between all three and Nelly, Castlemaine, and the Frenchwoman Louise de Kéroualle, whom we called Madame Carwell. So I bring the three on the stage to relieve the intellectual tension.

NEWTON'S RECTILINEAR UNIVERSE

There is another clash which is important and topical in view of the hold that professional science has gained on popular credulity since the middle of the nineteenth century. I mean the eternal clash between the artist and the physicist. I have therefore invented a collision between Newton and a personage whom I should like to have called Hogarth; for it was Hogarth who said "the line of beauty is a curve," and Newton whose first dogma it was that the universe is in principle rectilinear. He called straight lines right lines; and they were still so called in my school Euclid eighty years ago. But Hogarth could not by any magic be fitted into the year 1680, my chosen date; so I had to fall back on Godfrey Kneller. Kneller had not Hogarth's brains; but I have had to endow him with them to provide Newton with a victorious antagonist. In point of date Kneller just fitted in.

But I must make an exception to this general invitation. If by any chance you are a great mathematician or astronomer you had perhaps better stay away. I have made Newton aware of something wrong with the perihelion of Mercury. Not since Shakespear made Hector of Troy quote Aristotle has the stage perpetrated a more staggering anachronism. But I find the perihelion of Mercury so irresistible as a laugh catcher (like Weston-super-Mare) that I cannot bring myself to sacrifice it. I am actually prepared to defend it as a possibility. Newton was not only a lightning calculator with a monstrous memory: he was also a most ingenious and dexterous maker of apparatus. He made his own telescope; and when he wanted to look at Mercury without being dazzled by the sun he was quite clever enough to produce an artificial eclipse by putting an obturator into the telescope, though nobody else hit on that simple device until long after. My ignorance in these matters is stupendous; but I refuse to believe that Newton's system did not enable him to locate Mercury theoretically at its nearest point to the sun, and then to find out with his telescope that it was apparently somewhere else.

For the flash of prevision in which Newton foresees Einstein's curvilinear universe I make no apology. Newton's first law of motion is pure dogma. So is Hogarth's first law of design. The modern astronomers have proved, so far, that Hogarth was right and Newton wrong. But as the march of science during my long lifetime has played skittles with all the theories in turn I dare not say how the case will stand by the time this play of mine reaches its thousandth performance (if it ever does). Meanwhile let me admit that Newton in my play is a stage astronomer: that is, an astronomer not for an age but for all time. Newton as a man was the queerest of the prodigies; and I have chapter and verse for all his contradictions.

CHARLES'S GOLDEN DAYS

As to Charles, he adolesced as a princely cosmopolitan vagabond of curiously mixed blood, and ended as the first king in England whose kingship was purely symbolic, and who was clever enough to know that the work of the regicides could not be undone, and that he had to reign by his wits and not by the little real power they had left him. Unfortunately the vulgarity of his reputation as a Solomonic polygamist has not only obscured his political ability, but eclipsed the fact that he was the best of husbands. Catherine of Braganza, his wife, has been made to appear a nobody, and Castlemaine, his concubine, almost a great historical figure. When you have seen my play you will not make that mistake, and may therefore congratulate yourself on assisting at an act of historical justice.

Let us therefore drop the popular subject of The Merry Monarch and his women. On the stage, and indeed off it, he is represented as having practically no other interest, and being a disgracefully unfaithful husband. It is inferred that he was politically influenced by women, especially by Louise de Kéroualle, who, as an agent of Louis XIV, kept him under the thumb of that Sun of Monarchs as his secret pensioner. The truth is that Charles, like most English kings, was continually in money difficulties because the English people, having an insuperable dislike of being governed at all, would not pay taxes enough to finance an efficient civil and military public service. In Charles's day especially they objected furiously to a standing army, having had enough of that under Cromwell, and grudged their king even the lifeguards which were the nucleus of such an army. Charles, to carry on, had to raise the necessary money somewhere; and as he could not get it from the Protestant people of England he was clever enough to get it from the Catholic king of France; for, though head of the Church of England, he privately ranked Protestants as an upstart vulgar middle-class sect, and the Catholic Church as the authentic original Church of Christ, and the only possible faith for a gentleman. In achieving this he made use of Louise: there is no evidence that she made use of him. To the Whig historians the transaction makes Charles a Quisling in the service of Louis and a traitor to his own country. This is mere Protestant scurrility: the only shady part of it is that Charles, spending the money in the service of England, gave *le Roi Soleil* no value for it.

The other mistresses could make him do nothing that his goodnature did not dispose him to do, whether it was building Greenwich Hospital or making dukes of his bastards. As a husband he took his marriage very seriously, and his sex adventures as calls of nature on an entirely different footing. In this he was in the line of evolution, which leads to an increasing separation of the unique and intensely personal and permanent marriage relation from the carnal intercourse described in Shakespear's sonnet. This, being a response to the biological decree that the world must be peopled, may arise irresistibly between persons who could not live together endurably for a week but can produce excellent children. Historians who confuse Charles's feelings for his wife with his appetite for Barbara Villiers do not know chalk from cheese biologically.

The Future of Women in Politics

The establishment of representative government in England is assumed to have been completed by the enfranchisement of women in 1928. The enormous hiatus left by their previous disenfranchisement is supposed to have been filled up and finished with. As a matter of fact it has only reduced Votes For Women to absurdity; for the women immediately used their vote to keep women out of Parliament. After seventeen years of it the nation, consisting of men and women in virtually equal numbers, is misrepresented at Westminster by 24 women and 616 men. During the Suffragette revolt of 1913 I gave great offence to the agitators by forecasting this result, and urging that what was needed was not the vote, but a constitutional amendment enacting that all representative bodies shall consist of women and men in equal numbers, whether elected or nominated or co-opted or registered or picked up in the street like a coroner's jury.

The Coupled Vote

In the case of elected bodies the only way of effecting this is by the Coupled Vote. The representative unit must be not a man *or* a woman but a man *and* a woman. Every vote, to be valid, must be for a human pair, with the result that the elected body must consist of men and women in equal numbers. Until this is achieved it is idle to prate about political democracy as existing, or ever having existed, at any known period of English history.

It is to be noted that the half-and-half proportion is valid no matter what the proportion of women to men is in the population. It never varies considerably; but even if it did the natural unit would still be the complete couple and not its better (or worse) half.

The wisdom or expediency of this reform is questioned on various grounds. There are the people who believe that the soul is a masculine organ lacking in women, as certain physical organs are, and is the seat of male political faculty. But, so far, dissection, spectrum analysis, the electronic microscope, have failed to discover in either sex any specific organ or hormone that a biologist can label as the soul. So we christen it The Holy Ghost or The Lord of Hosts and dechristen it as a Life Force or Élan Vital. As this is shared by women and men, and, when it quits the individual, produces in both alike the dissolution we call death, democratic representation cannot be said to exist where women are not as fully enfranchised and qualified as men. So far no great harm has been done by their legal disabilities because men and women are so alike that for the purposes of our crude legislation it matters little whether juries and parliaments are packed with men or women; but now that the activities of government have been greatly extended, detailed criticism by women has become indispensable in Cabinets. For instance, the House of Lords is more representative than the House of Commons because its members are there as the sons of their fathers, which is the reason for all of us being in the world; but it would be a much more human body if it were half-and-half sons and daughters.

All this went on with the approval of the women, who formed half the community, and yet were excluded not only from the franchise but from the professions and public services, except the thrones. Up to a point this also did not matter much; for in oligarchies women exercise so much influence privately and irresponsibly that the cleverest of them are for giving all power to the men, knowing that they can get round them without being hampered by the female majority whose world is the kitchen, the nursery, and the drawingroom if such a luxury is within their reach.

But representation on merely plangent Parliamentary bodies
is not sufficient. Anybody can complain of a grievance; but its
remedy demands constructive political capacity. Now political
capacity is rare; but it is not rarer in women than in men. Nature's
supply of five per cent or so of born political thinkers and ad-
ministrators are all urgently needed in modern civilization; and if
half of that natural supply is cut off by the exclusion of women
from Parliament and Cabinets the social machinery will fall short
and perhaps break down for lack of sufficient direction. Competent
women, of whom enough are available, have their proper places
filled by incompetent men: there is no Cabinet in Europe that
would not be vitally improved by having its male tail cut off and
female heads substituted.

But how is this to be done? Giving all women the vote makes
it impossible because it only doubles the resistance to any change.
When it was introduced in England not a single woman was
returned at the ensuing General Election, though there were
women of proved ability in the field. They were all defeated by
male candidates who were comparative noodles and nobodies.

Therefore I suggest and advocate The Coupled Vote, making
all votes invalid except those for a bisexed couple, and thus ensur-
ing the return of a body in which men and women are present
in equal numbers. Until this is done, adult suffrage will remain
the least democratic of all political systems. I leave it to our old
parliamentary hands to devise a plan by which our electorate can
be side-tracked, humbugged, cheated, lied to, or frightened into
tolerating such a change. If it has to wait for their enlightenment
it will wait too long.

Malvern
1939

Ayot Saint Lawrence
1945

"IN GOOD KING CHARLES'S GOLDEN DAYS"

ACT I

The library in the house of Isaac Newton in Cambridge in the year 1680. It is a cheerful room overlooking the garden from the first floor through a large window which has an iron balcony outside, with an iron staircase down to the garden level. The division of the window to the left as you look out through it is a glass door leading to these stairs, making the room accessible from the garden. Inside the room the walls are lined with cupboards below and bookshelves above. To the right of the window is a stand-up writing desk. The cupboards are further obstructed by six chairs ranged tidily along them, three to the right of the window and three to the left (as you look out). Between them a table belonging to the set of chairs stands out in the middle with writing materials on it and a prodigious open Bible, made for a church lectern. A comfortable chair for the reader faces away from the window. On the reader's left is a handsome armchair, apparently for the accommodation of distinguished visitors to the philosopher.

Newton's housekeeper, a middle aged woman of very respectable appearance, is standing at the desk working at her accounts.

A serving maid in morning deshabille comes in through the interior door, which is in the side wall to the left of the window (again as you look out through it).

THE MAID. Please, Mrs Basham, a Mr Rowley wants to know when the master will be at home to receive him.

MRS BASHAM. Rowley? I dont know him. This is no hour to call on Mr Newton.

THE MAID. No indeed, maam. And look at me! not dressed to open the door to gentlefolk.

MRS BASHAM. Is he a gentleman? Rowley is not much of a name.

THE MAID. Dressed like a nobleman, maam. Very tall and very dark. And a lot of dogs with him, and a lackey. Not a person you could shut the door in the face of, maam. But very condescending, I must say.

MRS BASHAM. Well, tell him to come back at half past eleven; but I can't promise that Mr Newton will be in. Still, if he likes to come on the chance. And without his dogs, mind. Our Diamond would fight with them.

THE MAID. Yes, maam: I'll tell him [going].

MRS BASHAM. Oh, Sally, can you tell me how much is three times seven. You were at school, werent you?

SALLY. Yes, maam; but they taught the boys to read, write, and cipher. Us girls were only taught to sew.

MRS BASHAM. Well, never mind. I will ask Mr Newton. He'll know, if anybody will. Or stop. Ask Jack the fish hawker. He's paunching the rabbit in the kitchen.

SALLY. Yes, maam. [She goes].

MRS BASHAM. Three sixpences make one and sixpence and three eightpences make two shillings: they always do. But three sevenpences! I give it up.

Sally returns.

SALLY. Please, maam, another gentleman wants Mr Newton.

MRS BASHAM. Another nobleman?

SALLY. No, maam. He wears leather clothes. Quite out of the common.

MRS BASHAM. Did he give his name?

SALLY. George Fox, he said, maam.

MRS BASHAM. Why, thats the Quaker, the Man in Leather Breeches. He's been in prison. How dare he come here wanting to see Mr Newton? Go and tell him that Mr Newton is not at home to the like of him.

SALLY. Oh, he's not a person I could talk to like that, maam. I dursnt.

MRS BASHAM. Are you frightened of a man that would call a church a steeple house and walk into it without taking off his hat? Go this instant and tell him you will raise the street against him if he doesnt go away. Do you hear. Go and do as I tell you.

SALLY. I'd be afraid he'd raise the street against us. I will do my best to get rid of him without offence. [*She goes*].

MRS BASHAM [*calling after her*] And mind you ask Jack how much three times seven is.

SALLY [*outside*] Yes'm.

Newton, aged 38, comes in from the garden, hatless, deep in calculation, his fists clenched, tapping his knuckles together to tick off the stages of the equation. He stumbles over the mat.

MRS BASHAM. Oh, do look where youre going, Mr Newton. Someday youll walk into the river and drown yourself. I thought you were out at the university.

NEWTON. Now dont scold, Mrs Basham, dont scold. I forgot to go out. I thought of a way of making a calculation that has been puzzling me.

MRS BASHAM. And you have been sitting out there forgetting everything else since breakfast. However, since you have one of your calculating fits on I wonder would you mind doing a little sum for me to check the washing bill. How much is three times seven?

NEWTON. Three times seven? Oh, that is quite easy.

MRS BASHAM. I suppose it is to you, sir; but it beats me. At school I got as far as addition and subtraction; but I never could do multiplication or division.

NEWTON. Why, neither could I: I was too lazy. But they are quite unnecessary: addition and subtraction are quite sufficient. You add the logarithms of the numbers; and the antilogarithm of the sum of the two is the answer. Let me see: three times seven? The logarithm of three must be decimal four seven seven or thereabouts. The logarithm of seven is, say, decimal eight four five. That makes one decimal three two two, doesnt it? What's the antilogarithm of one decimal three two two? Well, it must be less than twentytwo and more than twenty. You will be safe if you put it down as—

Sally returns.

SALLY. Please, maam, Jack says it's twentyone.

NEWTON. Extraordinary! Here was I blundering over this

163

simple problem for a whole minute; and this uneducated fish hawker solves it in a flash! He is a better mathematician than I.

MRS BASHAM. This is our new maid from Woolsthorp, Mr Newton. You havnt seen her before.

NEWTON. Havnt I? I didnt notice it. [*To Sally*] Youre from Woolsthorp, are you? So am I. How old are you?

SALLY. Twentyfour, sir.

NEWTON. Twentyfour years. Eight thousand seven hundred and sixty days. Two hundred and ten thousand two hundred and forty hours. Twelve million six hundred and fourteen thousand, four hundred minutes. Seven hundred and fiftysix million eight hundred and sixtyfour thousand seconds. A long long life.

MRS BASHAM. Come now, Mr Newton: you will turn the child's head with your figures. What can one do in a second?

NEWTON. You can do, quite deliberately and intentionally, seven distinct actions in a second. How do you count seconds? Hackertybackertyone, hackertybackertytwo, hackertybackerty-three and so on. You pronounce seven syllables in every second. Think of it! This young woman has had time to perform more than five thousand millions of considered and intentional actions in her lifetime. How many of them can you remember, Sally?

SALLY. Oh sir, the only one I can remember was on my sixth birthday. My father gave me sixpence: a penny for every year.

NEWTON. Six from twentyfour is eighteen. He owes you one and sixpence. Remind me to give you one and sevenpence on your next birthday if you are a good girl. Now be off.

SALLY. Oh, thank you, sir. [*She goes out*].

NEWTON. My father, who died before I was born, was a wild, extravagant, weak man: so they tell me. I inherit his wildness, his extravagance, his weakness, in the shape of a craze for figures of which I am most heartily ashamed. There are so many more important things to be worked at: the transmutations of matter, the elixir of life, the magic of light and color, above all, the secret meaning of the Scriptures. And when I should be concentrating my mind on these I find myself wandering off into idle games of speculation about numbers in infinite series, and dividing curves into indivisibly short triangle bases. How silly! What a waste of time, priceless time!

MRS BASHAM. There is a Mr Rowley going to call on you at half past eleven.

NEWTON. Can I never be left alone? Who is Mr Rowley? What is Mr Rowley?

MRS BASHAM. Dressed like a nobleman. Very tall. Very dark. Keeps a lackey. Has a pack of dogs with him.

NEWTON. Oho! So that is who he is! They told me he wanted to see my telescope. Well, Mrs Basham, he is a person whose visit will be counted a great honor to us. But I must warn you that just as I have my terrible weakness for figures Mr Rowley has a very similar weakness for women; so you must keep Sally out of his way.

MRS BASHAM. Indeed! If he tries any of his tricks on Sally I shall see that he marries her.

NEWTON. He is married already. [*He sits at the table*].

MRS BASHAM. Oh! That sort of man! The beast!

NEWTON. Shshsh! Not a word against him, on your life. He is privileged.

MRS BASHAM. He is a beast all the same!

NEWTON [*opening the Bible*] One of the beasts in the Book of Revelation, perhaps. But not a common beast.

MRS BASHAM. Fox the quaker, in his leather breeches, had the impudence to call.

NEWTON [*interested*] George Fox? If he calls again I will see him. Those two men ought to meet.

MRS BASHAM. Those two men indeed! The honor of meeting you ought to be enough for them, I should think.

NEWTON. The honor of meeting me! Dont talk nonsense. They are great men in their very different ranks. I am nobody.

MRS BASHAM. You are the greatest man alive, sir. Mr Halley told me so.

NEWTON. It was very wrong of Mr Halley to tell you anything

of the sort. You must not mind what he says. He is always pestering me to publish my methods of calculation and to abandon my serious studies. Numbers! Numbers! Numbers! Sines, cosines, hypotenuses, fluxions, curves small enough to count as straight lines, distances between two points that are in the same place! Are these philosophy? Can they make a man great?

He is interrupted by Sally, who throws open the door and announces visitors.

SALLY. Mr Rowley and Mr Fox.

King Charles the Second, aged 50, appears at the door, but makes way for George Fox the Quaker, a big man with bright eyes and a powerful voice in reserve, aged 56. He is decently dressed; but his garments are made of leather.

CHARLES. After you, Mr Fox. The spiritual powers before the temporal.

FOX. You are very civil, sir; and you speak very justly. I thank you [*he passes in*].

Sally, intensely impressed by Mr Rowley, goes out.

FOX. Am I addressing the philosopher Isaac Newton?

NEWTON. You are, sir. [*Rising*] Will your noble friend do me the honor to be seated in my humble dwelling?

Charles bows and takes the armchair with easy grace.

FOX. I must not impose on you by claiming the gentleman as my friend. We met by chance at your door; and his favorite dog was kind enough to take a fancy to me.

CHARLES. She is never mistaken, sir. Her friends are my friends, if so damaged a character as mine can claim any friends.

NEWTON [*taking a chair from the wall and placing it near his table to his left*] Be seated, Mr Fox, pray.

FOX. George Fox at your service, not Mister. But I am very sensible of your civility. [*He sits*].

NEWTON [*resuming his seat at the table*] It seems that it is I who am at your service. In what way can I oblige you?

FOX. As you remind me, I have come here uninvited. My business will keep while you discharge yours with this nobleman— so called.

CHARLES. I also am uninvited, Pastor. I may address you so both truthfully and civilly, may I not?

FOX. You have found the right word. I tended my father's sheep when I was a child. Now I am a pastor of men's souls.

CHARLES. Good. Well, Pastor, I must inform you I have no business here except to waste our host's invaluable time and to improve my own, if he will be good enough to allow me such a liberty. Proceed then with your business; and take no notice of me. Unless, that is, you would prefer me to withdraw.

FOX. I have no business in this world that all men may not hear: the more the better.

CHARLES. I guessed as much; and confess to an unbounded curiosity to hear what George Fox can have to say to Isaac Newton. It is not altogether an impertinent curiosity. My trade, which is a very unusual one, requires that I should know what Tom, Dick and Harry have to say to oneanother. I find you two gentlemen much more interesting and infinitely more important.

MRS BASHAM [posted behind Newton's chair] What is your business, Mr Rowley? Mr Newton has much to do this morning. He has no time for idle conversation.

NEWTON. I had forgotten to make this lady known to you, gentlemen. Mrs Basham: my housekeeper, and the faithful guardian of my hours.

CHARLES. Your servant, Mistress Basham.

FOX. God be with you, woman.

NEWTON. Mr Rowley is a gentleman of great consequence, Mrs Basham. He must not be questioned as if he were Jack the fish hawker. His business is his father's business.

CHARLES. No, no. My father's business is abolished in England: he was executed for practising it. But we keep the old signboard up over the door of the old shop. And I stand at the shop door in my father's apron. Mrs Basham may ask me as many questions as she pleases; for I am far less important now in England than Jack the fish hawker.

MRS BASHAM. But how do you live, sir? That is all I meant to ask.

CHARLES. By my wits, Mistress Basham: by my wits. Come,

Pastor: enough of me. You are face to face with Isaac Newton. I long to hear what you have to say to him.

FOX. Isaac Newton: I have friends who belong to the new so-called Royal Society which the King has established, to enquire, it seems, into the nature of the universe. They tell me things that my mind cannot reconcile with the word of God as revealed to us in the Holy Scriptures.

NEWTON. What is your warrant for supposing that revelation ceased when King James's printers finished with the Bible?

FOX. I do not suppose so. I am not one of those priestridden churchmen who believe that God went out of business six thousand years ago when he had called the world into existence and written his book about it. We three sitting here together may have a revelation if we open our hearts and minds to it. Yes: even to you, Charles Stuart.

CHARLES. The mind of Charles Stuart is only too open, Pastor.

MRS BASHAM. What did you call the gentleman, Mr Fox?

CHARLES. A slip of the tongue, Mistress Basham. Nowhere in Holy writ, Pastor, will you find any disapproval of Paul when he changed his name from Saul. Need you be more scrupulous than the apostles?

FOX. It is against my sinful nature to disoblige any man; so Mr Rowley you shall be if you so desire. But I owed it to you to let you know that I was not deceived by your new name.

CHARLES. I thank you, Pastor. Your sinful nature makes you the best mannered man in the kingdom. And now, what about the revelations?

FOX. I am troubled. I cannot conceive that God should contradict himself. How must the revelation of today be received if it be contrary to the revelation of yesterday? If what has been revealed to you, Isaac Newton, be true, there is no heaven above us and no hell beneath us. The sun which stood still upon Gibeon and the moon in the Valley of Ajalon had stood still since the creation of the world.

NEWTON. Do not let that trouble you, Pastor. Nothing has ever stood still for an instant since the creation of the world:

168

neither the sun, the moon, the stars, nor the smallest particle of matter, except on two occasions.

CHARLES. Two! I remember only one.

NEWTON. Yes, sir: two. The first was when the sun stood still on Gibeon to give Joshua time to slaughter the Amorites. The second was when the shadow on the dial of Ahaz went ten degrees backward as a sign from God to good King Hezekiah who was dying of a boil until the prophet Isaiah made them put a lump of figs on it.

MRS BASHAM. There is nothing like a poultice of roasted figs to cure a gumboil. And to think that is because it is in the Holy Bible! I never knew it.

NEWTON. On reflection, the sun has stopped three times; for it must have stopped for an infinitesimal moment when it turned back, and again when it resumed its course.

FOX. I thank God that you are not an unbeliever and would not make me one.

NEWTON. My good friend, there is nothing so wonderful that a philosopher cannot believe it. The philosopher sees a hundred miracles a day where the ignorant and thoughtless see nothing but the daily round, the common task. Joshua was an ignorant soldier. Had he been a philosopher he would have known that to stop the nearest speck of dust would have served his turn as well as to stop the sun and moon; for it could not have stopped without stopping the whole machinery of the heavens. By the way, Mrs Basham, the fact that the sun and moon were visible at the same time may help me to fix the day on which the miracle occurred. [*To the others*] Excuse me, gentlemen: I have written a chronological history of the world; and the dates give me some trouble.

CHARLES. Did not the late Archbishop Ussher fix the dates of everything that ever happened?

NEWTON. Unfortunately he did not allow for the precession of the equinoxes. I had to correct some of his results accordingly.

CHARLES. And, saving the pastor's presence, what the divvle is the precession of the equinoxes?

M

FOX. I am sinful enough to be glad that you are as ignorant as myself. I suffer greatly from shame at my ignorance.

NEWTON. Shame will not help you, Pastor. I spend my life contemplating the ocean of my ignorance. I once boasted of having picked up a pebble on the endless beach of that ocean. I should have said a grain of sand.

CHARLES. I can well believe it. No man confronted with the enormity of what he does not know can think much of what he does know. But what is the precession of the equinoxes? If I fire off those words at court the entire peerage will be prostrate before the profundity of my learning.

MRS BASHAM. Oh, tell the gentlemen, Mr Newton; or they will be here all day.

NEWTON. It is quite simple: a child can understand it. The two days in the year on which the day and night are of equal duration are the equinoxes. In each successive sidereal year they occur earlier. You will see at once that this involves a retrograde motion of the equinoctial points along the ecliptic. We call that the precession of the equinoxes.

FOX. I thank you, Isaac Newton. I am as wise as I was before.

MRS BASHAM. You ought to be ashamed of yourself, Mr Newton, injuring the poor gentlemen's brains with such outlandish words. You must remember that everybody is not as learned as you are.

NEWTON. But surely it is plain to everybody—

MRS BASHAM. No: it isnt plain to anybody, Mr Newton.

SALLY [*bursting in*] Mr Rowley: theres a lady in a coach at the door wants to know are you ready to take a drive with her.

CHARLES. Any name?

SALLY. No, sir. She said youd know.

CHARLES. A duchess, would you say?

SALLY. Oh no, sir. Spoke to me quite familiar.

CHARLES. Nelly! Mr Newton: would you like to be introduced to Mistress Gwynn, the famous Drury Lane actress?

MRS BASHAM [*turning imperatively to Charles*] Oh, I couldnt allow that, Mr Rowley. I am surprised at you mentioning such a person in my presence.

CHARLES. I apologize. I did not know that you disapproved of the playhouse, Mrs Basham.

MRS BASHAM. I do not disapprove of the playhouse, sir. My grandfather, who is still alive and hearty, was befriended in his youth by Mr William Shakespear, a wellknown player and writer of comedies, tragedies, and the like. Mr Shakespear would have died of shame to see a woman on the stage. It is unnatural and wrong. Only the most abandoned females would do such a thing.

CHARLES. Still, the plays are more natural with real women in them, are they not?

MRS BASHAM. Indeed they are not, Mr Rowley. They are not like women at all. They are just like what they are; and they spoil the play for anyone who can remember the old actors in the women's parts. They could make you believe you were listening to real women.

CHARLES. Pastor Fox: have you ever spoken with a female player?

FOX [shuddering] I! No, sir: I do not frequent such company.

CHARLES. Why not, Pastor? Is your charity so narrow? Nell is no worse than Mary Magdalen.

MRS BASHAM. I hope Mary Magdalen made a good end and was forgiven; though we are nowhere told so. But I should not have asked her into my house. And at least she was not on the stage. [She retires behind Newton's chair].

CHARLES. What do you say, Pastor? Is Nelly not good enough for you?

FOX. Sir: there is nobody who is not good enough for me. Have I not warned our Christian friends who are now captives in Barbary not to forget that the life of God and the power of God are in their heathen masters the Turks and the Moors as well as in themselves? Is it any the less in this player woman than in a Turk or a Moor? I am not afraid of her.

CHARLES. And you, Mr Newton?

NEWTON. Women enter a philosopher's life only to disturb it.

They expect too much attention. However, Mistress Gwynn has called to take you away, not to interrupt my work on fluxions. And if you will condescend to go down to her she need not come up to us. [*He rises in dismissal of the King*].

CHARLES [*rising*] I see I must take my leave.

Nelly dashes in. Sally withdraws.

NELLY. Rowley darling: how long more are you going to keep me waiting in the street?

CHARLES. You are known to everyone present, Mistress Gwynn, I think. May I make our host known to you? The eminent philosopher, Mr Newton.

NELLY [*going past Charles to Newton*] I dont know what a philosopher is, Mr Newton; but you look one, every inch. Your servant, sir. [*She curtsies to him*].

NEWTON. Yours, madam. I am ashamed that you should have been kept waiting at the wrong side of my door.

NELLY. It is an honor to be seen at your door, Mr Newton. [*Looking round her*] And who keeps your house so beautifully? I thought philosophers were like Romish priests, not allowed to marry.

NEWTON. Is my house beautifully kept? I have never noticed it. This is Mrs Basham, my housekeeper. [*He sits resignedly*].

NELLY. You never noticed it! You dont deserve such a housekeeper. Your servant, Mrs Basham.

Mrs Basham bows stiffly, trying not to be flattered.

CHARLES. The other gentleman is the famous founder of the sect of Quakers.

FOX. Of Friends, Friend Rowley.

NELLY [*running to Fox*] I know. I know. The man in the leather breeches.

FOX [*stubbornly seated*] I am also known as George Fox.

NELLY [*clapping him on the shoulder*] What of that? Anybody might be George Fox; but there is only one man in the leather breeches. Your servant, George.

FOX. Yours, Nelly.

NELLY. There! Nelly! [*She goes to the wall for a chair and plants it at Fox's left, quite close*]. If I may add you to the list of my beaus I shall be the proudest woman in London.

FOX. I did not found the order of beaus. I founded that of Friends.

NELLY. Ten times better. Our beaus are our foes: they care for nothing but to steal our honor. Pray for me, Friend Fox: I think you have God by the ear closer than the bishops.

FOX. He is closer to you than you have placed yourself to me. Let no priest come between you.

CHARLES. We must not waste any more of Mr Newton's time, Mistress Gwynn. He is at work on fluxions.

NELLY. On what?

CHARLES. Fluxions I think you said, Mr Newton.

NELLY. What are fluxions?

CHARLES. Mr Newton will tell you. I should be glad to know, myself.

NEWTON. Fluxions, Madam, are the rates of change of continuously varying quantities.

NELLY. I must go home and think about that, Mr Philosopher.

NEWTON [*very seriously*] I shall be much indebted to you, madam, if you will communicate to me the result of your reflections. The truth is, I am not quite satisfied that my method— or perhaps I had better say the notation of my method—is the easiest that can be devised. On that account I have never cared to publish it.

NELLY. You really think I could teach you something, Mr Newton? What a compliment! Did you hear that, Rowley darling?

NEWTON. In these very simple matters one may learn from anyone. And you, Madam, must have very remarkable mental powers. You repeat long parts from memory in the theatre. I could not do that.

NELLY. Bless me, so I do, Mr Newton. You are the first man I ever met who did not think an actress must be an ignorant ninny —except schoolboys, who think she is a goddess. I declare you are the wisest man in England, and the kindest.

CHARLES. And the busiest, Nelly. Come. He has given us as much of his time as we have any right to ask for.

NELLY. Yes, I know. I am coming. [*She rises and goes to Charles, whose left arm she takes*]. May I come again, Mr Newton?

NEWTON [*rising*] No no no no no, Madam. I cannot entertain ladies. They do not fit into my way of life. Mr Rowley: you are well known to be as interested in ladies as I am interested in the Scriptures; and I thank you for bringing this very attractive sample for my diversion—

NELLY [*as if tasting a sweet*] Oh!

NEWTON [*continuing*]—but sufficient unto the day is the evil thereof—

NELLY [*in violent protest*] Oh!!!

NEWTON. —and I beg you will bring no more ladies here until I have time to set aside a day of relaxation for their reception.

NELLY. We must go, Rowley darling. He doesnt want us.

CHARLES. You are fortunate, Mr Newton, in suffering nothing worse than Nell. But I promise you your house shall be a monastery henceforth.

As Charles and Nell turn to the door to go out, the Duchess of Cleveland, 39, formerly Lady Castlemaine, and born Barbara Villiers, bursts into the room and confronts them in a tearing rage.

BARBARA. Ah! I have caught you, have I, with your trull. This is the scientific business which made it impossible for you to see me this morning.

CHARLES. Be silent for a moment, Barbara, whilst I present you to Mr Newton, the eminent philosopher, in whose house you are an uninvited guest.

BARBARA. A pretty house. A pretty philosopher. A house kept for you to meet your women in.

MRS BASHAM [*coming indignantly to the middle of the room*] Oh! Mr Newton: either this female leaves the house this instant or I do.

BARBARA. Do you know, woman, that you are speaking of the Duchess of Cleveland?

MRS BASHAM. I do not care who I am speaking of. If you are the

Duchess of Cleveland and this house were what you said it was you would be only too much at home in it. The house being what it is you are out of place in it. You go or I go.

BARBARA. You insolent slut, I will have you taken to the Bridewell and whipped.

CHARLES. You shall not, Barbara. If you do not come down with me to your carriage without another word, I will throw you downstairs.

BARBARA. Do. Kill me; and be happy with that low stage player. You have been unfaithful to me with her a thousand times.

NEWTON. Patience, patience, patience. Mrs Basham: the lady is not in a state of reason: I will prove to you that what she says has no sense and need not distress us. [*To Barbara*] Your Grace alleges that Mr Rowley has been unfaithful to you a thousand times.

BARBARA. A hundred thousand times.

NEWTON. For each unfaithfulness allow a day—or shall I say a night? Now one hundred thousand nights are almost two hundred and seventyfour years. To be precise, 273 years 287 days, allowing 68 days for Leap Year every four years. Now Mr Rowley is not 300 years old: he is only fifty, from which you must deduct at least fifteen years for his childhood.

BARBARA. Fourteen.

NEWTON. Let us say fourteen. Probably your Grace was also precocious. How many years shall we strike off your age for the days of your innocence?

NELL. Five at most.

BARBARA. Be silent, you.

NEWTON. Say twelve. That makes you in effect about twentyeight.

BARBARA. Have I denied it?

NELL. Flatterer!

NEWTON. Twentyeight to Mr Rowley's thirtysix. Your grace has been available since, say, the year 1652, twentyeight years ago. My calculation is therefore correct.

BARBARA. May I ask what you mean by available?

NEWTON. I mean that the number of occasions on which Mr Rowley could possibly be unfaithful to you is ten thousand two hundred and twenty plus seven for leap years. Yet you allege one hundred thousand occasions, and claim to have lived for nearly three centuries. As that is impossible, it is clear that you have been misinformed about Mistress Gwynn.

Nell claps vigorously.

BARBARA [*to Newton*] Are you mocking me, sir?

NEWTON. Figures cannot mock, because they cannot feel. That is their great quality, and their great fault. [*He goes to the door*]. And now may I have the honor of conducting your Grace to your coach—or is it one of those new fangled sedan chairs? Or would your Grace prefer to be thrown down my humble staircase by Mr Rowley? It has twentyfour steps, in two flights.

BARBARA. I will not leave this house until that player woman has gone first. [*She strides past them and plants herself in Newton's chair*].

NELL. After all, dear, it's Mr Newton's house and not ours. He was in the act of putting me out when you burst in. I stayed only because I wanted to see you in one of those tantrums of yours that Rowley so often tells me about. I might copy them on the stage.

BARBARA. He dares talk to you about me!!

NELL. He talks to me about everything, dear, because I let him get in a word occasionally, which is more than you do.

BARBARA [*to Charles*] Will you stand there and let me be insulted by this woman?

CHARLES [*with conviction*] Barbara: I am tired of your tantrums. I made you a duchess: you behave like a streetwalker. I pensioned you and packed you off to Paris; you have no business to be here. Pastor: what have you to say to all this? You are the oldest and wisest person present, are you not?

FOX. Fiftysix. And still a child in wisdom.

BARBARA [*contemptuously, noticing Fox for the first time*] What does this person know about women?

FOX. Only what the woman in myself teaches me.

NELL. Good for leather breeches! What do you think of her, George?

FOX. She prates overmuch about unfaithfulness. The man Rowley cannot be unfaithful to her because he has pledged no faith to her. To his wife only can he be unfaithful.

CHARLES. Wrong, Pastor. You do not know my wife. To her only I can never be unfaithful.

NELL. Yes: you are kind to us; but we are nothing to you. [*Sighing*] I would change places with her.

BARBARA. Will you order this common player to be silent in my presence?

NELL. It is not fair of her to keep mentioning my profession when I cannot decently mention hers.

With a scream of rage the duchess rises to fly at Nell, but is seized by Fox, who drags down her raised fists and throws her back into the chair.

FOX [*sternly*] Woman: behave yourself. In any decent English village you would go to the ducking stool to teach you good manners and gentle speech. You must control yourself—

He is interrupted by the clangor of a church bell, which has a terrible effect on him.

FOX [*in a thundering voice, forgetting all about the duchess*] Ha! I am called: I must go.

He makes for the door but is stopped by Charles, who, releasing Nell, shuts it quickly and posts himself with his back to it.

CHARLES. Stop. You are going to brawl in church. You will be thrown into prison; and I shall not be able to save you.

FOX. The bell, the bell. It strikes upon my life. I am called. Earthly kings cannot stay me. Let me pass.

CHARLES. Stand back, Mr Fox. My person is sacred.

NEWTON. What is the matter?

CHARLES. The church bell: it drives him mad. Someone send and stop it.

The bell stops.

FOX. God has stopped it. [*He falls on his knees and collapses,*

177

shivering like a man recovering from a fit.

Charles and Newton help him to his feet and lead him back to his chair.

FOX [*to Charles*] Another stroke, and I should not have answered for your life.

BARBARA. You must control yourself, preacher. In any decent English village you would be put in the stocks to teach you good manners.

FOX. Woman: I have been put in the stocks; and I shall be put there again. But I will continue to testify against the steeple house and the brazen clangor of its belfries.

MRS BASHAM. Now Mr Fox. You must not say such things here.

FOX. I tell you that from the moment you allow this manmade monster called a Church to enter your mind your inner light is like an extinguished candle; and your soul is plunged in darkness and damned. There is no atheist like the Church atheist. I have converted many a poor atheist who would have been burnt or hanged if God had not sent him into my hands; but I have never converted a churchman: his answer to everything is not his God, but the Church, the Church, the Church. They burn each other, these churchmen: they persecute: they do wickednesses of which no friend of God would be capable.

MRS BASHAM. The Popish Church, not the Protestant one, Mr Fox.

FOX. All, all, all of them. They are all snares of the devil. They stand between Man and his Maker, and take on themselves divine powers when they lack divine attributes. Am I to hold my peace in the face of this iniquity? When the bell rings to announce some pitiful rascal twaddling in his pulpit, or some fellow in a cassock pretending to bind and loose, I hear an Almighty Voice call "George Fox, George Fox: rise up: testify: unmask these impostors: drag them down from their pulpits and their altars; and let it be known that what the world needs to bring it back to God is not Churchmen but Friends, Friends of God, Friends of man, friendliness and sincerity everywhere, superstition and pulpit playacting nowhere."

CHARLES. Pastor: it is not given to every man as it has been to you to make a religion for himself. A readymade Church is an indispensable convenience for most of us. The inner light must express itself in music, in noble architecture, in eloquence: in a word, in beauty, before it can pass into the minds of common men. I grant you the clergy are mostly dull dogs; but with a little disguise and ritual they will pass as holy men with the ignorant. And there are great mysteries that must be symbolized, because though we feel them we do not know them, Mr Newton having not yet discovered their nature, in spite of all his mathematics. And this reminds me that we are making a most unwarrantable intrusion on our host's valuable time. Mr Newton: on my honor I had no part in bringing upon you this invasion of womanhood. I hasten to take them away, and will wait upon you at some happier moment. Come, ladies: we must leave Mr Newton to his mathematics. [*He is about to go to the door. Barbara rises to accompany him*].

NEWTON [*stopping him*] I must correct that misunderstanding, sir. I would not have you believe that I could be so inhospitable as to drive away my guests merely to indulge in the trifling pursuit of mathematical calculation, which leads finally nowhere. But I have more serious business in hand this morning. I am engaged in a study of the prophecies in the book of Daniel. [*He indicates the Bible*]. It may prove of the greatest importance to the world. I beg you to allow me to proceed with it in the necessary solitude. The ladies have not wasted my time: I have to thank her Grace of Cleveland for some lights on the Book of Revelation suggested to me by her proceedings. But solitude—solitude absolutely free from the pleasant disturbance of ladies' society—is now necessary to me; and I must beg you to withdraw.

Sally, now dressed in her best, throws the door open from without, and proudly announces—

SALLY. Her Grace the Duchess of Portsmouth.

Louise de Kéroualle, a Frenchwoman who at 30 retains her famous babyish beauty, appears on the threshold.

NEWTON [*beside himself*] Another woman! Take her away.

179

Take them all away. [*He flings himself into his chair at the table and buries his face in his hands*].

CHARLES. Louise: it is unlike you to pursue me. We are unwelcome here.

LOUISE [*coming over to him*] Pursue you! But I have never been so surprised in my life as to find you here. And Nelly! And her Grace of Cleveland back from Paris! What are you all doing here? I came to consult Mr Newton, the alchemist. [*Newton straightens up and stares*]. My business with him is private: it is with him, not with you, chéri. I did not know he was holding a reception.

CHARLES. Mr Newton is not an alchemist.

LOUISE. Pardon me: he is.

CHARLES. Mr Newton: are you an alchemist?

NEWTON. My meditations on the ultimate constitution of matter have convinced me that the transmutation of metals, and indeed of all substances, must be possible. It is occurring every day. I understand that you, Mr Rowley, have a private laboratory at Whitehall, in which you are attempting the fixation of mercury.

CHARLES. Without success, Mr Newton. I shall give it up and try for the philosopher's stone instead.

FOX. Would you endanger your souls by dabbling in magic? The scripture says "Thou shalt not suffer a witch to live." Do you think that God is fonder of sorcerers and wizards than of witches? If you count the wrath of God as nothing, and are above the law by your rank, are you not ashamed to believe such old wives' tales as the changing of lead into gold by the philosopher's stone?

NEWTON. Pastor Fox: I thank you for your wellmeant warning. Now let me warn you. The man who begins by doubting the possibility of the philosopher's stone soon finds himself beginning to doubt the immortality of the soul. He ends by doubting the existence of the soul. There is no witchcraft about these things. I am as certain of them as I am of the fact that the world was created four thousand and four years before the birth of our Lord.

FOX. And what warrant have you for that? The Holy Bible says nothing of your four thousand and four. It tells us that the world was created "in the beginning": a mighty word. "In the beginning"! Think of it if you have any imagination. And because some fool in a steeplehouse, dressed up like a stage player in robes and mitre, dares to measure the days of the Almighty by his kitchen clock, you take his word before the word of God! Shame on you, Isaac Newton, for making an idol of an archbishop! There is no credulity like the credulity of philosophers.

NEWTON. But the archbishop has counted the years! My own chronology of the world has been founded on his calculation. Do you mean to tell me that all the labor I have bestowed on that book has been wasted?

FOX. Sinfully wasted.

NEWTON. George Fox: you are an infidel. Leave my house.

FOX [rising] Your philosophy has led you to the conclusion that George Fox is an infidel. So much the worse for your philosophy! The Lord does not love men that count numbers. Read second Samuel, chapter twentyfour: the book is before you. Good morning; and God bless you and enlighten you. [He turns to go].

CHARLES. Stay, Pastor. [He makes Fox sit down again and goes to Newton, laying a hand on his shoulder]. Mr Newton: the word infidel is not one to be used hastily between us three. Old Tom Hobbes, my tutor, who was to me what Aristotle was to Alexander the Great, was called an infidel. You yourself, in spite of your interest in the book of Daniel, have been suspected of doubting whether the apple falls from the tree by the act of God or by a purely physical attraction. Even I, the head of the Church, the Defender of the Faith, stand between the Whigs who suspect me of being a Papist and the Tories who suspect me of being an atheist. Now the one thing that is true of all three of us is that if the common people knew our real minds they would hang us and bury us in unconsecrated ground. We must stand together, gentlemen. What does it matter to us whether the world is four thousand years old, or, as I should guess, ten thousand?

NEWTON. The world ten thousand years old! Sir: you are mad.

NELL [*shocked*] Rowley darling: you mustnt say such things.

BARBARA. What business is it of yours, pray? He has always defied God and betrayed women. He does not know the meaning of the word religion. He laughed at it in France. He hated it in Scotland. In England he believes nothing. He loves nothing. He fears nothing except having to go on his travels again, as he calls it. What are ten thousand years to him, or ten million?

FOX. Are ten million years beyond the competence of Almighty God? They are but a moment in His eyes. Four thousand years seem an eternity to a mayfly, or a mouse, or a mitred fool called an archbishop. Are we mayflies? Are we mice? Are we archbishops?

MRS BASHAM. Mr Fox: I have listened to too much blasphemy this morning. But to call an archbishop a mitred fool and compare him to a mouse is beyond endurance. I cannot believe that God will ever pardon you for that. Have you no fear of hell?

FOX. How shall I root out the sin of idolatry from this land? Worship your God, woman, not a dressed-up priest.

MRS BASHAM. The archbishop is not a graven image. And when he is officiating he is not in the likeness of anything in the heavens above or on the earth beneath. I am afraid you do not know your catechism, Mr Fox.

CHARLES [*laughing*] Excellent, Mrs Basham. Pastor: she has gravelled you with the second commandment. And she has put us to shame for quarrelling over a matter of which we know nothing. By the way, where were we when we began to quarrel? I have clean forgotten.

LOUISE. It was my business with Mr Newton, I think. Nellie: will you take our sovereign lord away and leave me to speak with the alchemist in private?

CHARLES. Mr Newton: not for worlds would I deprive you of a *tête-à-tête* with her Grace of Portsmouth. Pastor: you will accompany us. Nellie: you will come with the pastor. But first I must throw the Duchess of Cleveland downstairs [*moving towards her*].

BARBARA [*screaming and making for the door*] Coward! Help! Murder! [*She rushes out*].

CHARLES. Your servant, Mrs Basham.

Mrs Basham curtsies. Charles salutes her and goes out.

NELL [*beckoning to Fox*] Come on, leather breeches.

FOX [*rising and going towards the door*] Well, what you are, God made you. I am bound to be your friend.

NELL [*taking his arm as he passes*] I am proud of your friendship, George.

They go out arm in arm.

Louise, being now the person of highest rank present, follows them as far as the armchair, in which she seats herself with distinguished elegance.

LOUISE [*to Mrs Basham*] Madam: may I have a moment alone with the alchemist?

NEWTON. You certainly may not, your Grace. I will not have Mr Locke and his friends accuse me of having relations with women. If your business cannot be discussed before Mrs Basham it cannot be discussed with me. And you will please not speak of me as "the alchemist" as you might speak of the apothecary or the chimney sweep. I am by profession—if it can be called a profession—a philosopher.

LOUISE. Pardon: I am not habituated to your English manners. It is strange to me that a philosopher should need a chaperon. In France it is I who should need one.

NEWTON. You are quite safe with me and Mrs Basham, madam. What is your business?

LOUISE. I want a love charm.

NEWTON. A what?

LOUISE. A love charm. Something that will make my lover faithful to me if I drop it into his tay. And mind! it must make him love me, and not love everybody. He is far too amorous already of every pretty woman he meets. I make no secret of who he is: all the world knows it. The love charm must not do him any harm; for if we poison the king we shall be executed in the most horrible manner. It must be something that will be good for him.

NEWTON. And peculiar to yourself? Not to Mistress Gwynn?

LOUISE. I do not mind Nellie: she is a dear, and so helpful when there is any trouble or illness. He picked her up out of the gutter; but the good God sometimes drops a jewel there: my nurse, a peasant woman, was worth a thousand duchesses. Yes: he may have Nellie: a change is sometimes good for men.

MRS BASHAM [*fearfully shocked*] Oh! Mr Newton: I must go. I cannot stay and listen to this French lady's talk. [*She goes out with dignity*].

LOUISE. I shall never understand the things that Englishwomen are prudish about. And they are so extraordinarily coarse in other things. May I stay, now that your chaperon has gone?

NEWTON. You will not want to stay when I tell you that I do not deal in love potions. Ask the nearest apothecary for an aphrodisiac.

LOUISE. But I cannot trust a common apothecary: it would be all over the town tomorrow. Nobody will suspect you. I will pay any price you like.

NEWTON. I tell you, madam, I know nothing about such things. If I wished to make you fall in love with me—which God forbid! —I should not know how to set about it. I should learn to play some musical instrument, or buy a new wig.

LOUISE. But you are an alchemist: you must know.

NEWTON. Then I am not an alchemist. But the changing of Bodies into Light and Light into Bodies is very conformable to the Course of Nature, which seems delighted with Transmutations.

LOUISE. I do not understand. What are transmutations?

NEWTON. Never mind, madam. I have other things to do than to peddle love charms to the King's ladies.

LOUISE [*ironically*] Yes: to entertain the Duchess of Cleveland and Mistress Gwynn, and hire a mad preacher to amuse them! What else have you to do that is more important than my business with you?

NEWTON. Many other things. For instance, to ascertain the exact distance of the sun from the earth.

LOUISE. But what a waste of time! What can it possibly matter whether the sun is twenty miles away or twentyfive?

NEWTON. Twenty or twentyfive!!! The sun is millions and millions of miles from the earth.

LOUISE. Oh! Oh!! Oh!!! You are quite mad, Monsieur Nieuton. At such a distance you could not see it. You could not feel its heat. Well, you cannot see it so plainly here as in France, nor so often; but you can see it quite plainly sometimes. And you can feel its heat. It burns your skin, and freckles you if you are sandy-haired. And then comes a little cloud over it and you shiver with cold. Could that happen if it were a thousand miles away?

NEWTON. It is very very large, madam. It is one million three hundred thousand times heavier than the earth.

LOUISE. My good Monsieur Nieuton: do not be so fanciful. [*Indicating the window*] Look at it. Look at it. It is much smaller than the earth. If I hold up a sou—what you call a ha-pen-ny—before my eye, it covers the sun and blots it out. Let me teach you something, Monsieur Nieuton. A great French philosopher, Blaise Pascal, teached me this. You must never let your imagination run away with you. When you think of grandiose things—hundreds of millions and things like that—you must continually come down to earth to keep sane. You must see: you must feel: you must measure.

NEWTON. That is very true, madam. Above all, you must measure. And when you measure you find that many things are bigger than they look. The sun is one of them.

LOUISE [*rising and going to the table to coax him*] Ah! You are impossible. But you will make me a love potion, will you not?

NEWTON. I will write you a prescription, madam.

He takes a sheet of paper and writes the prescription. Louise watches as he writes.

LOUISE. Aqua? But aqua is only water, monsieur.

NEWTON. Water with a cabalistic sign after it, madam.

LOUISE. Ah, parfaitement. And this long magical word, what is it? Mee-kah-pah-nees. What is that?

NEWTON. Mycapaynis, madam. A very powerful lifegiving substance.

LOUISE. It sounds wonderful. Is it harmless?

NEWTON. The most harmless substance in the world, madam, and the most precious.

LOUISE. Truly you are a great man, Monsieur Nieuton, in spite of your millions oı miles. And this last word here?

NEWTON. Only sugar, to sweeten the micapanis, but with the cabalistic sign after it. Here is your love charm, madam. But it is not a potion: the apothecary will make it into pills for you.

LOUISE [*taking the paper and tucking it into the bosom of her dress*] Good. That is better, much better. It is so much easier to make men take pills than drink potions. And now, one thing more. You must swear to give this prescription to no other woman of the court. It is for me alone.

NEWTON. You have my word of honor, madam.

LOUISE. But a word of honor must be a gentleman's word of honor. You, monsieur, are a bourgeois. You must swear on your Bible.

NEWTON. My word is my word, madam. And the Bible must not be mixed up with the magic of micapanis.

LOUISE. Not black magic, is it? I could not touch that.

NEWTON. Neither black nor white, madam. Shall we say grey? But quite harmless, I assure you.

LOUISE. Good. And now I must make you a little present for your pills. How much shall it be?

NEWTON. Keep your money for the apothecary, madam: he will be amply satisfied with five shillings. I am sufficiently rewarded by the sound scientific advice you have given me from your friend Blaise Pascal. He was anticipated by an Englishman named Bacon, who was, however, no mathematician. You owe me nothing.

LOUISE. Shall I give one of the new golden guineas to the lady I shocked if I meet her on the stairs?

NEWTON. No. She would not take it.

LOUISE. How little you know the world, Monsieur! Nobody refuses a golden guinea.

NEWTON. You can try the experiment, madam. That would be

the advice of your friend Pascal. [*He goes to the door, and opens it for her*].

LOUISE. Perhaps I had better make it two guineas. She will never refuse that.

NEWTON [*at the door, calling*] Sally!

LOUISE [*with a gracious inclination of her head*] Monsieur—

NEWTON. I wish your Grace good morning.

SALLY [*at the door*] Yes, sir?

NEWTON. Shew her Grace the Duchess of Portsmouth to her chair or whatever it is.

LOUISE. Au plaisir de vous revoir, Monsieur le philosophe.

The Duchess goes out, Sally making her a rustic curtsey as she passes, and following her out, leaving Newton alone.

NEWTON [*greatly relieved*] Ouf!

He returns to his place at the table and to his Bible, which, helped by a marker, he opens at the last two chapters of the book of Daniel. He props his head on his elbows.

NEWTON. Twelve hundred and ninety days. And in the very next verse thirteen hundred and thirtyfive days. Five months difference! And the king's daughter of the south: who was she? And the king of the south? And he that cometh against him? And the vile person who obtains the kingdom by flatteries? And Michael? Who was Michael? [*He considers this a moment; then suddenly snatches a sheet of paper and writes furiously*].

SALLY [*throwing open the door, bursting with pride*] His Royal Highness the Duke of York.

The Duke, afterwards James II, comes in precipitately.

JAMES [*imperiously*] Where is his Majesty the King?

NEWTON [*rising in ungovernable wrath*] Sir: I neither know nor care where the King is. This is my house; and I demand to be left in peace in it. I am engaged in researches of the most sacred importance; and for them I require solitude. Do you hear, sir? solitude!

JAMES. Sir: I am the Duke of York, the King's brother.

NEWTON. I am Isaac Newton, the philosopher. I am also an Englishman; and my house is my castle. At least it was until this morning, when the whole court came here uninvited. Are there not palaces for you and the court to resort to? Go away.

JAMES. I know you. You are a follower of the arch infidel Galileo!

NEWTON. Take care, sir. In my house the great Galileo shall not be called an infidel by any Popish blockhead, prince or no prince. Galileo had more brains in his boots than you have in your whole body.

JAMES. Had he more brains in his boots than the Catholic Church? Than the Pope and all his cardinals, the greatest scholars of his day? Is there more learning in your head than in the libraries of the Vatican?

NEWTON. Popes and cardinals are abolished in the Church of England. Only a fool would set up these superstitious idolaters against the Royal Society, founded by your royal brother for the advancement of British science?

JAMES. A club of damnable heretics. I shall know how to deal with them.

NEWTON [*rising in a fury and facing him menacingly*] Will you leave my house, or shall I throw you out through the window?

JAMES. You throw me out! Come on, you scum of a grammar school.

They rush at one another, and in the scuffle fall on the floor, Newton uppermost. Charles comes in at this moment.

CHARLES. Odsfish, Mr Newton, whats this? A wrestling match?

Newton hastily rolls off James. The two combatants remain sitting on the floor, staring up at Charles.

CHARLES. And what the divvle are you doing here, Jamie? Why arnt you in Holland?

JAMES. I am here where I have been thrown by your friend and protégé, the infidel philosopher Newton.

CHARLES. Get up, man: dont play the fool. Mr Newton: your privilege with me does not run to the length of knocking my brother down. It is a serious matter to lay hands on a royal personage.

NEWTON. Sir: I had no intention of knocking your royal

brother down. He fell and dragged me down. My intention was only to throw him out of the window.

CHARLES. He could have left by the door, Mr Newton.

NEWTON. He could; but he would not, in spite of my repeated requests. He stayed here to heap insults on the immortal Galileo, whose shoe latchet he is unworthy to unloose.

He rises and confronts the King with dignity.

CHARLES. Will you get up, Jamie, and not sit on the floor grinning like a Jackanapes. Get up, I tell you.

JAMES [*rising*] You see what comes of frequenting the houses of your inferiors. They forget themselves and take liberties. And you encourage heretics. I do not.

CHARLES. Mr Newton: we are in your house and at your orders. Will you allow my brother and myself to have this room to ourselves awhile?

NEWTON. My house is yours, sir. I am a resolute supporter of the Exclusion Bill because I hope to prove that the Romish Church is the little horn of the fourth beast mentioned by the prophet Daniel. But the great day of wrath is not yet come. Your brother is welcome here as long as you desire it.

Newton goes out. Charles takes the armchair. When he is seated James takes Newton's chair at the table.

JAMES. That fellow is crazy. He called me a Popish blockhead. You see what comes of encouraging these Protestants. If you had a pennorth of spunk in you you would burn the lot.

CHARLES. What I want to know is what you are doing here when you should be in Holland. I am doing what I can to stop this Exclusion Bill and secure the crown for you when I die. I sent you to Holland so that your talent for making yourself unpopular might be exercised there and not here. Your life is in danger in London. You had no business to come back. Why have you done it?

JAMES. Charles: I am a prince.

CHARLES. Oh, do I not know it, God help you!

JAMES. Our father lost his head by compromising with Protestants, Republicans, Levellers and Atheists. What did he gain by it? They beheaded him. I am not going to share his fate by repeating that mistake. I am a Catholic; and I am civil to none but Catholics, however unpopular it may make me. When I am king—as I shall be, in my own right, and not by the leave of any Protestant parliamentary gang—I shall restore the Church and restore the monarchy: yes, the monarchy, Charles; for there has been no real Restoration: you are no king, cleverly as you play with these Whigs and Tories. That is because you have no faith, no principles: you dont believe in anything; and a man who doesnt believe in anything is afraid of everything. Youre a damned coward, Charles. I am not. When I am king I shall reign: these fellows shall find what a king's will is when he reigns by divine right. They will get it straight in the teeth then; and Europe will see them crumble up like moths in a candle flame.

CHARLES. It is a funny thing, Jamie, that you, who are clever enough to see that the monarchy is gone and that I keep the crown by my wits, are foolish enough to believe that you have only to stretch out your clenched fist and take it back again. I sometimes ask myself whether it would not be far kinder of me to push the Exclusion Bill through and save you from the fate of our father. They will have your head off inside of five years unless you jump into the nearest fishing smack and land in France.

JAMES. And leave themselves without a king again! Not they: they had enough of that under old Noll's Major-Generals. Noll knew how to rule: I will say that for him; and I thank him for the lesson. But when he died they had to send for us. When they bully you you give in to them and say that you dont want to go on your travels again. But by God, if they try to bully me I will threaten to go on my travels and leave them without a king. That is the way to bring them down on their marrowbones.

CHARLES. You could not leave them without a king. Protestant kings—Stuart kings—are six a penny in Europe today. The Dutch lad's grandfather-in-law was our grandfather. Your daughter Mary is married to him. The Elector of Hanover has the same hook on to grandfather James. Both of them are rank Protestants and hardened soldiers, caring for nothing but fighting the French. Besides Mary there is her sister Anne, Church of England to the backbone. With the Protestants you do not succeed by divine right: they take their choice and send for you, just as they sent for me.

JAMES. Yes, if you look at it in that way and let them do it. Charles: you havnt the spirit of a king: that is what is the matter with you. As long as they let you have your women, and your dogs, and your pictures, and your music, and your chemical laboratory, you let them do as they like. The merry monarch: thats what you are.

CHARLES. Something new in monarchs, eh?

JAMES. Psha! A merry monarch is no monarch at all.

CHARLES. All the same, I must pack you off to Scotland. I cannot have you here until I prorogue parliament to get rid of the Exclusion Bill. And you will have to find a Protestant husband for Anne: remember that.

JAMES. You pretend you are packing me off to save me from my Catholic unpopularity. The truth is you are jealous of my popularity.

CHARLES. No, Jamie: I can beat you at that game. I am an agreeable sort of fellow: old Newcastle knocked that into me when I was a boy. Living at the Hague on two hundred and forty pounds a year finished my education in that respect. Now you, Jamie, became that very disagreeable character a man of principle. The people, who have all sorts of principles which they havnt gathered out of your basket, will never take to you until you go about shouting No Popery. And you will die rather than do that: wont you?

JAMES. Certainly I shall; and so, I trust, would you. Promise me you will die a Catholic, Charles.

CHARLES. I shall take care not to die in an upstart sect like the Church of England, and perhaps lose my place in Westminster Abbey when you are king. Your principles might oblige you to throw my carcase to the dogs. Meanwhile, however popular you may think yourself, you must go and be popular in Scotland.

JAMES. I am popular everywhere: thats what you dont understand because you are not a fighting man; and I am. In the British Isles, Charles, nothing is more popular than the navy; and nobody is more popular than the admiral who has won a great naval victory. Thats what I have done, and you havnt. And that puts me ahead of you with the British people every time.

CHARLES. No doubt; but the British people do not make kings in England. The crown is in the hands of the damned Whig squirearchy who got rich by robbing the Church, and chopped off father's head, crown and all. They care no more for your naval victory than for a bunch of groundsel. They would not pay for the navy if we called it ship money, and let them know what they are paying for.

JAMES. I shall make them pay. I shall not be their puppet as you are. Do you think I will be in the pay of the king of France, whose bitter bread we had to eat in our childhood, and who left our mother without firewood in the freezing winter? And all this because these rebellious dogs will not disgorge enough of their stolen wealth to cover the cost of governing them! If you will not teach them their lesson they shall learn it from me.

CHARLES. You will have to take your money where you can get it, Jamie, as I do. French money is as good as English. King Louis gets little enough for it: I take care of that.

JAMES. Then you cheat him. How can you stoop?

CHARLES. I must. And I know that I must. To play the king as you would have me I should need old Noll's army; and they took good care I should not have that. They grudge me even the guards.

JAMES. Well, what old Noll could do I can do; and so could you if you had the pluck. I will have an army too.

CHARLES. Of Protestants?

JAMES. The officers will be Catholics. The rank and file will be what they are ordered to be.

CHARLES. Where will you get the money to pay them? Old Noll had the city of London and its money at his back.

JAMES. The army will collect the taxes. How does King Louis do it? He keeps the biggest army in Europe; and he keeps you

192

into the bargain. He hardly knows what a parliament is. He dragoons the Protestants out of France into Spitalfields. I shall dragoon them out of Spitalfields.

CHARLES. Where to?

JAMES. To hell, or to the American plantations, whichever they prefer.

CHARLES. So you are going to be the English Louis, the British Roi Soleil, the sun king. This is a deuced foggy climate for sun kings, Jamie.

JAMES. So you think, Charles. But the British climate has nothing to do with it. What is it that nerves Louis to do all these things? The climate of the Catholic Church. His foot is on the rock of Saint Peter; and that makes him a rock himself.

CHARLES. Your son-in-law Dutch Billy is not afraid of him. And Billy's house is built, not on a rock, not even on the sands, but in the mud of the North Sea. Keep your eye on the Orangeman, Jamie.

JAMES. I shall keep my eye on your Protestant bastard Monmouth. Why do you make a pet of that worthless fellow? Know you not he is longing for your death so that he may have a try for the crown while this rascally Popish plot is setting the people against me?

CHARLES. For my death! What a thought! I grant you he has not the makings of a king in him: I am not blind to his weaknesses. But surely he is not heartless.

JAMES. Psha! there is not a plot in the kingdom to murder either of us that he is not at the bottom of.

CHARLES. He is not deep enough to be at the bottom of anything, Jamie.

JAMES. Then he is at the top. I forgive him for wanting to make an end of me: I am no friend of his. But to plot against you, his father! you, who have petted him and spoilt him and forgiven him treason after treason! for that I shall not forgive him, as he shall find if ever he falls into my hand.

CHARLES. Jamie: this is a dreadful suspicion to put into my mind. I thought the lad had abused my affection until it was exhausted; but it still can hurt. Heaven keep him out of your hand! that is all I can say. Absalom! O Absalom: my son, my son!

JAMES. I am sorry, Charles; but this is what comes of bringing up your bastards as Protestants and making dukes of them.

CHARLES. Let me tell you a secret, Jamie: a king's secret. Peter the fisherman did not know everything. Neither did Martin Luther.

JAMES. Neither do you.

CHARLES. No; but I must do the best I can with what I know, and not with what Peter and Martin knew. Anyhow, the long and the short of it is that you must start for Scotland this very day, and stay there until I send you word that it is safe for you to come back.

JAMES. Safe! What are you afraid of, man? If you darent face these Protestant blackguards, is that any reason why I should run away from them?

CHARLES. You were talking just now about your popularity. Do you know who is the most popular man in England at present?

JAMES. Shaftesbury, I suppose. He is the Protestant hero just as Nelly is the Protestant whoor. I tell you Shaftesbury will turn his coat as often as you crack your whip. Why dont you crack it?

CHARLES. I am not thinking of Shaftesbury.

JAMES. Then who?

CHARLES. Oates.

JAMES. Titus Oates! A navy chaplain kicked out of the service for the sins of Sodom and Gomorrah! Are you afraid of him?

CHARLES. Yes. At present he is the most popular man in the kingdom. He is lodged in my palace at Whitehall with a pension of four hundred pounds a year.

JAMES. What!!!

CHARLES. And I, who am called a king, cannot get rid of him. This house is Isaac Newton's; and he can order you out and throw you out of the window if you dont go. But my house must harbor the vilest scoundrel in Europe while he parades in lawn sleeves through the street with his No Popery mob at his heels, and murders our best Catholic families with his brazen perjuries and his silly Popish plot that should not impose on a rabbit. No man with eyes in his head could look at the creature for an instant without seeing that he is only half human.

JAMES. Flog him through the town. Flog him to death. They can if they lay on hard enough and long enough. The same mob that now takes him for a saint will crowd to see the spectacle and revel in his roarings.

CHARLES. That will come, Jamie. I am hunting out his record; and your man Jeffries will see to it that the poor divvle shall have no mercy. But just now it is not Oates that we have to kill: the people would say that he was murdered by the Catholics and run madder than ever. They blame the Catholics now for the Great Fire of London and the plague. We must kill the Popish Plot first. When we have done that, God help Titus Oates! Meanwhile, away with you to Scotland and try your cat-o-ninetails on the Covenanters there.

JAMES. Well, I suppose I must, since England is governed by its mob instead of by its king. But I tell you, Charles, when I am king there shall be no such nonsense. You jeer at me and say that I am the protector of your life, because nobody will kill you to make me king; but I take that as the highest compliment you could pay me. This mob that your Protestant Republicans and Presbyterians and Levellers call the people of England will have to choose between King James the Second and King Titus Oates. And James and the Church—and there is only one real Church of God—will see to it that their choice will be Hobson's choice.

CHARLES. The people of England will have nothing to do with it. The real Levellers today, Jamie, are the lords and the rich squires—Cromwell's sort—and the moneyed men of the city. They will keep the people's noses to the grindstone no matter what happens. And their choice will be not between you and Titus Oates, but between your daughter Mary's Protestant husband and you.

JAMES. He will have to cross the seas to get here. And I, as Lord High Admiral of England, will meet him on the seas and

sink him there. He is no great general on land: on water he is
nothing. I have never been beaten at sea.

CHARLES. Jamie, Jamie: nothing frightens me so much as your
simple stupid pluck, and your faith in Rome. You think you will
have the Pope at your back because you are a Catholic. You are
wrong: in politics the Pope is always a Whig, because every
earthly monarch's court is a rival to the Vatican.

JAMES. Do you suppose that if Orange Billy, the head of the
Protestant heresy in Europe, the anti-Pope you might call him,
dared to interfere with me, a Catholic king, the Pope could take
his part against me in the face of all Europe! How can you talk
such nonsense? Do you think Mary would share the crown if he
tore it from her father's head? Rochester called you the king
that never said a foolish thing and never did a wise one; but it
seems to me that you talk silly-clever nonsense all day, though
you are too wise: that is, too big a coward, ever to risk a fight
with the squirearchy. What are they in France? Lackeys round
the throne at Versailles: not one of them dare look King Louis
straight in the face. But in France there is a real king.

CHARLES. He has a real army and real generals. And taxes
galore. Old Noll went one better than Louis: he was a general
himself. And what a general! Preston, Dunbar, Worcester: we
could do nothing against him though we had everything on our
side, except him. I have been looking for his like ever since we
came back. I sometimes wonder whether Jack Churchill has any
military stuff in him.

JAMES. What! That henpecked booby! I suppose you know
that he got his start in life as your Barbara's kept man?

CHARLES. I know that the poor lad risked breaking his bones
by jumping out of Barbara's window when she was seducing him
and I came along unexpectedly. I have always liked him for that.

JAMES. It was worth his while. She gave him five thousand
pounds for it.

CHARLES. Yes: I had to find the money. I was tremendously
flattered when I heard of it. I had no idea that Barbara put so high
a price on my belief in her faithfulness, in which, by the way, I

did not believe. Poor Barbara was never alone with a pretty fellow for five minutes without finding out how much of a man he was. I threw Churchill in her way purposely to keep her in good humor. What struck me most in the affair was that Jack bought an annuity with the money instead of squandering it as any other man of his age would have done. That was a sign of solid ability. He may be henpecked: what married man is not? But he is no booby.

JAMES. Meanness. Pure meanness. The Churchills never had a penny to bless themselves with. Jack got no more education than my groom.

CHARLES. Latin grammar is not much use on the battlefield, as we found out. Turenne found Jack useful enough in Spain; and Turenne was supposed to be France's greatest general. Your crown may depend on Jack: by the time I die he will be as old a soldier as Oliver was at Dunbar.

JAMES. Never fear. I shall buy him if he's worth it.

CHARLES. Or if you are worth it. Jack is a good judge of a winner.

JAMES. He has his price all the same.

CHARLES. All intelligent men have, Jamie.

JAMES. Psha! Dont waste your witticisms on me: they butter no parsnips. If he can pick a winner he had better pick me.

CHARLES. There are only two horses in the race now: the Protestant and the Catholic. I have to ride both at once.

JAMES. That was what Father tried to do. See what he got by it!

CHARLES. See what I get by it! Not much, perhaps; but I keep my head on my shoulders. It takes a man of brains to do that. Our father unfortunately tried his hand at being also a man of blood, as Noll called him. We Stuarts are no good at that game: Noll beat us at it every time. I hate blood and battles: I have seen too much of them to have any dreams of glory about them. I am, as you say, no king. To be what you call a king I lack military ambition; and I lack cruelty. I have to manage Protestants who are so frightfully cruel that I dare not interfere with Protestant judges who are merciless. The penalty for high treason is so abominable that only a divvle could have invented it, and a nation of divvles crowd to see it done. The only time I risked my crown was when I stopped them after they had butchered ten of the regicides: I could bear no more. They were not satisfied: they dug up the body of old Noll, and butchered it rather than have their horrible sport cut short.

JAMES. Serve the rascals right! A good lesson for them and their like. Dont be such a mollycoddle, Charles. What you need is a bit of my sea training to knock the nonsense out of you.

CHARLES. So you will try your luck as a man of blood, will you?

JAMES. I will do what is necessary. I will fight my enemies if they put me to it. I will take care that those who put me to it shall not die easy deaths.

CHARLES. Well, that will seem very natural to the mob. You will find plenty of willing tools. But I would not light the fires of Smithfield again if I were you. Your pet Jeffries would do it for you and enjoy it; but Protestants do not like being burnt alive.

JAMES. They will have to lump it if they fly in the face of God.

CHARLES. Oh, go to Scotland: go to Jericho. You sicken me. Go.

JAMES. Charles! We must not part like this. You know you always stand by me as far as you dare. I ought not to talk to you about government and kingcraft: you dont understand these matters and never will; and I do understand them. I have resolved again and again not to mention them to you; for after all we are brothers; and I love you in spite of all the times you have let me down with the Protestants. It is not your fault that you have no head for politics and no knowledge of human nature. You need not be anxious about me. I will leave for Scotland tomorrow. But I have business in London tonight that I will not postpone for fifty thousand Titus Oateses.

CHARLES. Business in London tonight! The one redeeming point in your character, Jamie, is that you are not a man of principle in the matter of women.

JAMES. You are quite wrong there: I am in all things a man of principle and a good Catholic, thank God. But being human I am also a man of sin. I confess it; and I do my penances!

CHARLES. The women themselves are worse penances than any priest dare inflict on you. Try Barbara: a week with her is worse than a month in hell. But I have given up all that now. Nelly is a good little soul who amuses me. Louise manages my French affairs. She has French brains and manners, and is always a lady. But they are now my friends only: affectionate friends, family friends, nothing else. And they alone are faithful to the elderly king. I am fifty, Jamie, fifty: dont forget that. And women got hold of me when I was fourteen, thirtysix years ago. Do you suppose I have learnt nothing about women and what you call love in that time? You still have love affairs: I have none. However, I am not reproaching you: I am congratulating you on being still young and green enough to come all the way from Holland for a night in London.

Mrs Basham returns, much perturbed.

MRS BASHAM. Mr Rowley: I must tell you that I cannot receive any more of your guests. I have not knives nor plates nor glasses enough. I have had to borrow chairs from next door. Your valet, Mr Chiffinch, tells who ever has any business with you this morning to come on here. Mr Godfrey Kneller, the new Dutch painter, with a load of implements connected with his trade, had got in in spite of me: he heard the noise your people were making. There are the two ladies and the player woman, and yourself and your royal brother and Mr Fox and the painter. That makes seven; and Mr Newton makes eight and I make nine. I have nothing to offer them but half a decanter of sherry that was opened last Easter, and the remains of a mouldy cake. I have sent Sally out with orders that will run away with a fortnight's housekeeping money; and that wont be half what theyll expect. I thought they were all going away when they came downstairs; but the French lady wanted to look through Mr Newton's telescope; and the jealous lady wouldnt leave until the French lady left; and the player woman is as curious as a magpie and makes herself as much at home as if she lived here. It has ended in their all staying. And now Mr Newton is explaining everything and shewing off his telescope and never thinking what I am to do with them! How am I to feed them?

CHARLES. Dont feed them, Mrs Basham. Starve them out.

MRS BASHAM. Oh no: I cant do that. What would they think of us? Mr Newton has his position to keep up.

CHARLES. It is the judgment of heaven on you for turning away my pretty spaniels from your door this morning.

MRS BASHAM. There were twelve of them, sir.

CHARLES. You would have found them much better company than nine human beings. But never mind. Sally will tell all the tradesmen that Mr Newton is entertaining me and my brother. They will call themselves Purveyors to his Majesty the King. Credit will be unlimited.

JAMES. Remember that this is Friday: a fast day. All I need is three or four different kinds of fish.

MRS BASHAM. No, sir: in this house you will have to be content with a Protestant dinner. Jack the fish hawker is gone. But he left us a nice piece of cod; and thats all youll get, sir.

CHARLES. Jamie: we must clear out and take the others with us. It seems we cannot visit anyone without ruining them.

JAMES. Pooh! What can a few pounds more or less matter to anybody?

CHARLES. I can remember when they meant a divvle of a lot to me, and to you too. Let us get back to Newmarket.

MRS BASHAM. No, sir: Mr Newton would not like that: he knows his duties as your host. And if you will excuse me saying so, sir: you all look as if a plain wholesome dinner would do you no harm for once in a way. By your leave I will go to look after it. I must turn them all out of the laboratory and send them up here while I lay the table there.

She goes out.

JAMES. "A nice piece of cod!" Among nine people!

CHARLES. "Isnt that a dainty dish to set before a king?" Your fast will be a real fast, Jamie, for the first time in your life.

JAMES. You lie. My penances are all real.

CHARLES. Well, a hunk of bread, a lump of cheese, and a bottle of ale are enough for me or for any man at this hour.

All the rest come back except Mrs Basham, Barbara, and Newton. Fox comes first.

FOX. I have made eight new friends. But has the Lord sent them to me? Such friends! [*He takes his old seat, much perplexed*].

NELL [*coming in*] Oh, Rowley darling, they want me to recite my big speech from The Indian Emperor. But I cant do that without proper drapery: its classical. [*Going to the Duke*] And what is my Jamie doing here?

LOUISE [*taking a chair from the wall and planting it at Charles's right, familiarly close*] Why not give us a prologue? Your prologues are your best things. [*She sits*].

CHARLES and JAMES. Yes, yes: a prologue.

All are now seated, except Nell.

NELL. But I cant do a prologue unless I am in breeches.

FOX [*rising*] No. Eleanor Gwyn: how much more must I endure from you? I will not listen to a prologue that can be spoken only by a woman in breeches. And I warn you that when I raise my voice to heaven against mummery, whether in playhouse or steeplehouse, I can drown and dumb the loudest ribald ranter.

CHARLES. Pastor: Mistress Gwyn is neither a ribald nor a ranter. The plays and prologues in which she is famous are the works of the greatest poet of the age: the poet Laureate, John Dryden.

FOX. If he has given to the playhouse talents that were given to him for the service of God, his guilt is the deeper.

CHARLES. Have you considered, Pastor, that the playhouse is a place where two or three are gathered together?

NELL. Not when I am playing, Rowley darling. Two or three hundred, more likely.

FOX [*resuming his seat in the deepest perplexity*] Sir: you are upsetting my mind. You have forced me to make friends with this player woman; and now you would persuade me that the playhouse is as divine as my meeting house. I find your company agreeable to me, but very unsettling.

CHARLES. The settled mind stagnates, Pastor. Come! Shall I give you a sample of Mr Dryden at his best?

NELL. Oh yes, Rowley darling: give us your pet speech from Aurengzebe.

LOUISE. Yes yes. He speaks it beautifully. He is almost as good an actor as King Louis; and he has really more of the grand air.

CHARLES. Thank you, Louise. Next time leave out the almost. My part is more difficult than that of Louis.

JAMES. Pray silence for his Majesty the King, who is going to make a fool of himself to please the Quaker.

CHARLES. Forgive Jamie, ladies and gentlemen. He will give you his own favorite recitation presently; but the King comes first. Now listen. [*He rises. They all rise, except Fox*]. No, pray. My audience must be seated. [*They sit down again*].

Charles recites the pessimistic speech from Aurengzebe as follows:

When I consider life, 'tis all a cheat;
Yet, fooled with hope, men favor the deceit;
Trust on, and think tomorrow will repay:
Tomorrow's falser than the former day;
Lies worse; and, while it says we shall be blest
With some new choice, cuts off what we possessed.
Strange cozenage! None would live past years again;
Yet all hope pleasure in what yet remain;
And from the dregs of life think to receive
What the first sprightly running could not give.
I'm tired of waiting for this chemic gold
Which fools us young, and beggars us when old.

Nell and Louise applaud vigorously.

CHARLES. What do you think of that, Pastor? [*He sits*].

FOX. It is the cry of a lost soul from the bottomless blackness of its despair. Never have I heard anything so terrible. This man has never lived. I must seek him out and shew him the light and the truth.

NELL. Tut tut, George! The man in the play is going to be killed. To console himself he cries Sour Grapes: that is all. And now what shall I give you?

JAMES. Something oldfashioned. Give him a bit of Shakespear.

NELL. What! That author the old actors used to talk about. Kynaston played women in his plays. I dont know any. We cannot afford them nowadays. They require several actors of the first quality; and—would you believe it, George?—those laddies will not play now for less than fifteen shillings a week.

FOX [*starting up again*] Fifteen shillings a week to a player when the servants of God can scarce maintain themselves alive by working at mechanical trades! Such wickedness will bring a black judgment on the nation. Charles Stuart: have you no regard for your soul that you suffer such things to be done?

CHARLES. You would not grudge these poor fellows their fifteen shillings if you knew what women cost.

FOX. What manner of world is this that I have come into? Is virtue unknown here, or is it despised? [*He gives it up, and relapses into his seat*].

JAMES. Mr Dryden has an answer for that. [*He recites, seated*].
How vain is virtue which directs our ways
Through certain danger to uncertain praise!
The world is made for the bold impious man
Who stops at nothing, seizes all he can.
Justice to merit does weak aid afford;
She trusts her balance, and ignores her sword.
Virtue is slow to take whats not her own,
And, while she long consults, the prize is gone.

FOX. I take no exception to this. I have too good reason to know that it is true. But beware how you let these bold impious fellows extinguish hope in you. Their day is short; but the inner light is eternal.

JAMES. I am safe in the bosom of my Church, Pastor.

LOUISE. Take the gentleman's mind off his inner light, Nell. Give us a speech.

NELL. They dont want a speech from me. Rowley began talking about speeches because he wanted to do one himself. And now His Highness the Duke of York must have his turn.

JAMES. Are we poor devils of princes not to have any of the

good things, nor do any of the pleasant things, because we are Royal Highnesses? Were you not freer and happier when you sold oranges in Drury Lane than you are now as a court lady?

FOX. Did you sell oranges in Drury Lane?

NELL. They say I did. The people like to believe I did. They love me for it. I say nothing.

CHARLES. Come! Give us one of Cydara's speeches from The Indian Emperor. It was in that that you burst on the world as the ambitious orange girl.

NELL. A wretched part: I had to stand mum on the stage for hours while the others were spouting. Mr Dryden does not understand how hard that is. Just listen to this, the longest speech I had.

> May I believe my eyes! What do I see?
> Is this her hate to him? her love to me?
> 'Tis in my breast she sheathes her dagger now.
> False man: is this thy faith? Is this thy vow?

Then somebody says something.

CHARLES.

> What words, dear saint, are these I hear you use?
> What faith? what voice? are those which you accuse?

NELL. "Those which you accuse": thats my cue.

> More cruel than the tiger o'er his spile
> And falser than the weeping crocodile
> Can you add vanity to guilt, and take
> A pride to hear the conquests which you make?
> Go: publish your renown: let it be said
> The woman that you love you have betrayed—

Rowley darling: I cannot go on if you keep laughing at me. If only Mr Dryden had given me some really great lines, like the ones he gave to Montezuma. Listen.

> Still less and less my boiling spirits flow
> And I grow stiff, as cooling metals do.
> Farewell, Almira.

FOX. Now do you tell me that living men and women, created by God in His likeness and not in that of gibbering apes, can be bribed to utter such trash, and that others will pay to hear them do it when they will not enter a meeting house for a penny in the plate to hear the words of God Himself? What society is this I am in? I must be dreaming that I am in hell.

NELL. George: you are forgetting yourself. You should have applauded me. I will recite no more for you. [*She takes a chair from the wall and seats herself beside Louise, on her right*].

CHARLES. He does not understand, Nell. Tell him the story of the play, and why Montezuma says such extravagant things.

NELL. But how can I, Rowley darling? I dont know what it is all about: I know only my part and my cue. All I can say is that when Montezuma speaks those lines he drops dead.

FOX. Can you wonder that he does so? I should drop dead myself if I heard such fustian pass my lips.

JAMES. Is it worse than the fustian that passes the lips of the ranters in your conventicles?

FOX. I cannot deny it: the preachers are a greater danger than the players. I had not thought of this before. Again you unsettle my mind. There is one Jeremy Collier who swears he will write such a book on the profaneness and immorality of the stage as will either kill the theatre or shame it into decency; but these lines just uttered by Eleanor Gwyn are not profane and immoral: they are mad and foolish.

LOUISE. All the less harmful, monsieur. They are not meant to be taken seriously; and no one takes them so. But your Huguenot ranters pretend to be inspired; and foolish people are deluded by them. And what sort of world would they make for us if they got the upper hand? Can you name a single pleasure that they would leave us to make life worth living?

FOX. It is not pleasure that makes life worth living. It is life that makes pleasure worth having. And what pleasure is better than the pleasure of holy living?

JAMES. I have been in Geneva, blasphemously called the City of God under that detestable Frenchman Calvin, who, thank God, has by now spent a century in hell. And I can testify that he left the wretched citizens only one worldly pleasure.

CHARLES. Which one was that?

JAMES. Moneymaking.

CHARLES. Odsfish! that was clever of him. It is a very satisfying pleasure, and one that lasts til death.

LOUISE. It does not satisfy me.

CHARLES. You have never experienced it, Louise. You spend money: you do not make it. You spend ten times as much as Nelly; but you are not ten times as happy. If you made ten times as much as she, you would never tire of it and never ask for anything better.

LOUISE. Charles: if I spent one week making money or even thinking about it instead of throwing it away with both hands all my charm would be gone. I should become that dull thing, a plain woman. My face would be full of brains instead of beauty. And you would send me back to France by the next ship, as you sent Barbara.

CHARLES. What if I did? You will soon be tired of me; for I am an ugly old fellow. But you would never tire of moneymaking.

NELL. Now the Lord be praised, my trade is one in which I can make money without losing my good looks!

LOUISE [to Charles] If you believe what you say, why do you not make money yourself instead of running after women?

CHARLES. Because there is a more amusing occupation for me.

LOUISE. I have not seen you practise it, Charles. What is it?

CHARLES. Kingcraft.

JAMES. Of which you have not the faintest conception.

CHARLES. Like Louise, you have not seen me practise it. But I am King of England; and my head is still on my shoulders.

NELL. Rowley darling: you must learn to keep King Charles's head out of your conversation. You talk too much of him.

CHARLES. Why is it that we always talk of my father's head and never of my great grandmother's? She was by all accounts a pretty woman; but the Protestants chopped her head off in spite of Elizabeth. They had Strafford's head off in spite of my father. And then they had his own off. I am not a bit like him;

but I have more than a touch in me of my famous grandfather Henry the Fourth of France. And he died with a Protestant's dagger in his heart: the deadliest sort of Protestant: a Catholic Protestant. There are such living paradoxes. They burnt the poor wretch's hand off with the dagger in it, and then tore him to pieces with galloping horses. But Henry lay dead all the same. The Protestants will have you, Jamie, by hook or crook: I foresee that: they are the real men of blood. But they shall not have me. I shall die in my bed, and die King of England in spite of them.

FOX. This is not kingcraft: it is chicanery. Protestantism gives the lie to itself: it overthrows the Roman Church and immediately builds itself another nearer home and makes you the head of it, though it is now plain to me that your cleverness acknowledges no Church at all. You are right there: Churches are snares of the divvle. But why not follow the inner light that has saved you from the Churches? Be neither Catholic nor Protestant, Whig nor Tory: throw your crown into the gutter and be a Friend: then all the rest shall be added to you.

They all laugh at him except Charles.

CHARLES. A crown is not so easy to get rid of as you think, Pastor. Besides, I have had enough of the gutter: I prefer Whitehall.

JAMES [*to Fox*] You would like to have a king for your follower, eh?

FOX. I desire Friends, not followers. I am simple in my tastes. I am not schooled and learned as you two princes are.

CHARLES. Thank your stars for that, Pastor: you have nothing to unlearn.

FOX. That is well said. Too often have I found that a scholar is one whose mind is choked with rubbish that should never have been put there. But how do you come to know this? Things come to my knowledge by the grace of God; yet the same things have come to you who live a most profane life and have no sign of grace at all.

CHARLES. You and I are mortal men, Pastor. It is not possible for us to differ very greatly. You have to wear leather breeches lest you be mistaken for me.

Barbara storms in with a sheet of drawing paper in her hand.

BARBARA [*thrusting the paper under Charles's nose*] Do you see this?

CHARLES [*scrutinizing it admiringly*] Splendid! Has Mr Kneller done this? Nobody can catch a likeness as he can.

BARBARA. Likeness! You have bribed him to insult me. It makes me look a hundred.

CHARLES. Nonsense, dear. It is you to the life. What do you say, Jamie? [*He hands the drawing to James*].

JAMES. It's you, duchess. He has got you, wrinkle for wrinkle.

BARBARA. You say this to my face! You, who have seen my portrait by Lilly!

NELL. You were younger then, darling.

BARBARA. Who asked you for your opinion, you jealous cat?

CHARLES. Sit down; and dont be silly, Barbara. A woman's face does not begin to be interesting until she is our age.

BARBARA. Our age! You old wreck, do you dare pretend that you are as young as I am?

CHARLES. I am only fifty, Barbara. But we are both getting on.

BARBARA. Oh! [*With a scream of rage she tears the drawing to fragments and stamps on them*].

CHARLES. Ah, that was wicked of you: you have destroyed a fine piece of work. Go back to France. I tell you I am tired of your tantrums.

Barbara, intimidated, but with a defiant final stamp on the drawing, flings away behind James to one of the chairs against the cupboards, and sits there sulking.

Newton comes in from the garden, followed by Godfrey Kneller, a Dutchman of 34, well dressed and arrogant. They are both almost as angry as Barbara.

NEWTON. Mr Kneller: I will dispute with you no more. You do not understand what you are talking about.

KNELLER. Sir: I must tell you in the presence of His Majesty you are a most overweening, a most audacious man. You presume to teach me my profession.

CHARLES. What is the matter, Mr Newton?

NEWTON. Let it pass, Mr Rowley. This painter has one kind of understanding: I have another. There is only one course open to us both; and that is silence. [*Finding his chair occupied by the Duke of York he takes another from beside Barbara and seats himself at the side of the table on the Duke's left*].

CHARLES. Mr Newton is our host, Mr Kneller; and he is a very eminent philosopher. Will you not paint his picture for me? That can be done in silence.

KNELLER. I will paint his picture if your Majesty so desires. He has an interesting head: I should have drawn it this morning had not Her Grace of Cleveland insisted on my drawing her instead. But how can an interesting head contain no brain: that is the question.

CHARLES. Odsfish, man, he has the greatest brain in England.

KNELLER. Then he is blinded by his monstrous conceit. You shall judge between us, sir. Am I or am I not the greatest draughtsman in Europe?

CHARLES. You are certainly a very skilful draughtsman, Mr Kneller.

KNELLER. Can anyone here draw a line better than I?

CHARLES. Nobody here can draw a line at all, except the Duchess of Cleveland, who draws a line at nothing.

BARBARA. Charles—

CHARLES. Be quiet, Barbara. Do not presume to contradict your King.

KNELLER. If there is a science of lines, do I not understand it better than anyone?

CHARLES. Granted, Mr Kneller. What then?

KNELLER. This man here, this crazy and conceited philosopher, dares to assert in contradiction of me, of ME! that a right line is a straight line, and that everything that moves moves in a straight line unless some almighty force bends it from its path. This, he says, is the first law of motion. He lies.

CHARLES. And what do you say, Mr Kneller?

209

KNELLER. Sir: I do not say: I know. The right line, the line of beauty, is a curve. My hand will not draw a straight line: I have to stretch a chalked string on my canvas and pluck it. Will you deny that your duchess here is as famous for her beauty as the Psyche of the divine Raphael? Well, there is not a straight line in her body: she is all curves.

BARBARA [*outraged, rising*] Decency, fellow! How dare you?

CHARLES. It is true, Barbara. I can testify to it.

BARBARA. Charles: you are obscene. The impudence! [*She sits*].

KNELLER. The beauty, madam. Clear your mind of filth. There is not a line drawn by the hand of the Almighty, from the rainbow in the skies to the house the snail carries on his back, that is not a curve, and a curve of beauty. Your apple fell in a curve.

NEWTON. I explained that.

KNELLER. You mistake explanations for facts: all you science-mongers do. The path of the world curves, as you yourself have shewn; and as it whirls on its way it would leave your apple behind if the apple fell in a straight line. Motion in a curve is the law of nature; and the law of nature is the law of God. Go out into your garden and throw a stone straight if you can. Shoot an arrow from a bow, a bullet from a pistol, a cannon ball from the mightiest cannon the King can lend you, and though you had the strength of Hercules, and gunpowder more powerful than the steam which hurls the stones from Etna in eruption, yet cannot you make your arrow or your bullet fly straight to its mark.

NEWTON [*terribly perturbed*] This man does not know what he is saying. Take him away; and leave me in peace.

CHARLES. What he says calls for an answer, Mr Newton.

JAMES. The painter is right. A cannon ball flies across the sea in curves like the arches of a bridge, hop, hop, hop. But what does it matter whether it flies straight or crooked provided it hits between wind and water?

NEWTON. To you, admiral, it matters nothing. To me it makes the difference between reason and madness.

JAMES. How so?

NEWTON. Sir: if what this man believes be true, then not only

210

is the path of the cannon ball curved, but space is curved; time is curved; the universe is curved.

KNELLER. Of course it is. Why not?

NEWTON. Why not! Only my life's work turned to waste, vanity, folly. This comes of admitting strangers to break into my holy solitude with their diabolical suggestions. But I am rightly rebuked for this vice of mine that led me to believe that I could construct a universe with empty figures. In future I shall do nothing but my proper work of interpreting the scriptures. Leave me to that work and to my solitude. [*Desperately, clutching his temples*] Begone, all of you. You have done mischief enough for one morning.

CHARLES. But, Mr Newton, may we not know what we have done to move you thus? What diabolical suggestions have we made? What mischief have we done?

NEWTON. Sir: you began it, you and this infidel quaker. I have devoted months of my life to the writing of a book—a chronology of the world—which would have cost any other man than Isaac Newton twenty years hard labor.

CHARLES. I have seen that book, and been astounded at the mental power displayed in every page of it.

NEWTON. You may well have been, Mr Rowley. And now what have you and Mr Fox done to that book? Reduced it to a monument of the folly of Archbishop Ussher, who dated the creation of the world at four thousand and four, B.C., and of my stupidity in assuming that he had proved his case. My book is nonsense from beginning to end. How could I, who have calculated that God deals in millions of miles of infinite space, be such an utter fool as to limit eternity, which has neither beginning nor end, to a few thousand years? But this man Fox, without education, without calculation, without even a schoolboy's algebra, knew this when I, who was born one of the greatest mathematicians in the world, drudged over my silly book for months, and could not see what was staring me in the face.

JAMES. Well, why howl about it? Bring out another edition and confess that your Protestant mathematics are a delusion and a snare, and your Protestant archbishops impostors.

NEWTON. You do not know the worst, sir. I have another book in hand: one which should place me in line with Kepler, Copernicus, and Galileo as a master astronomer, and as the completer of their celestial systems. Can you tell me why the heavenly bodies in their eternal motion do not move in straight lines, but always in ellipses?

CHARLES. I understand that this is an unsolved problem of science. I certainly cannot solve it.

NEWTON. I have solved it by the discovery of a force in nature which I call gravitation. I have accounted for all the celestial movements by it. And now comes this painter, this ignorant dauber who, were it to save his soul—if he has a soul—could not work out the simplest equation, or as much as conceive an infinite series of numbers! this fellow substitutes for my first law of motion—straight line motion—motion in a curve.

JAMES. So bang goes your second volume of Protestant philosophy! Squashed under Barbara's outlines.

BARBARA. I will not have my outlines discussed by men. I am not a heathen goddess: I am a Christian lady. Charles always encourages infidels and libertines to blaspheme. And now he encourages them to insult me. I will not bear it.

CHARLES. Do not be an idiot, Barbara: Mr Kneller is paying you the greatest compliment in taking you for a model of the universe. The choice would seem to be between a universe of Barbara's curves and a universe of straight lines seduced from their straightness by some purely mathematical attraction. The facts seem to be on the side of the painter. But in a matter of this kind can I, as founder of the Royal Society, rank the painter as a higher authority than the philosopher?

KNELLER. Your Majesty: the world must learn from its artists because God made the world as an artist. Your philosophers steal all their boasted discoveries from the artists; and then pretend they have deduced them from figures which they call equations, invented for that dishonest purpose. This man talks of Copernicus, who pretended to discover that the earth goes round the sun instead of the sun going round the earth. Sir: Copernicus was a painter before he became an astronomer. He found astronomy easier. But his discovery was made by the great Italian painter Leonardo, born twentyone years before him, who told all his intimates that the earth is a moon of the sun.

NEWTON. Did he prove it?

KNELLER. Man: artists do not prove things. They do not need to. They KNOW them.

NEWTON. This is false. Your notion of a spherical universe is borrowed from the heathen Ptolemy, from all the magicians who believed that the only perfect figure is the circle.

KNELLER. Just what such blockheads would believe. The circle is a dead thing like a straight line: no living hand can draw it: you make it by twirling a pair of dividers. Take a sugar loaf and cut it slantwise, and you will get hyperbolas and parabolas, ellipses and ovals, which Leonardo himself could not draw, but which any fool can make with a knife and a lump of sugar. I believe in none of these mechanical forms. The line drawn by the artist's hand, the line that flows, that strikes, that speaks, that reveals! that is the line that shews the divine handiwork.

CHARLES. So you, too, are a philosopher, Mr Kneller!

KNELLER. Sir: when a man has the gift of a painter, that qualification is so magical that you cannot think of him as anything else. Who thinks of Leonardo as an engineer? of Michael Angelo as an inventor or a sonneteer? of me as a scholar and a philosopher? These things are all in our day's work: they come to us without thinking. They are trifles beside our great labor of creation and interpretation.

JAMES. I had a boatswain once in my flagship who thought he knew everything.

FOX. Perhaps he did. Divine grace takes many strange forms. I smell it in this painter. I have met it in common sailors like your boatswain. The cobbler thinks there is nothing like leather—

NELL. Not when you make it into breeches instead of boots, George.

BARBARA. Be decent, woman. One does not mention such

213

garments in well-bred society.

NELL. Orange girls and players and such like poor folk think nothing of mentioning them. They have to mend them, and sometimes to make them; so they have an honest knowledge of them, and are not ashamed like fine ladies who have only a dishonest knowledge of them.

CHARLES. Be quiet, Nelly: you are making Barbara blush.

NELL. Thats more than you have ever been able to do, Rowley darling.

BARBARA. It is well for you that you have all these men to protect you, mistress. Someday when I catch you alone I'll make you wish you had ten pairs of leather breeches on you.

CHARLES. Come come! no quarrelling.

NELL. She began it, Rowley darling.

CHARLES. No matter who began it, no quarrelling, I command.

LOUISE. Charles: the men have been quarrelling all the morning. Does your command apply to them too?

CHARLES. Their quarrels are interesting, Louise.

NELL. Are they? They bore me to distraction.

CHARLES. Much blood has been shed for them; and much more will be after we are gone.

BARBARA. Oh, do not preach, Charles. Leave that to this person who is dressed partly in leather. It is his profession: it is not yours.

CHARLES. The Protestants will not let me do anything else, my dear. But come! Mr Newton has asked us to leave his house many times. And we must not forget that he never asked us to come into it. But I have a duty to fulfil before we go. I must reconcile him with Mr Kneller, who must paint his portrait to hang in the rooms of the Royal Society.

KNELLER. It is natural that your Majesty should desire a work of mine for the Society. And this man's head is unusual, as one would expect from his being a philosopher: that is, half an idiot. I trust your Majesty was pleased with my sketch of Her Grace of Cleveland.

BARBARA. Your filthy caricature of Her Grace of Cleveland is under your feet. You are walking on it.

KNELLER [*picking up a fragment and turning it over to identify it*] Has the King torn up a work of mine? I leave the country this afternoon.

CHARLES. I would much sooner have torn up Magna Carta. Her Grace tore it up herself.

KNELLER. It is a strange fact, your Majesty, that no living man or woman can endure his or her portrait if it tells all the truth about them.

BARBARA. You lie, you miserable dauber. When our dear Peter Lilly, who has just died, painted me as I really am, did I destroy his portrait? But he was a great painter; and you are fit only to whitewash unmentionable places.

CHARLES. Her Grace's beauty is still so famous that we are all tired of it. She is the handsomest woman in England. She is also the stupidest. Nelly is the wittiest: she is also the kindest. Louise is the loveliest and cleverest. She is also a lady. I should like to have portraits of all three as they are now, not as Lilly painted them.

LOUISE. No, Charles: I do not want to have the whole truth about me handed down to posterity.

NELL. Same here. I prefer the orange girl.

KNELLER. I see I shall not succeed in England as a painter. My master Rembrandt did not think a woman worth painting until she was seventy.

NELL. Well, you shall paint me when I am seventy. In the theatre the young ones are beginning to call me Auntie! When they call me Old Mar Gwyn I shall be ready for you; and I shall look my very best then.

CHARLES. What about your portrait, Mr Fox? You have been silent too long.

FOX. I am dumbfounded by this strange and ungodly talk. To you it may seem mere gossip; but to me it is plain that this painter claims that his hand is the hand of God.

KNELLER. And whose hand is it if not the hand of God? You need hands to scratch your heads and carry food to your mouths.

That is all your hands mean to you. But the hand that can draw the images of God and reveal the soul in them, and is inspired to do this and nothing else even if he starves and is cast off by his father and all his family for it: is not his hand the hand used by God, who, being a spirit without body, parts or passions, has no hands?

FOX. So the men of the steeplehouse say; but they lie. Has not God a passion for creation? Is He not all passion of that divine nature?

KNELLER. Sir: I do not know who you are; but I will paint your portrait.

CHARLES. Bravo! We are getting on. How about your portrait, Mr Newton?

NEWTON. Not by a man who lives in a curved universe. He would distort my features.

LOUISE. Perhaps gravitation would distort them equally, Mr Newton.

CHARLES. That is very intelligent of you, Louise.

BARBARA. It takes some intelligence to be both a French spy and a bluestocking. I thank heaven for my stupidity, as you call it.

CHARLES. Barbara: must I throw you downstairs?

LOUISE. In France they call me the English spy. But this is the first time I have been called a bluestocking. All I meant was that Mr Kneller and Mr Newton seem to mean exactly the same thing; only one calls it beauty and the other gravitation; so they need not quarrel. The portrait will be the same both ways.

NEWTON. Can he measure beauty?

KNELLER. No. I can paint a woman's beauty; but I cannot measure it in a pint pot. Beauty is immeasurable.

NEWTON. I can measure gravitation. Nothing exists until it is measured. Fine words are nothing. Do you expect me to go to the Royal Society and tell them that the orbits of a planet are curved because painters think them prettier so? How much are they curved? This man cannot tell you. I can. Where will they be six months hence? He cannot tell you. I can. All he has to say is that the earth is a moon of the sun and that the line of beauty is a curve. Can he measure the path of the moon? Can he draw the curve?

KNELLER. I can draw your portrait. Can you draw mine?

NEWTON. Yes, with a camera obscura; and if I could find a chemical salt sensitive to light I could fix it. Some day portraits will be made at the street corners for sixpence apiece.

KNELLER. A looking glass will make your portrait for nothing. It makes the duchess's portrait fifty times a day.

BARBARA. It does not. I dont look at myself in the glass fifty times a day. Charles never passes one without looking at himself. I have watched him.

CHARLES. It rebukes my vanity every time, Barbara. I am an ugly fellow; yet I always think of myself as an Adonis.

LOUISE. You are not so ugly as you think, Charles. You were an ugly baby; and your wicked mother told you so. You have never got over it. But when I was sent to England to captivate you with my baby face, it was you who captivated me with your seventy inches and your good looks.

BARBARA. Ay, flatter him, flatter him: he loves it.

CHARLES. I cannot bear this. The subject is to be dropped.

LOUISE. But, Charles—

CHARLES. No, no, No. Not a word more. The King commands it.

Dead silence. They sit as if in church, except Fox, who chafes at the silence.

FOX. In the presence of this earthly king all you great nobles become dumb flunkeys. What will you be when the King of Kings calls you from your graves to answer for your lives?

NELL. Trust you, George, to put in a cheerful word. Rowley darling: may we all stop being dumb flunkeys and be human beings again?

CHARLES. Mr Rowley apologizes for his lapse into royalty. Only, the King's person is not to be discussed.

LOUISE. But, Charles, I love you when you put on your royalty. My king, Louis Quatorze, le grand monarque, le roi soleil, never puts off his royalty for a moment even in the most ridiculous circumstances.

BARBARA. Yes; and he looks like a well-to-do grocer, and will never look like anything else.

LOUISE. You would not dare to say so at Versailles, or even to think so. He is always great; and his greatness makes us great also. But it is true that he is not six feet high, and that the grand manner is not quite natural to him. Charles can do it so much better when he chooses. Charles: why dont you choose?

CHARLES. I prefer to keep the crown and the grand manner up my sleeve until I need them. Louis and I played together when we were boys. We know each other too well to be pleasant company; so I take care to keep out of his way. Besides, Louise, when I make you all great you become terrible bores. I like Nelly because nothing can make a courtier of her. Do you know why?

BARBARA. Because the orange girl has the gutter in her blood.

CHARLES. Not at all. Tell her the reason, Nell.

NELL. I dont know it, Rowley darling. I never was an orange girl; but I have the gutter in my blood all right. I think I have everything in my blood; for when I am on the stage I can be anything you please, orange girl or queen. Or even a man. But I dont know the reason why. So you can tell it to her, Rowley darling, if you know it.

CHARLES. It is because in the theatre you are a queen. I tell you the world is full of kings and queens and their little courts. Here is Pastor Fox, a king in his meeting house, though his meetings are against the law. Here is Mr Newton, a king in the new Royal Society. Here is Godfrey Kneller: a king among painters. I can make you duchesses and your sons dukes; but who would be mere dukes or duchesses if they could be kings and queens?

NELL. Dukes will be six a penny if you make all Barbara's sons dukes.

BARBARA. Oh! My sons have gentle blood in their veins, not gutter dirt.

CHARLES. For shame, Nelly! It was illbred of you to reproach her Grace for the most amiable side of her character.

NELL. I beg pardon. God forgive me, I am no better myself.

BARBARA. No better! You impudent slut.

NELL. Well, no worse, if you like. One little duke is enough for me.

LOUISE. Change the subject, Charles. What you were saying about little kings and queens being everywhere was very true. You are very spiritual.

BARBARA. Ha ha! Ha ha ha! He spiritual!

LOUISE. Clever, you call it. I am always in trouble with my English. And Charles is too lazy to learn French properly, though he lived in France so long.

BARBARA. If you mean clever, he is as clever as fifty foxes.

FOX. He may be fifty times as clever as I; but so are many of the blackest villains. Value him rather for his flashes of the inner light. Did he not stop the butchering of the regicides on the ground that if he punished them they could never punish themselves? That was what made me his loyal subject.

BARBARA. I did not mean fifty of you: I meant real foxes. He is so clever that he can always make me seem stupid when it suits him: that is, when I want anything he wont give me. He is as stingy as a miser.

CHARLES. You are like a dairymaid: you think there is no end to a king's money. Here is my Nelly, who is more careful of my money than she is of her own. Well, when I am dying, and all the rest of you are forgotten, my last thought will be of Nelly.

NELL. Rowley darling: dont make me cry. I am not the only one. Louise is very thoughtful about money.

BARBARA. Yes: she knows exactly how much he has: she gets it for him from the King of France.

LOUISE. This subject of conversation is in the worst possible taste. Charles: be a king again; and forbid it.

CHARLES. Nobody but Barbara would have introduced it. I forbid it absolutely.

Mrs Basham returns.

MRS BASHAM. Mr Newton: dinner is served.

BARBARA. You should address yourself to His Majesty. Where are your manners, woman?

MRS BASHAM. In this house Mr Newton comes first. Come along quick, all of you; or your victuals will be cold.

NEWTON [*rising*] Mr Kneller: will you take her Grace of Cleveland, as you are interested in her curves?

BARBARA [*violently*] No. I am the senior duchess: it is my right to be taken in by the King.

CHARLES [*rising and resignedly giving her his arm*] The Duke of York will follow with the junior duchess. Happy man!

All rise, except Fox.

BARBARA. Brute! [*She tries to disengage herself*].

CHARLES [*holding her fast*] You are on the King's arm. Behave yourself. [*He takes her out forcibly*].

MRS BASHAM. Now, your Highness. Now, Madam Carwell.

JAMES [*taking Louise*] You have remembered, I hope, that Madam Carwell is a Catholic?

MRS BASHAM. Yes: there will be enough cod for the two of you.

LOUISE. Provided Charles does not get at it first. Let us hurry. [*She hurries James out*].

MRS BASHAM. Will you take the player woman, Mr Kneller?

NELL. No no. The player woman goes with her dear old Fox. [*She swoops on the Quaker and drags him along*] George: today you will dine with publicans and sinners. You will say grace for them.

FOX. You remind me that where my Master went I must follow. [*They go out*].

MRS BASHAM. There is no one left for you to take in, Mr Kneller. Mr Newton must take me in and come last.

KNELLER. I will go home. I cannot eat in this house of straight lines.

MRS BASHAM. You will do nothing of the sort, Mr Kneller. There is a cover laid for you; and the King expects you.

NEWTON. The lines are not straight, Mr Kneller. Gravitation bends them. And at bottom I know no more about gravitation than you do about beauty.

KNELLER. To you the universe is nothing but a clock that an almighty clockmaker has wound up and set going for all eternity.

NEWTON. Shall I tell you a secret, Mr Beautymonger? The clock does not keep time. If it did there would be no further need for the Clockmaker. He is wiser than to leave us to our foolish selves in that fashion. When He made a confusion of tongues to prevent the Tower of Babel from reaching to heaven He also contrived a confusion of time to prevent us from doing wholly without Him. The sidereal clock, the clock of the universe, goes wrong. He has to correct it from time to time. Can you, who know everything because you and God are both artists, tell me what is amiss with the perihelion of Mercury?

KNELLER. The what?

NEWTON. The perihelion of Mercury.

KNELLER. I do not know what it is.

NEWTON. I do. But I do not know what is amiss with it. Not until the world finds this out can it do without the Clockmaker in the heavens who can set the hands back or forward, and move the stars with a touch of His almighty finger as He watches over us in the heavens.

KNELLER. In the heavens! In your universe there is no heaven. You have abolished the sky.

NEWTON. Ignoramus: there may be stars beyond our vision bigger than the whole solar system. When I have perfected my telescope it will give you your choice of a hundred heavens.

MRS BASHAM. Mr Kneller: your dinner will be cold; and you will be late for grace. I cannot have any more of this ungodly talk. Down with you to your dinner at once.

KNELLER. In this house, you said, Mr Newton comes first. But you take good care that he comes last. The mistress of this and every other house is she who cooks the dinner. [*He goes out*].

MRS BASHAM [*taking Newton out*] Thats a funny fellow, sir. But you really should not begin talking about the stars to people just as they are going away quietly. It is a habit that is growing on

you. What do they know or care about the perry healing of
Mercury that interests you so much? We shall never get these
people out of the house if— [*They pass out of hearing*].

There is peace in the deserted room.

ACT II

The boudoir of Catherine of Braganza, Charles's queen, in his not too palatial quarters in Newmarket late in the afternoon on the same day. A prie-dieu, and the pictures, which are all devotional, are signs of the queen's piety. Charles, in slippers and breeches, shirt and cravat, wrapped in an Indian silk dressing gown, is asleep on a couch. His coat and boots are on the carpet where he has thrown them. His hat and wig are on a chair with his tall walking stick. The door, opening on a staircase landing, is near the head of the couch, between it and the prie-dieu. There is a clock in the room.

Catherine, aged 42, enters. She contemplates her husband and the untidiness he has made. With a Portuguese shake of the head (about six times) she sets to work to put the room in order by taking up the boots and putting them tidily at the foot of the couch. She then takes out the coat and hangs it on the rail of the landing. Returning, she purposely closes the door with a bang sufficient to wake Charles.

CHARLES. How long have I been asleep?

CATHERINE. I not know. Why leave you your things about all over my room? I have to put them away like a chambermaid.

CHARLES. Why not send for Chiffinch? It is his business to look after my clothes.

CATHERINE. I not wish to be troubled with Chiffinch when we are alone.

CHARLES [*rising*] Belovéd: you should make me put away my clothes myself. Why should you do chambermaid's work for me? [*His "beloved" always has three syllables*].

CATHERINE. I not like to see you without your wig. But I am your wife and must put up with it.

CHARLES [*getting up*] I am your husband; and I count it a great privilege. [*He kisses her*].

CATHERINE. Yes yes; but why choose you my boudoir for your siesta?

CHARLES. Here in our Newmarket lodging it is the only place

where the women cannot come after me.

CATHERINE. A wife is some use then, after all.

CHARLES. There is nobody like a wife.

CATHERINE. I hear that Cleveland has come back from Paris. Did you send for her?

CHARLES. Send for her! I had as soon send for the divvle. I finished with Barbara long ago.

CATHERINE. How often have you told me that you are finished with all women! Yet Portsmouth keeps her hold on you, and Nellie the player. And now Cleveland comes back.

CHARLES. Beloved: you do not understand. These women do not keep their hold on me: I keep my hold on them. I have a bit of news for you about Louise. What do you think I caught her at this morning?

CATHERINE. I had rather not guess.

CHARLES. Buying a love potion. That was for me. I do not make love to her enough, it seems. I hold her because she is intelligent and ladylike and keeps me in touch with France and the French court, to say nothing of the money I have to extract from Louis through her.

CATHERINE. And Nelly? She can play the fine lady; but is she one?

CHARLES. Nelly is a good creature; and she amuses me. You know, beloved, one gets tired of court ladies and their conversation, always the same.

CATHERINE. And you really did not send for Cleveland to come back?

CHARLES. Beloved: when I was young I thought that there was only one unbearable sort of woman: the one that could think of nothing but her soul and its salvation. But in Barbara I found something worse: a woman who thought of nothing but her body and its satisfaction, which meant men and money. For both, Barbara is insatiable. Grab, grab, grab. When one is done with Barbara's body—a very fine body, I admit—what is there left?

CATHERINE. And you are done with Barbara's body?

CHARLES. Beloved: I am done with all bodies. They are all alike:

all cats are grey in the dark. It is the souls and the brains that are different. In the end one learns to leave the body out. And then Barbara is packed off to Paris, and is not asked back by me, though I have no doubt there is some man in the case.

CATHERINE. Why spend you so much time with me here—so much more than you used to?

CHARLES. Beloved: do I plague you? I am off.

He makes for the door: she runs to it and bars his egress.

CATHERINE. No: that is not what I meant. Go back and sit down.

Charles obediently goes back to the couch, where they sit side by side.

CHARLES. And what did you mean, beloved?

CATHERINE. You spend too much time away from court. Your brother is stealing the court away from you. When he is here his rooms are crowded: yours are empty.

CHARLES. I thank heaven for it. The older I grow, the less I can endure that most tiresome of all animals, the courtier. Even a dissolute court, as they say mine is—I suppose they mean a court where bawdy stories are told out loud instead of whispered—is more tedious than a respectable one. They repeat themselves and repeat themselves endlessly. And I am just as bad with my old stories about my flight after the battle of Worcester. I told the same one twice over within an hour last Tuesday. This morning Barbara called me an old wreck.

CATHERINE [*flaming up*] She dared! Send her to the Tower and let her rot there.

CHARLES. She is not so important as that, beloved. Nor am I. And we must forgive our enemies when we can afford to.

CATHERINE. I forgive my enemies, as you well know, Charles. It is my duty as a Catholic and a Christian. But it is not my duty to forgive your enemies. And you never forgive mine.

CHARLES. An excellent family arrangement for a royal pair. We can exchange our revenges and remain good Christians. But Barbara may be right. When a king is shunned, and his heir is courted, his death is not far off.

CATHERINE. You must not say things like that: I not can bear it. You are stronger in your mind than ever; and nobody can keep up with you walking.

CHARLES. Nevertheless, beloved, I shall drop before you do. What will happen to you then? that is what troubles me. When I am dead you must go back to Portugal, where your brother the king will take care of you. You will never be safe here, because you are a Catholic queen.

CATHERINE. I not think I shall care what becomes of me when you are gone. But James is a Catholic. When he is king what have I to fear? Or do you believe your son Monmouth will prevent him from succeeding you and become a Protestant king?

CHARLES. No. He will try, poor boy; but Jamie will kill him. He is his mother's son; and his mother was nothing. Then the Protestants will kill Jamie; and the Dutch lad will his chance and take it. He will be king: a Protestant king. So you must make for Portugal.

CATHERINE. But such things not could happen. Why are you, who are afraid of nothing else, so afraid of the Protestants?

CHARLES. They killed my great grandmother. They killed my father. They would kill you if I were not a little too clever for them: they are trying hard enough, damn them! They are great killers, these Protestants. Jamie has just one chance. They may call in Orange Billy before they kill him; and then it will hardly be decent for Billy to kill his wife's father. But they will get rid of Jamie somehow; so you must make for home the moment I have kissed you goodbye for the last time.

CATHERINE [almost in tears] You not must talk of it—[She breaks down].

CHARLES [caressing her] Beloved: you will only lose the worst of husbands.

CATHERINE. That is a lie: if anyone else said it I would kill her. You are the very best husband that ever lived.

CHARLES [laughing] Oh! Oh! Oh! The merry monarch! Beloved: can anything I can ever do make up to you for my unfaithfulness?

CATHERINE. People think of nothing but that, as if that were the whole of life. What care I about your women? your concubines? your handmaidens? the servants of your common pleasures? They have set me free to be something more to you than they are or can ever be. You have never been really unfaithful to me.

CHARLES. Yes, once, with the woman whose image as Britannia is on every British penny, and will perhaps stay there to all eternity. And on my honor nothing came of that: I never touched her. But she had some magic that scattered my wits: she made me listen for a moment to those who were always pressing me to divorce my patient wife and take a Protestant queen. But I could never have done it, though I was furious when she ran away from me and married Richmond.

CATHERINE. Oh, I know, I know: it was the only time I ever was jealous. Well, I forgive you: why should a great man like you be satisfied with a little thing like me?

CHARLES. Stop. I cannot bear that. I am not a great man; and neither are you a little woman. You have more brains and character than all the rest of the court put together.

CATHERINE. I am nothing except what you have made me. What did I know when I came here? Only what the nuns teach a Portuguese princess in their convent.

CHARLES. And what more had I to teach you except what I learnt when I was running away from the battle of Worcester? And when I had learnt that much there was an end of me as a king. I knew too much.

CATHERINE. With what you have taught me I shall govern Portugal if I return to it?

CHARLES. I have no doubt of it, beloved; but whether that will make you any happier I have my doubts. I wish you could govern the English for me.

CATHERINE. No one can govern the English: that is why they will never come to any good. In Portugal there is the holy Church: we know what we believe; and we all believe the same things. But here the Church itself is a heresy; and there are a thousand other heresies: almost as many heresies as there are people. And if you ask any of them what his sect believes he does not know: all he can say is that the men of the other sects should be hanged and their women whipped through the town at the cart's tail. But they are all against the true Church. I do not understand the English; and I do not want to govern them.

CHARLES. You are Portuguese. I am Italian, French, Scottish, hardly at all English. When I want to know how the great lump of my subjects will take anything I tell it to Barbara. Then I tell it to Chiffinch. Then I tell it to Jamie. When I have the responses of Barbara, Chiffinch, and Jamie, I know how Tom, Dick and Harry will take it. And it is never as I take it.

CATHERINE. In Portugal we not have this strange notion that Tom, Dick and Harry matter. What do they know about government?

CHARLES. Nothing; but they hate it. And nobody teaches them how necessary it is. Instead, when we teach them anything we teach them grammar and dead languages. What is the result? Protestantism and parliaments instead of citizenship.

CATHERINE. In Portugal, God be praised, there are no Protestants and no parliaments.

CHARLES. Parliaments are the very divvle. Old Noll began by thinking the world of parliaments. Well, he tried every sort of parliament, finishing with a veritable reign of the saints. And in the end he had to turn them all out of doors, neck and crop, and govern through his major-generals. And when Noll died they went back to their parliament and made such a mess of it that they had to send for me.

CATHERINE. Suppose there had been no you?

CHARLES. There is always somebody. In every nation there must be the makings of a capable council and a capable king three or four times over, if only we knew how to pick them. Nobody has found out how to do it: that is why the world is so vilely governed.

CATHERINE. But if the rulers are of noble birth—

CHARLES. You mean if they are the sons of their fathers. What good is that?

CATHERINE. You are king because you are the son of your father. And you are the best of kings.

CHARLES. Thank you. And your brother Alfonso was king of Portugal because he was the son of his father. Was he also the best of kings?

CATHERINE. Oh, he was dreadful. He was barely fit to be a stable boy; but my brother Pedro took his crown and locked him up; and Pedro also is my father's son.

CHARLES. Just so: six of one and half a dozen of the other. Heredity is no use. Learning Latin is no use: Jack Churchill, who is an ignoramus, is worth fifty scholars. If Orange Billy dies and one of my nieces succeeds him Jack will be King of England.

CATHERINE. Perhaps the Church should select the king—or the queen.

CHARLES. The Church has failed over and over again to select a decent Pope. Alexander Borgia was a jolly fellow; and I am the last man alive to throw stones at him; but he was not a model Pope.

CATHERINE. My father was a great king. He fought the Spaniards and set Portugal free from their yoke. And it was the people who chose him and made him do it. I have sometimes wondered whether the people should not choose their king.

CHARLES. Not the English people. They would choose Titus Oates. No, beloved: the riddle of how to choose a ruler is still unanswered; and it is the riddle of civilization. I tell you again there are in England, or in any other country, the makings of half a dozen decent kings and councils; but they are mostly in prison. If we only knew how to pick them out and label them, then the people could have their choice out of the half dozen. It may end that way, but not until we have learnt how to pick the people who are fit to be chosen before they are chosen. And even then the picked ones will be just those whom the people will not choose. Who is it that said that no nation can bear being well governed for more than three years? Old Noll found that out. Why am I a popular king? Because I am a lazy fellow. I enjoy myself and let the people see me doing it, and leave things as they are, though things as they are will not bear thinking of by those who know what they are. That is what the people like. It is what they would do if they were kings.

CATHERINE. You are not lazy: I wish you were: I should see more of you. You take a great deal too much exercise: you walk and walk and nobody can keep up with you; you are always gardening or sailing or building and talking to gardeners and sailors and shipwrights and bricklayers and masons and people like that, neglecting the court. That is how your brother gathers the court round him and takes it away from you.

CHARLES. Let him. There is nothing to be learnt at court except that a courtier's life is not a happy one. The gardeners and the watermen, the shipwrights and bricklayers and carpenters and masons, are happier and far far more contented. It is the worst of luck to be born a king. Give me a skilled trade and eight or ten shillings a week, and you and I, beloved, would pig along more happily than we have ever been able to do as our majesties.

CATHERINE. I not want to pig along. I was born to rule; and if the worst comes to the worst and I have to go back to my own country I shall shew the world that I can rule, and that I am not the ninny I am made to look like here.

CHARLES. Why dont you do it, beloved? I am not worth staying with.

CATHERINE. I am torn ten different ways. I know that I should make you divorce me and marry a young Protestant wife who would bring you a son to inherit the crown and save all this killing of Monmouth and James and the handing over of your kingdom to the Hollander. I am tempted to do it because then I should return to my own beautiful country and smell the Tagus instead of the dirty Thames, and rule Portugal as my mother used to rule over the head of my worthless brother. I should be somebody then. But I cannot bring myself to leave you: not for all the thrones in the world. And my religion forbids me to put a Protestant on the throne of England when the rightful heir to it is a good Catholic.

CHARLES. You shall not, beloved. I will have no other widow but you.

CATHERINE. Ah! you can coax me so easily.

CHARLES. I treated you very badly when I was a young man because young men have low tastes and think only of themselves. Besides, odsfish! we could not talk to oneanother. The English they taught you in Portugal was a tongue that never was spoke on land or sea; and my Portuguese made you laugh. We must forget our foolish youth: we are grown-up now.

CATHERINE. Happy man! You forget so easily. But think of the difference in our fortunes! All your hopes of being a king were cut off: you were an exile, an outcast, a fugitive. Yet your kingdom dropped into your mouth at last; and you have been a king since you were old enough to use your power. But I! My mother was determined from my birth that I should be a queen: a great queen: Queen of England. Well, she had her way: we were married; and they call me queen. But have I ever reigned? Am I not as much an exile and an outcast as ever you were? I am not Catherine of England: I am Catherine of Bragança: a foreign woman with a funny name that they cannot pronounce. Yet I have the blood of rulers in my veins and the brains of rulers in my head.

CHARLES. They are no use here: the English will not be ruled; and there is nothing they hate like brains. For brains and religion you must go to Scotland; and Scotland is the most damnable country on earth: never shall I forget the life they led me there with their brains and their religion when they made me their boy king to spite Old Noll. I sometimes think religion and brains are the curse of the world. No, beloved, England for me, with all its absurdities!

CATHERINE. There can be only one true religion; and England has fifty.

CHARLES. Well, the more the merrier, if only they could let oneanother live. But they will not do even that.

CATHERINE. Have you no conscience?

CHARLES. I have; and a very troublesome one too. I would give a dukedom to any doctor that would cure me of it. But somehow it is not a conscience of the standard British pattern.

CATHERINE. That is only your witty nonsense. Our consciences, which come from God, must be all the same.

CHARLES. They are not. Do you think God so stupid that he could invent only one sort of conscience?

CATHERINE [*shocked*] What a dreadful thing to say! I must not listen to you.

CHARLES. No two consciences are the same. No two love affairs are the same. No two marriages are the same. No two illnesses are the same. No two children are the same. No two human beings are the same. What is right for one is wrong for the other. Yet they cannot live together without laws; and a law is something that obliges them all to do the same thing.

CATHERINE. It may be so in England. But in Portugal the Holy Church makes all Catholics the same. My mother ruled them though she was a Spaniard. Why should I not do what my mother did?

CHARLES. Why not, indeed? I daresay you will do it very well, beloved. The Portuguese can believe in a Church and obey a king. The English robbed the Church and destroyed it: if a priest celebrates Mass anywhere in England outside your private chapel he is hanged for it. My great grandmother was a Catholic queen: rather than let her succeed to the throne they chopped her head off. My father was a Protestant king: they chopped his head off for trying to govern them and asking the Midlands to pay for the navy. While the Portuguese were fighting the Spaniards the English were fighting oneanother. You can do nothing with the English. How often have I told you that I am no real king: that the utmost I can do is to keep my crown on my head and my head on my shoulders. How often have you asked me to do some big thing like joining your Church, or some little thing like pardoning a priest or a Quaker condemned to some cruel punishment! And you have found that outside the court, where my smiles and my frowns count for everything, I have no power. The perjured scoundrel, Titus Oates, steeped in unmentionable vices, is lodged in my palace with a pension. If I could have my way he would be lodged on the gallows. There is a preacher named Bunyan who has written a book about the Christian life that is being read, they tell me, all the world over; and I could not release him from Bedford Gaol, where he rotted for years. The world will remember Oates and Bunyan; and I shall be The Merry Monarch. No: give me English birds and English trees, English dogs and Irish horses, English rivers and English ships; but English men! No, NO, NO.

CATHERINE. And Englishwomen?

CHARLES. Ah! there you have me, beloved. One cannot do without women: at least I cannot. But having to manage rascals like Buckingham and Shaftesbury, and dodgers like Halifax, is far worse than having to manage Barbara and Louise.

CATHERINE. Is there really any difference? Shaftesbury is trying to have me beheaded on Tower Hill on a charge of plotting to poison you sworn to by Titus Oates. Barbara is quite ready to support him in that.

CHARLES. No, beloved. The object of having you beheaded is to enable me to marry a Protestant wife and have a Protestant heir. I have pointed out to Barbara that the Protestant wife would not be so kind to her as you are, and would have her out of the kingdom before she could say Jack Robinson. So now she has thrown over Shaftesbury; and when I have thrown him over, as I shall know how to do presently, there will be an end of him. But he will be succeeded by some stupider rascal, or, worse still, some stupid fellow who is not a rascal. The clever rascals are all for sale; but the honest dunderheads are the very divvle.

CATHERINE. I wish you were not so clever.

CHARLES. Beloved: you could not do without my cleverness. That is why you must go back to Portugal when I am gone.

CATHERINE. But it makes your mind twist about so. You are so clever that you think you can do without religion. If only I could win you to the Church I should die perfectly happy; and so would you.

CHARLES. Well, I promise you I will not die a Protestant. You must see to that when the hour strikes for me: the last hour. So my very belovedest will die happy; and that is all I care about. [*Caressing her*] Does that satisfy you?

CATHERINE. If only I could believe it.

CHARLES. You mean I am the king whose word no man relies on.

CATHERINE. No: you are not that sort of king for me. But will it be a real conversion? I think you would turn Turk to please me.

CHARLES. Faith I believe I would. But there is more in it than that. It is not that I have too little religion in me for the Church: I have too much, like a queer fellow I talked with this morning. [*The clock strikes five*]. Odsfish! I have a Council meeting. I must go. [*He throws off his dressing gown*]. My boots! What has become of my boots?

CATHERINE. There are your boots. And wait until I make you decent.

Whilst he pulls his boots on, she fetches his coat and valets him into it. He snatches up his hat and stick and puts the hat on.

CATHERINE. No no: you have forgotten your wig. [*She takes his hat off and fetches the wig*]. Fancy your going into the Council Chamber like that! Nobody would take you for King Charles the Second without that wig. Now. [*She puts the wig on him; then the hat. A few final pats and pulls complete his toilet*]. Now you look every inch a king. [*Making him a formal curtsey*] Your Majesty's visit has made me very happy. Long live the King!

CHARLES. May the Queen live for ever!

He throws up his arm in a gallant salute and stalks out. She rises and throws herself on her knees at her prie-dieu.